RODOLPHE LANDEMAINE
RECIPES AND INSTRUCTIONS

THE COMPLETE GUIDE TO BAKING

BREAD, BRIOCHE AND OTHER GOURMET TREATS

PHOTOGRAPHY BY JOERG LEHMANN
ILLUSTRATIONS BY YANNIS VAROUTSIKOS
SCIENTIFIC EXPLANATIONS BY ANNE CAZOR

hardie grant books

ABOUT MAISON LANDEMAINE

Originally from Mayenne, Rodolphe Landemaine completed apprenticeships for his two professions of baker and pastry chef with Les Compagnons du Devoir et du Tour de France. To perfect his knowledge, he then joined the teams of renowned restaurants Ladurée in Paris, working alongside Pierre Hermé; Paul Bocuse in Lyon; the Parisian gourmet restaurant Lucas Carton; and even the Bristol Hotel in Paris. In 2007, he and his wife, Yoshimi, opened the first of their Maison Landemaine bakeries, in the 9th arrondissement of Paris, before expanding into other quarters of the capital.

Maison Landemaine rests on three strong values: work, excellence and pleasure. Its products are created using the best raw materials – Label Rouge or organic flour, certified regional butter, fresh in-season fruit and vegetables – with artisanal techniques based on natural sourdoughs and slow fermentation as specialties of the house, values that inspire all its Parisian teams. Recently, the adventure has also extended to Japan, with a baker training school and a first shop in the heart of Tokyo.

This book is the culmination of ten years of constantly renewed work and improvement to offer products of excellent quality to everyone, every day. Maison Landemaine reveals the secrets of its recipes along with explanations and the tricks of the baker's trade. And now over to you: happy baking and bon appétit!

CONTENTS

HOW TO USE THIS BOOK

BASICS

Discover all the ingredients, techniques and base recipes for baking breads,
from wheat flour and kneading to baking and layered doughs.
For each basic: a diagram and explanations of the
specifics of the technique or the mixture.

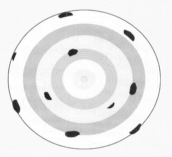

RECIPES

Put the base recipes to work to make breads, Viennese pastries,
brioches, tarts and cakes. For each recipe: cross-references to the basics,
a diagram to understand the concept of the recipes, and step-by-step
photos to follow the stages involved in making your masterpiece.

ILLUSTRATED GLOSSARY

Enrich your knowledge with illustrations of the main
techniques and details on the use of ingredients.

CHAPTER I
THE BASICS OF BREADMAKING

WHEAT FLOUR

Understand

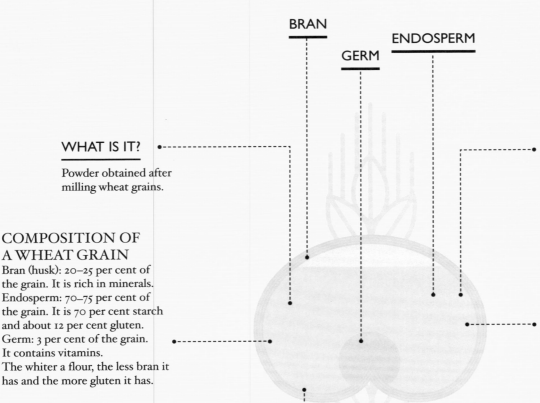

BRAN

GERM

ENDOSPERM

WHAT IS IT?

Powder obtained after
milling wheat grains.

COMPOSITION OF A WHEAT GRAIN

Bran (husk): 20–25 per cent of
the grain. It is rich in minerals.
Endosperm: 70–75 per cent of
the grain. It is 70 per cent starch
and about 12 per cent gluten.
Germ: 3 per cent of the grain.
It contains vitamins.
The whiter a flour, the less bran it
has and the more gluten it has.

FROM WHEAT TO FLOUR

The wheat is crushed, sifted, separated and
crushed again until the flour produced is
refined to the desired degree (white, semi-
wholemeal, brown, wholemeal . . .).

STONE-GROUND FLOUR

This is flour crushed between two millstones
(rather than metal cylinders). This traditional
technique allows the germ and all or some
of the bran to be preserved. The flour
retains most of its nutritional richness.

FLOURS RICH IN BRAN

The bran is the protective outer later of
the wheat grain. During milling, the bran
is separated from the endosperm. Then,
depending on the flour being produced, part
of these husks is returned to the flour. The
more bran in the flour, the less the bread
dough will rise (the flour is coarser, which
makes the formation of the gluten network
more difficult), and the denser the crumb will
be. A flour rich in bran is rich in fibre, protein,
vitamins and minerals. It has a rustic taste.

WHAT IS THE 'T' OF A FLOUR?

*French flour is classified using T numbers.
They correspond to the mineral (i.e. ash)
content in 100 g flour. The more refined
a flour, the whiter it is, and the less
bran and therefore minerals it contains:
from 0.45 per cent for a T45 flour
to 1.5 per cent for a T150 flour.*
Flour with a low T number (strong)
*Appearance: white, fine
Mineral content: low
Gluten content: high to very high
Uses: white bread, brioches, Viennese pastries
Produces: elastic dough that rises
quickly, airy easy-to-chew crumb,
thin crust, simple flavours.*

Flour with a high T number (weak)
*Appearance: shades of grey, grainy
Mineral content: high
Gluten content: low
Uses: rustic breads, specialty breads
Produces: fragile, less elastic dough
because the gluten network plays less of a
role, dense crumb. The breads are tastier,
because the flour contains more bran.*

*In Australia, we have fewer flour varieties.
French T55 flour is the equivalent of
Australian plain flour; higher T numbers
represent darker flours. Combine
white and wholemeal flours to make
'intermediate' flour types, such as T80.*

WHAT IS GLUTEN ?

*Gluten is a protein in flour. During
kneading, bonds form between the gluten
proteins, creating a tight mesh (the gluten
network). If the dough is overworked (or
not kneaded for long enough), this mesh
won't be tight enough, and will be too
porous. It won't retain enough of the gas
produced during rising to allow the dough
to prove properly. Gluten is thus the main
element that allows dough to rise. The
higher the gluten content of a flour, the
easier the dough will rise. We call gluten-
free flours non-breadmaking flours.*

Learn

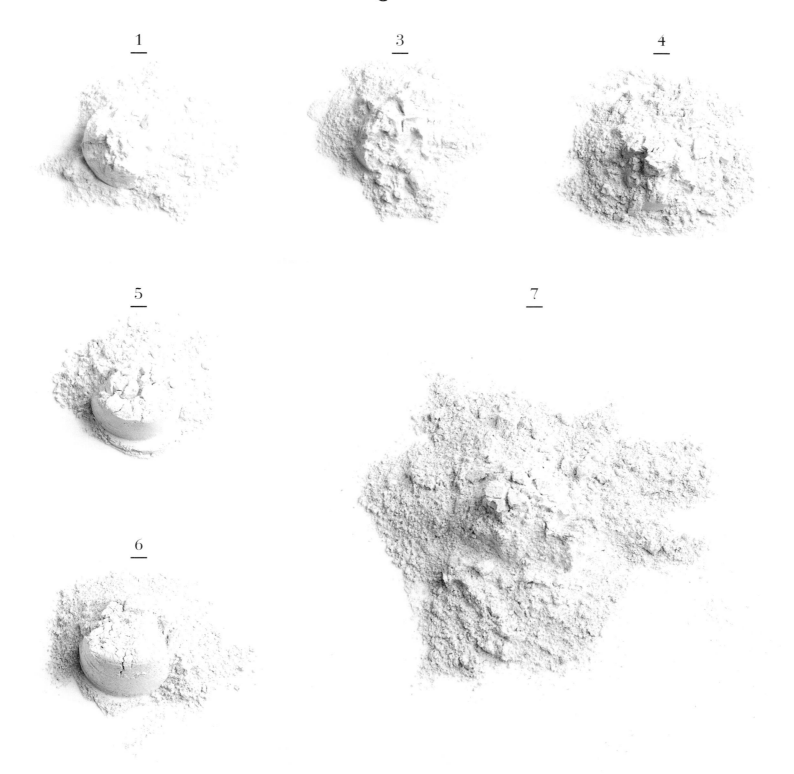

1

3

4

5

7

6

1 T45: PASTRY FLOUR

The result of milling high-quality wheat very rich in protein, it contains more gluten than standard flour.
Appearance: white, fine
Mineral content: 0.45 per cent
Gluten content: very high
Uses: brioches, Viennese pastries

2 T55: PLAIN FLOUR

Appearance: white, fine
Mineral content: 0.55 per cent
Gluten content: high
Uses: white bread, tart pastry, pizza dough, pâtisserie

3 T65: STRONG FLOUR

Appearance: white, medium grain
Mineral content: 0.65 per cent
Gluten content: medium
Uses: country bread, tart pastry, pizza dough, pâtisserie

4 T65: BAKER'S FLOUR

Guaranteed without additives (*Bread Decree 1993*)
Appearance: white, medium grain
Mineral content: 0.65 per cent
Gluten content: medium
Uses: traditional breads

5 T80: SEMI-WHOLEMEAL OR HALF FLOUR

Appearance: light grey, medium grain
Mineral content: 0.80 per cent
Gluten content: medium
Uses: specialty breads, pâtisserie

6 T110: LIGHT WHOLEMEAL FLOUR

Appearance: grey, coarse grain
Mineral content: 1.10 per cent
Gluten content: low
Use: brown bread

7 T150: WHOLEMEAL FLOUR

Appearance: grey, coarse grain
Mineral content: 1.50 per cent
Gluten content: low
Use: bran bread

OTHER
FLOURS

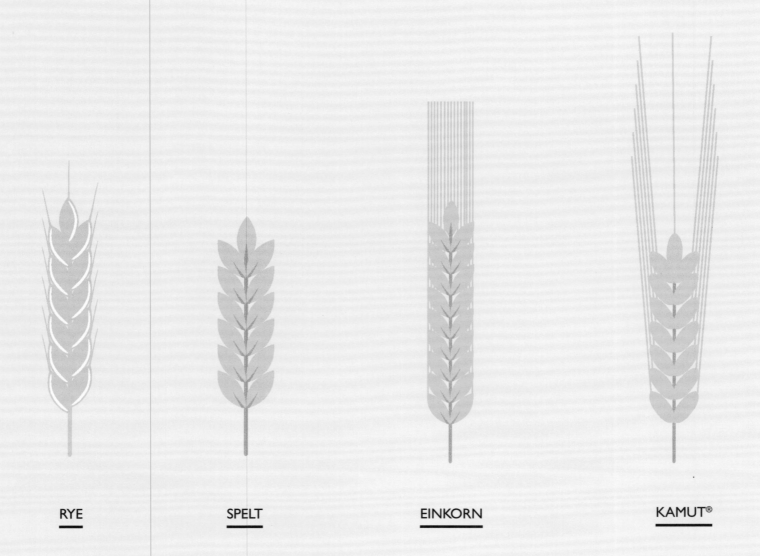

RYE   SPELT   EINKORN   KAMUT®

WHY MUST THESE FLOURS BE MIXED WITH
WHILE FLOUR TO MAKE BREAD?

*Because they don't contain enough gluten for the gluten network
to form correctly. Mixing with wheat flour (which is rich in gluten)
produces a dough with more volume and an airier crumb.*

1 SPELT FLOUR

Produced by milling grains from spelt.
This soft subspecies is the ancestor of wheat.
Composition: 12 per cent gluten,
rich in bran and nutrients.
Uses: intermediate between wheat
flour and einkorn flour. Can be
used alone to make bread.
Result: denser crumb than
wheat flour, darker colour (light
brown). Quite strong taste.

1

2

3

4

2 EINKORN FLOUR

Produced by milling grains of einkorn wheat. This ancient cereal variety only exists in organic farming.
Composition: 7 per cent gluten, very easily digested. Suits people who are sensitive to gluten.
Use: can be used alone to make bread, but is more often mixed with wheat flour (use 50–70 per cent einkorn flour).
Result: dense yellow crumb. Delicate, slightly sweet taste.

3 KAMUT® FLOUR

Produced by milling grains of khorasan wheat (ancestor of wheat). Originally from Egypt, it only exists in organic farming. The trademark Kamut® comes from an Egyptian word meaning 'wheat'.
Composition: 10–12 per cent gluten, easily digested. Suits people who are sensitive to gluten.
Use: can be used alone to make bread, but is more often mixed with wheat flour (use 50–70 per cent Kamut® flour).
Result: tight crumb. Delicate taste but stronger than wheat. Light aroma of dried fruit.

4 RYE FLOUR

Produced by milling rye grains. A cereal from northern Europe.
Composition: contains a type of gluten that isn't good for breadmaking; fragile, less elastic than wheat, forming only a weak gluten network.
Use: can be used alone to make bread, but is easier to work with when mixed with wheat flour (use 20–50 per cent rye flour).
Result: tight, dense crumb, dark brown, lots of bite. Strong taste.

GLUTEN-FREE FLOURS

Understand

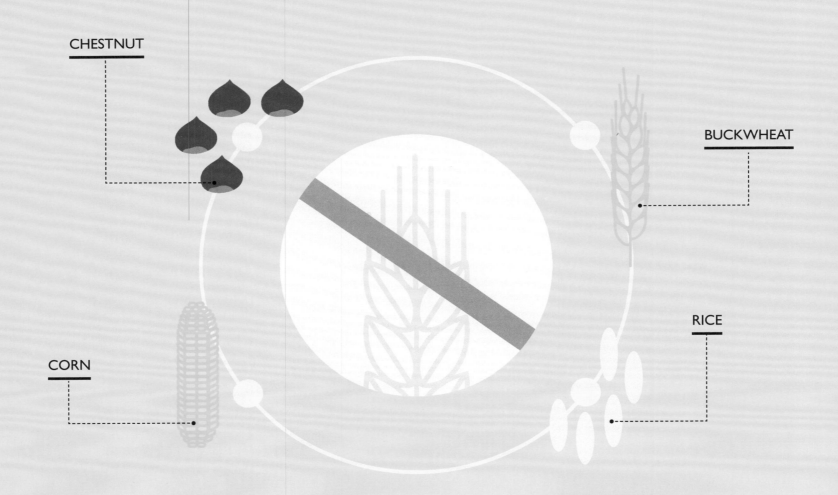

CHESTNUT

BUCKWHEAT

CORN

RICE

WHAT IS A GLUTEN-FREE FLOUR?

A flour devoid of gluten. Without gluten, it's impossible to form a gluten network, that tight mesh that holds the gases produced by fermentation and makes the dough rise. As there is no rising phase, we say that bread doesn't form. You can nevertheless make a loaf, but it will be very dense.

1 CHESTNUT FLOUR

Made by grinding chestnuts.
Composition: 0 per cent gluten.
Use: non-breadmaking flour; must be mixed with wheat flour (use 5–20 per cent chestnut flour).
Result: tight beige crumb. Sweet, intense taste.

2 CORNFLOUR

Made by grinding corn kernels.
Composition: 0 per cent gluten, grainy texture.
Use: non-breadmaking flour; must be mixed with wheat flour (use 5–20 per cent cornflour).
Result: very yellow crumb. Sweet taste.

3 BUCKWHEAT FLOUR

Produced by crushing buckwheat seeds, a grey cereal originally from north-east Asia.
Composition: 0 per cent gluten.
Use: non-breadmaking flour; must be mixed with wheat flour (use 5–20 per cent buckwheat flour).
Result: grey crumb, tight. Slightly acidic taste.

4 RICE FLOUR

Produced by crushing rice grains.
Composition: 0 per cent gluten, rich in starch.
Use: non-breadmaking flour; must be mixed with wheat flour (use 5–10 per cent rice flour).
Result: grainy crumb. Slightly sweet taste.

FRESH
BAKER'S YEAST

Understand

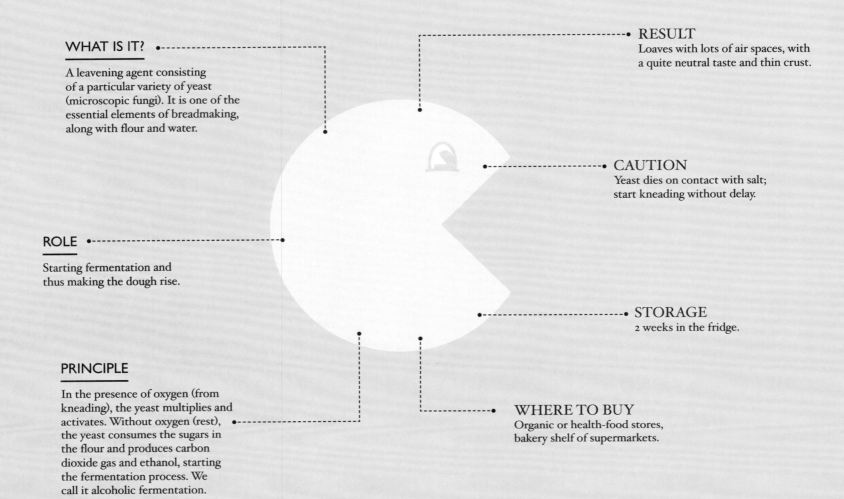

WHAT IS IT?

A leavening agent consisting of a particular variety of yeast (microscopic fungi). It is one of the essential elements of breadmaking, along with flour and water.

ROLE

Starting fermentation and thus making the dough rise.

PRINCIPLE

In the presence of oxygen (from kneading), the yeast multiplies and activates. Without oxygen (rest), the yeast consumes the sugars in the flour and produces carbon dioxide gas and ethanol, starting the fermentation process. We call it alcoholic fermentation.

RESULT

Loaves with lots of air spaces, with a quite neutral taste and thin crust.

CAUTION

Yeast dies on contact with salt; start kneading without delay.

STORAGE

2 weeks in the fridge.

WHERE TO BUY

Organic or health-food stores, bakery shelf of supermarkets.

WHY USE BAKER'S YEAST RATHER THAN SOURDOUGH?

Baker's yeast produces more rapid and more even fermentation. It can be used immediately. Being formed into a small cube prevents oxidation. It crumbles easily.

CAN YOU USE DRIED YEAST INSTEAD?

Dried yeast has the same composition as fresh baker's yeast, but has been dehydrated to make a powder and is sold in sachets or containers. It is more complicated to get the amount right; it is more concentrated, which means you need to add less than fresh yeast to the same weight of flour. It keeps better than fresh yeast.

SOURDOUGH STARTER

Understand

WHAT IS IT?

Natural living leavening agent obtained by culturing wild yeast and lactobacteria, starting with an equal mixture of warm water and flour. It is one of the essential ingredients of breadmaking, with flour and water.

ROLE

Starting fermentation and thus making the dough rise.

PRINCIPLE

The natural wild yeasts and bacteria that occur in this mixture consume the sugars in the flour and start the fermentation process of the whole mixture. This creates the 'sourdough starter'. Then, to avoid too great an acidity, we refresh the starter regularly by adding fresh water and flour. After a few days (or weeks) of refreshing and resting in a warm place, the sourdough is ready.

RESULT

Dense crumb, with a rustic taste and a thick crust.

TWO TYPES OF SOURDOUGH

Liquid starter: refreshed with more water. It promotes lactic fermentation by the bacteria. Firm starter: refreshed with more flour. It promotes acetic fermentation by the yeast.

WHICH TO CHOOSE: LIQUID OR FIRM STARTER?

Taste: gentle, lactic with a liquid starter; pronounced, acetic with a firm starter. Crust: crunchy with a liquid starter; crunchy and thick with a firm starter. Crumb: honeycombed with a liquid starter; dense with a firm starter (because the acidity, which has a tendency to tighten the crumb, plays a bigger role). Storage: longer with a firm starter.

WHY USE SOURDOUGH RATHER THAN BAKER'S YEAST?

The sourdough yields a more rustic bread with a more acidic taste. It is richer in nutrients. Bread made with it will keep for longer.

WHY IS THE RESULTANT DOUGH ACIDIC?

The particular composition of sourdough (bacteria plus wild yeast) promotes acidic fermentation, which lends the dough a certain acidity.

...AND DRIED YEAST?

It is sold powdered in sachets or containers. It is less effective than natural sourdough. It creates less acidity and thus less flavour. In contrast, it is more practical and keeps better.

MAKING A LIQUID
SOURDOUGH STARTER

Understand

WATER

FLOUR

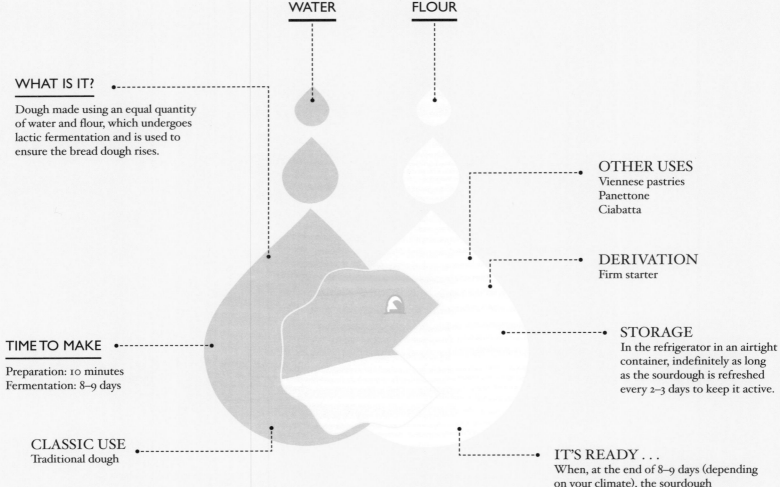

WHAT IS IT?
Dough made using an equal quantity of water and flour, which undergoes lactic fermentation and is used to ensure the bread dough rises.

OTHER USES
Viennese pastries
Panettone
Ciabatta

DERIVATION
Firm starter

TIME TO MAKE
Preparation: 10 minutes
Fermentation: 8–9 days

STORAGE
In the refrigerator in an airtight container, indefinitely as long as the sourdough is refreshed every 2–3 days to keep it active.

CLASSIC USE
Traditional dough

IT'S READY . . .
When, at the end of 8–9 days (depending on your climate), the sourdough doubles in volume in 8 hours: we call this the 'sourdough starter'. Appearance: like a beige–cream yoghurt.

ADVANTAGES OVER FRESH BAKER'S YEAST
Slightly acidic taste
Larger palette of aromas and tastes
Crunchier crust
Longer storage

WHY MUST THE SOURDOUGH BE 'REFRESHED'?
During fermentation, the yeasts and bacteria consume the sugars in the flour. Once all the sugar has been consumed, fermentation stops. If the starter hasn't been fed with enough sugar, it will be too acidic and the bread will be sour.

WHY ADD HONEY?
To accelerate the proliferation of the microorganisms and to make the dough rise faster.

WHY MUST IT BE RESTED IN A WARM PLACE?
So the microorganisms can grow and multiply sufficiently to 'work' effectively. If this doesn't occur, the starter will be too acidic and the taste of the bread will be too strong.

TRICKY ASPECT
Storage. If the dough is refreshed too often and the temperature of the resting place isn't high enough, the sourdough will ferment less, the dough will rise less, and the bread will be less acidic and less rich in aromas and flavours. In contrast, if the sourdough is fermented for too long between refreshing or the temperature of the resting place is too high, the sourdough will be too acidic and the taste of the bread too aggressive.

TIP
The sourdough must be given enough time to become active. It is better to wait longer than not long enough.

MAKES 300 G

TO BEGIN (FIRST STAGE)

100 g organic T65 flour
100 g water at 50°C
10 g organic honey

TO REFRESH (EVERY 36 OR 48 HOURS)

100 g water
100 g organic T65 strong flour

DAY 1

Mix the flour, warm water and honey in a round-bottomed bowl. Transfer the mixture to an airtight container and leave to rest in a warm place (at least 25°C: on top of the refrigerator or over a central-heating radiator, for example) for 48 hours.

DAY 3

When small bubbles have formed, remove 100 g of the mixture to a round-bottomed bowl and discard the rest. Refresh the dough by adding 100 g water and 100 g flour. Mix with a wooden spoon. Transfer to the airtight container and leave in a warm place for about 36 hours.

DAY 5

Repeat the previous step. Again leave to rest for about 36 hours in a warm place.

DAY 6 OR 7

Repeat the refreshment step one last time. Again leave to rest for about 36 hours in a warm place.

The starter will be ready to use at the end of 8 or 9 days. (Note that in some climates, where warm places are hard to find or are everywhere, the sourdough may mature more slowly or more quickly.)

MAKING A FIRM
SOURDOUGH STARTER

Understand

WATER   FLOUR

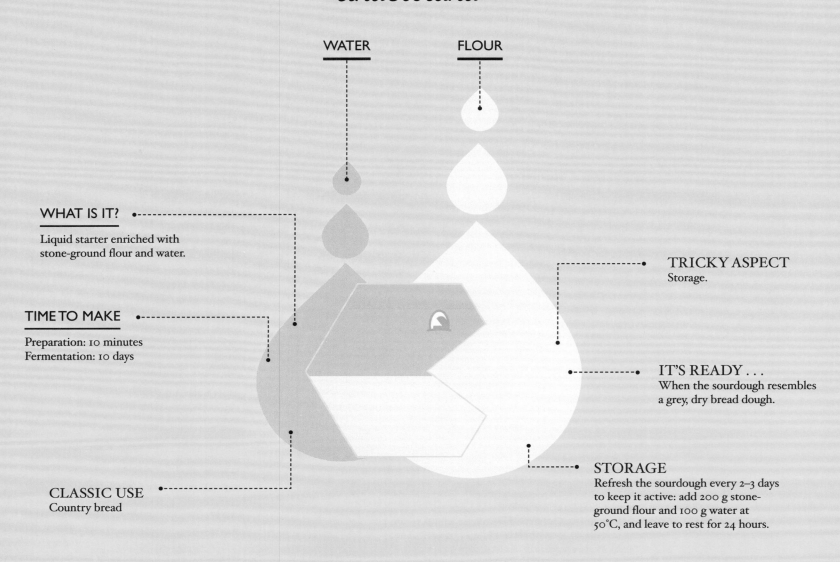

WHAT IS IT?

Liquid starter enriched with
stone-ground flour and water.

TIME TO MAKE

Preparation: 10 minutes
Fermentation: 10 days

CLASSIC USE
Country bread

TRICKY ASPECT
Storage.

IT'S READY . . .
When the sourdough resembles
a grey, dry bread dough.

STORAGE
Refresh the sourdough every 2–3 days
to keep it active: add 200 g stone-
ground flour and 100 g water at
50°C, and leave to rest for 24 hours.

**WHY USE A FIRM STARTER RATHER
THAN A LIQUID STARTER?**

*Thick and crunchy crust.
Strong and pronounced flavour.
Longer storage.*

WHAT MAKES THEM DIFFERENT?

*A firm starter gives a thicker crust
and a tighter crumb because the
dough is denser, and a stronger
taste because it is more acidic.*

MAKES 400 G

TO BEGIN (FIRST STAGE)

100 g organic T65 strong flour
100 g water at 50°C
10 g organic honey

TO REFRESH (EVERY
36 OR 48 HOURS)

100 g water
100 g organic T65 strong flour

DAY I

Mix the flour, warm water and honey in a round-bottomed bowl. Transfer the mixture to an airtight container and leave to rest in a warm place (at least 25°C: on top of the refrigerator or over a central-heating radiator, for example) for 48 hours.

DAY 3

When small bubbles have formed, remove 100 g of the mixture to a round-bottomed bowl and discard the rest. Add 100 g water and 100 g flour, then mix with a wooden spoon. Cover with plastic wrap, with the plastic touching the surface of the mixture, and leave to rest in a warm place for 36 hours.

DAY 5

Repeat the previous step. Again leave to rest for about 36 hours in a warm place.

DAY 6 OR 7

Repeat the refreshment step one last time. Again leave to rest for about 36 hours in a warm place.

TO TRANSFORM LIQUID STARTER INTO FIRM STARTER

200 g stone-ground T80 semi-wholemeal or T110 light wholemeal flour

50 g water at 50°C

DAY 8 OR 9

Remove 100 g of liquid starter (starter culture), and place it in the bowl of an electric mixer with the dough hook attached. Add the stone-ground flour and the warm water, and knead for 5 minutes at the lowest speed. Transfer the dough to an airtight container and leave to rest in the refrigerator for 24 hours before using.

POOLISH STARTER

Understand

WHAT IS IT

Mixture of equal quantities of flour and water, enlivened with fresh baker's yeast. A kind of 'express' sourdough (10 hours rather than 8 days).

RESULT

Gives a more pronounced, interesting flavour than straight baker's yeast, but is less acidic than sourdough. The crumb is rough (as with sourdough) and the crust is thin (as with baker's yeast).

TIME TO MAKE

Preparation: 5 minutes
Fermentation: 10 hours

ROLE

Like sourdough and yeast, it is a leavening agent. It ensures fermentation and that the dough will rise.

CLASSIC USES

White bread
Viennese pastry (helps the base dough rise during cooking)

ADVANTAGES OVER SOURDOUGH

Easy to get going.
No need to produce a starter culture.
It can be made only several hours before kneading.

ADVANTAGES OVER FRESH BAKER'S YEAST

The dough is tastier. Because the fermentation time is longer, the flavours have more time to develop.
It relaxes the gluten and improves the flexibility of the dough.
It keeps better.

TRICKY ASPECT

Using the poolish when it is mature: at the very moment it sinks again (it will sag in the middle); too early and the dough will be insufficiently fermented and will lack taste; too late and it will be acidic.

TIP

Use warm water to accelerate fermentation.

TO MAKE 200 G

pinch of fresh baker's yeast
100 g warm water
100 g T65 baker's flour

1 Dissolve the crumbled yeast in the water.

2 Pour in the flour and whisk to obtain a smooth mixture.

3 Cover with plastic wrap or a clean tea towel.

4 Leave to rest at room temperature for about 10 hours.

5 Mix the poolish with the other ingredients at the beginning of kneading.

WATER

Understand

WHAT IS IT?

Indispensable ingredient, with flour and leavening agents, for making bread.

A GOOD TEMPERATURE

The temperature of the water is the main parameter we can control to obtain a dough with the right temperature (23–24°C).

ROLES

Hydrating flour (to form a dough): use 600–700 g water for each 1 kg flour. Dissolving salt and yeast. Assisting in the formation of the gluten network. Making gluten supple, to give the dough its characteristic elasticity. Creating the indispensable humid environment the yeasts need to be active.

WHY IS THE TEMPERATURE OF THE DOUGH SO IMPORTANT?

Because the yeasts in the dough require a particular temperature (23–24°C) to be active enough to transform the sugars into carbon dioxide. If the dough is too warm or too cold, the fermentation won't be optimal. The bread won't be 'good'.

HOW DO WE WORK OUT THE BEST WATER TEMPERATURE?

The base temperature (T°) must be 55–65°C.
base T° = water T° + room T° + flour T°
The temperatures of the room and the flour are generally the same. Simply add them together, then do the following subtraction:
base T° – (T° flour + T° room) = T° water

WHAT HAPPENS IF THE WATER IS TOO COLD?

The base temperature will be too low. As a result, fermentation won't be optimal. The dough will be weaker, the crumb less developed and the crust irregular.

WHAT HAPPENS IF THE WATER IS TOO HOT?

The base temperature will be too high. As a result, the dough will be too strong and sticky, the texture of the bread will be grainier and the crust dull.

WHAT IS THE RATE OF HYDRATION?

This is the quantity of water incorporated into the flour during kneading to form the dough. For 100 g flour, it should be 55–75 g water. It influences the moistness of the crumb and affects the crust: the less water the dough contains, the faster the surface dries out during cooking. The crust thus has more time to form and will be thicker.

SALT

Understand

WHAT IS IT?

Last indispensable ingredient,
with flour, leavening agents
and water, for making bread.

WHICH TO USE

Table salt or sea salt.
Proportion: 9–10 g salt
per 500 g flour.

ROLES IN THE DOUGH

Tightening the dough: it creates bonds
between the proteins, which ensures
better stability in the gluten.
Regulating fermentation: it limits the
activity of the leavening agent; without
salt, a dough ferments much faster.

ROLES IN THE COOKED BREAD

Enhancing taste.
Contributing to the
colouration of the crust.
Retaining a moist crumb, thanks to its
hygroscopic properties: it helps keep the
crumb soft during and after cooking.

CAUTIONS

Yeast dies on contact with salt;
start kneading without delay.

WHY DOES YEAST DIE ON CONTACT WITH SALT?

*Because the salt absorbs the water in the yeast cells, causing them
to dehydrate. This renders them inactive, or even kills them.*

FATS AND OILS
MILK

Understand

FATS AND OILS

WHAT ARE THEY?

Fatty acids of animal or plant origin.

ROLES

Fat diminishes the formation of the gluten network, which impacts the crust and the crumb: silky and melt-in-the-mouth crumb, thin crust.

USES

Viennese pastries
Brioches
Italian breads

TIPS

Use butter and margarine at room temperature to make them easier to incorporate.

TOURAGE OR DRY BUTTER

Butter richer in fat and thus lower in water content than classic butter, used for making puff pastry and croissants. Advantages: it is easier to work with because as it contains less water it melts faster. It doesn't 'mix' into the surrounding dough during cooking, which makes it easier to retain the different layers of the pastry.

OILS

Vegetable fats that provide greater hydration than an equal quantity of butter, and that make a dough less heavy. Used most often for salted baked goods.

MILK

WHAT IS IT?

If it is used in this book without any other qualification, it indicates full-fat cow's milk. It is 87 per cent water and 4 per cent fat.

ROLES

Contributing to the hydration of the dough due to its high water content. Adding moistness thanks to its fat content. Influencing the colour and taste of baked goods.

CLASSIC USES

Vienna dough
Viennese pastries
Brioches

PLANT-BASED MILKS

They can be substituted for cow's milk in the same quantities.
For a neutral taste: soy, rice or oat milk.
For a more distinctive taste: hazelnut, almond or spelt milk.

SUGAR
EGGS

Understand

SUGAR

WHAT IS IT?

Product extracted from
sugar cane or sugar beet.

ROLES

Giving good mechanical and physical
tolerance to doughs: the sugar
diminishes the formation of the
gluten network; doughs containing
sugar are easier to work.
Improving fermentation: sugar
is fermentable, i.e. directly
absorbed by yeast.
Adding to the aromas,
improving the taste.
Promoting colouration during
cooking, thanks to the Maillard
reactions (see page 285).

WHICH TO USE

Caster sugar: the sugar
most used in baking.
Icing sugar: sugar ground very
finely into a completely smooth
powder, used for pâtisserie
because it mixes in more easily.

EGGS

WHAT ARE THEY?

In baking, only chicken eggs are used.
1 medium egg = 50 g
32 g white: rich in water
18 g yolk: rich in proteins

ROLES

Colouring doughs.
Glazing before cooking.
Drawing out flavours, along
with sugar and fat.
Great at binding.
Allowing greater aeration of doughs.

CLASSIC USES

Brioches
Glazing
Pâtisserie

WHY DO EGGS PROMOTE
HONEYCOMBING IN DOUGHS?

*The proteins in eggs have surfactant
properties that promote the incorporation
of air in doughs. In fact, they can bind
water and air at the same time.*

KNEADING
BY HAND

Understand

WHAT IS IT?

Mixing all the dough ingredients together by hand.

TRICKY ASPECTS

Keeping the dough at the right temperature (23–24°C).
Kneading for long enough: the gluten must be well stretched and the dough elastic, or the gas could escape and the dough won't rise.

ROLES

Activating and promoting the growth of the yeast thanks to incorporation of air in the dough. We call this the 'aerobic' phase. Developing the gluten network in the dough: the movement of kneading promotes the formation of bonds between the gluten proteins. These bonds are what allows the gluten network to form. The dough thus develops 'strength' and is ready for the fermentation phase.

TIP

Pull on a small piece of the dough at the end of kneading; the dough is ready if it doesn't tear (the gluten resists).

TIME TO MAKE

15 minutes

EQUIPMENT

Thermometer

IT'S READY . . .

When the dough is smooth, elastic and no longer sticky.

WHAT HAPPENS WHEN WE KNEAD FOR TOO LONG?

The bonds between the proteins start to break: the dough weakens and becomes sticky.

WHAT HAPPENS WHEN WE DON'T KNEAD FOR LONG ENOUGH?

The gluten network won't be strong enough to hold the gas during fermentation and cooking. The bread won't rise as much.

WHY MUST THE DOUGH BE AT 23–24°C?

The cells in the yeast are living organisms. They consume the sugars in the flour to produce carbon dioxide during fermentation. They do this best at 23–24°C.

Learn

INGREDIENTS

salt
leavening agent
water
flour

1 Dissolve the salt and the leavening agent in the water in a round-bottomed bowl.

2 Mound the flour on a clean work surface and make a well in the centre. Pour the water mixture into the well and gradually incorporate the flour. This mixing stage is called 'frasage'.

3 Make a rough rectangle with all the dough. Cut off a quarter, starting from the left-hand side.

4 Stick the dough piece back on at the right-hand side of the main dough rectangle. Do this several times for about 3 minutes. The aim is to stretch the gluten and make the dough elastic. These stages are called 'découpage' (cutting) and 'passage en tête' (bringing to the head).

5 Remove a large piece of the dough and throw it violently against the work surface. Fold the dough on itself to trap as much air in the middle as possible. These stages are called 'étirage' (drawing out) and 'soufflage' (blowing into).

6 Using a thermometer, check that the temperature of the dough is at 23–24°C.

31

MECHANICAL KNEADING

Understand

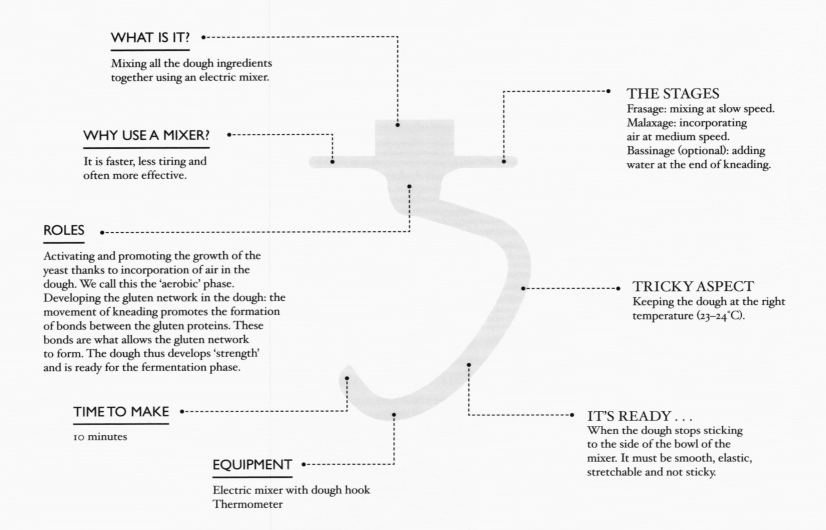

WHAT IS IT?

Mixing all the dough ingredients together using an electric mixer.

WHY USE A MIXER?

It is faster, less tiring and often more effective.

ROLES

Activating and promoting the growth of the yeast thanks to incorporation of air in the dough. We call this the 'aerobic' phase. Developing the gluten network in the dough: the movement of kneading promotes the formation of bonds between the gluten proteins. These bonds are what allows the gluten network to form. The dough thus develops 'strength' and is ready for the fermentation phase.

TIME TO MAKE

10 minutes

EQUIPMENT

Electric mixer with dough hook
Thermometer

THE STAGES

Frasage: mixing at slow speed.
Malaxage: incorporating air at medium speed.
Bassinage (optional): adding water at the end of kneading.

TRICKY ASPECT

Keeping the dough at the right temperature (23–24°C).

IT'S READY...

When the dough stops sticking to the side of the bowl of the mixer. It must be smooth, elastic, stretchable and not sticky.

DO YOU GET THE SAME RESULT BY HAND AND WITH A MIXER?

During kneading, the dough is subjected to forces of stretching and compression. These forces are greater with mechanical kneading. We obtain a more elastic dough that bears the rising phase of fermentation better because the gluten network is better developed.

WHY IS THE LENGTH OF THE KNEADING TIME IMPORTANT?

It must be adapted according to the desired result. A short kneading time allows preservation of the flour flavours but not the optimal development of the gluten network – however, this is counterbalanced by a long pointage (bulk fermentation), with a rabat (folding) that strengthens the dough. This is done for large loaves, when aiming for a particular flavour. A long kneading time gives the dough lots of strength but it loses taste. The pointage is short because the dough doesn't need to regain its strength. This is the case with baguettes, where the aim is a neutral taste and lots of honeycombing.

WHAT IS 'BASSINAGE'?

This is extra water incorporated at the end of kneading to soften an overly firm dough. It allows a thinner crust to form (the more water in a dough, the slower it dries out and the less time the crust has to form) and a more risen bread.

WHY KNEAD AT LOW THEN MEDIUM SPEED?

The first kneading allows the ingredients to mix: it must be slow to give a smooth dough. The second kneading promotes development of the gluten network and incorporates air. This is possible at medium speed.

INGREDIENTS

flour
water
leavening agent
salt

1   Put all the ingredients in the bowl of
an electric mixer and using the dough hook
attachment mix them well at the lowest speed for
4 minutes. This mixing stage is called 'frasage'.

2   Increase the speed of the mixer to medium and
continue to knead until the dough is smooth and pulls
away from the side of the bowl, about 6 minutes. This
massaging and softening stage is called 'malaxage'.

3   Using a thermometer, check that the
temperature of the dough is at 23–24°C.

FERMENTATION

Understand

WHAT IS IT?

Transformation of the sugars in the flour into carbon dioxide and ethanol through the action of the microorganisms in the leavening agent (baker's yeast or sourdough). The release of the gas makes the dough swell up.

FERMENTATION TEMPERATURE

The dough must be at a temperature of 23–24˚C for the microorganisms in the leavening agent to develop. It's also the temperature at which the flavours can develop optimally.

ROLES

Allowing optimal rising of the dough.
Providing the bread with flavours and aromas.

WHICH LEAVENING AGENT FOR WHICH TYPE OF FERMENTATION?

– *Fermentation with baker's yeast: the rising stage is important and rapid because the yeast produces lots of carbon dioxide. It also produces ethanol (which evaporates). We call this alcoholic fermentation. The crumb is airy, the taste neutral.*
– *Fermentation with liquid sourdough starter: the rising stage is slow and difficult (often assisted by the addition of baker's yeast), and requires heat and humidity. We call this lactic fermentation (it produces acid). It creates more flavours.*
– *Fermentation with firm sourdough starter: the rising stage is even longer, and occurs in the refrigerator. We call this acetic fermentation. The taste is rustic and sour.*

Learn

1 KNEADING

Activation of leavening agents in the presence of oxygen.

2 POINTAGE (BULK FERMENTATION)

Anaerobic phase: in the absence of oxygen, the microorganisms consume the sugars in the flour and produce carbon dioxide. The release of gas causes the first rise.

3 RABAT (FOLDING)

Reactivation of the leavening agents during pointage, by incorporating more air (oxygen) into the dough.

4 POINTAGE (FINAL STAGE)

Anaerobic phase: having consumed all the oxygen, the microorganisms start consuming sugars again. The dough continues to rise.

5 PRE-SHAPING

Pre-cutting the dough with a view to forming the desired bread shape, in which the dough will finish rising in situ.

6 REST

Necessary phase before shaping so that the dough is relaxed enough not to tear.

7 SHAPING

Forming the dough into a shape, such as a ball or loaf.

8 FINAL PROOF

Second rise – same process as during pointage, but the bread is in its final form.

FERMENTATION
POINTAGE

Understand

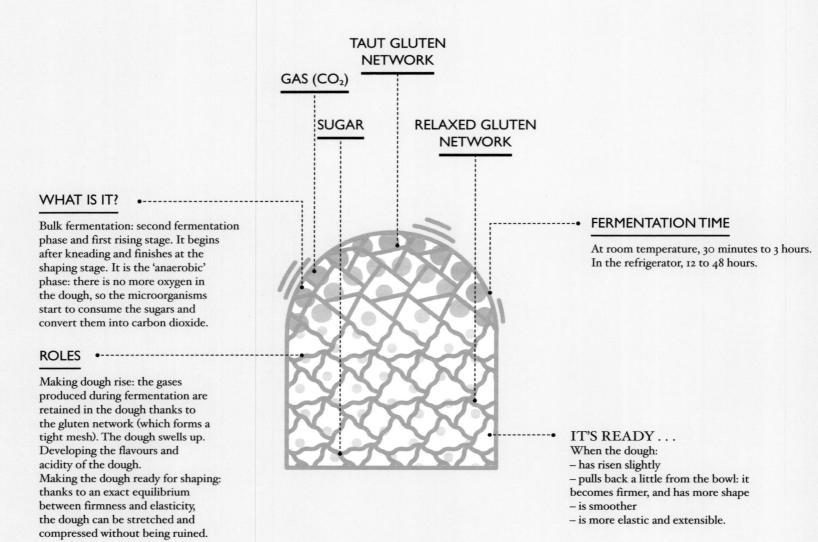

GAS (CO$_2$)

TAUT GLUTEN NETWORK

SUGAR

RELAXED GLUTEN NETWORK

WHAT IS IT?

Bulk fermentation: second fermentation phase and first rising stage. It begins after kneading and finishes at the shaping stage. It is the 'anaerobic' phase: there is no more oxygen in the dough, so the microorganisms start to consume the sugars and convert them into carbon dioxide.

ROLES

Making dough rise: the gases produced during fermentation are retained in the dough thanks to the gluten network (which forms a tight mesh). The dough swells up. Developing the flavours and acidity of the dough.
Making the dough ready for shaping: thanks to an exact equilibrium between firmness and elasticity, the dough can be stretched and compressed without being ruined.

FERMENTATION TIME

At room temperature, 30 minutes to 3 hours. In the refrigerator, 12 to 48 hours.

IT'S READY . . .
When the dough:
– has risen slightly
– pulls back a little from the bowl: it becomes firmer, and has more shape
– is smoother
– is more elastic and extensible.

WHY DO POINTAGE IN THE REFRIGERATOR IN SOME CASES?

To develop the flavours: fermentation is slower, more qualitative, and the leavening agents have time to grow to full size.
To develop the gluten network: the cold tightens the 'mesh' of the network.
To increase the rate of hydration of the bread to achieve better honeycombing and a thinner crust. The cold will allow the dough to tighten and to hold its shape better during cooking.
To be less dependent on the rising of the bread: there's more flexibility regarding when to put it in the oven.

WHY DOES THE POINTAGE TIME VARY FROM DOUGH TO DOUGH?

This depends on the rate of hydration and the quantity of fermenting microorganisms in the dough.
The fewer fermenting organisms there are, the longer the pointage stage will be (because there are few of them they take more time to consume the sugars; the dough thus takes longer to rise). Likewise, if the dough contains lots of water, it will be weaker. A long pointage phase gives it time to strengthen.

CONDITIONS FOR DOUGH FERMENTATION
Directly in the bowl of an electric mixer. Covered with plastic wrap or a clean tea towel, protected from the air (to avoid a crust developing on the dough and disruption of fermentation).
At room temperature.

FERMENTATION
RABAT (FOLDING)

Understand

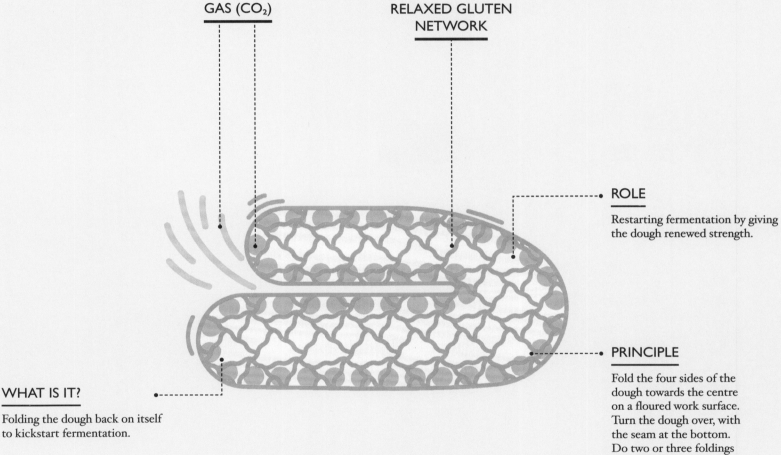

GAS (CO₂)

RELAXED GLUTEN NETWORK

ROLE

Restarting fermentation by giving the dough renewed strength.

PRINCIPLE

Fold the four sides of the dough towards the centre on a floured work surface. Turn the dough over, with the seam at the bottom. Do two or three foldings during pointage.

WHAT IS IT?

Folding the dough back on itself to kickstart fermentation.

HOW DOES FOLDING GET FERMENTATION GOING AGAIN?

During pointage, the activity of the leavening agents gradually slows down. Folding the dough will:
– remove excess carbon dioxide, which will bring the microorganisms closer together and make them multiply (by division); this will restart the fermenting activity
– tighten the gluten network: the dough is very loose, so folding will make it more elastic and give it better form (firmness). The dough regains its strength and pointage can restart.

FERMENTATION
RELAXATION

Understand

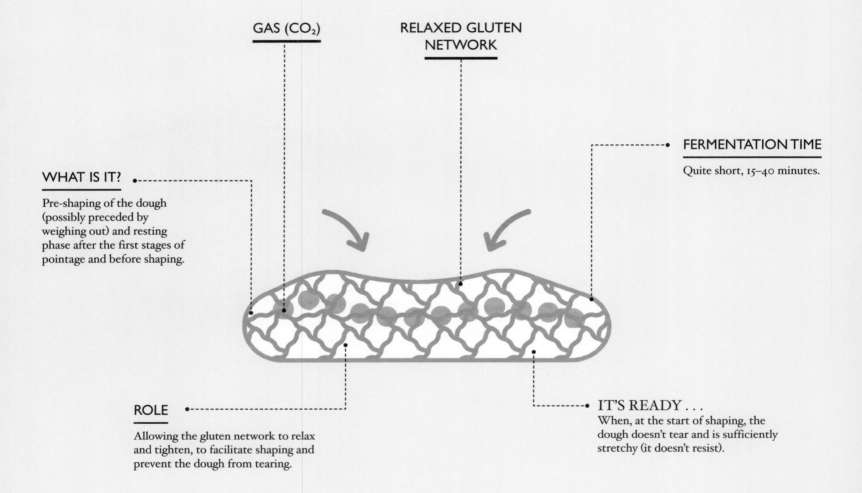

GAS (CO$_2$)

RELAXED GLUTEN NETWORK

FERMENTATION TIME
Quite short, 15–40 minutes.

WHAT IS IT?
Pre-shaping of the dough (possibly preceded by weighing out) and resting phase after the first stages of pointage and before shaping.

ROLE
Allowing the gluten network to relax and tighten, to facilitate shaping and prevent the dough from tearing.

IT'S READY . . .
When, at the start of shaping, the dough doesn't tear and is sufficiently stretchy (it doesn't resist).

PRE-SHAPING INTO A BALL
For round or slightly elongated loaves, the dough must be formed into a ball after pointage, to relax it. Bring the edges of the dough towards the centre. Turn the ball over. Pinch the dough under the ball with your hands, to tighten the top.

PRE-SHAPING INTO A LOG
For baguettes, French sticks or wheat-stalk bread, the dough must be formed into an elongated shape after pointage, to relax it. Make a ball with the dough, then gently roll it on a floured work surface under the palm of your hand to elongate it.

WHY IS IT IMPERATIVE NOT TO TEAR THE DOUGH?
If the dough is torn, the gas escapes, and the dough won't rise any more. The bread will be dense.

CONDITIONS FOR RELAXING
Seam side down, under a clean tea towel on a floured work surface, or in a round-bottomed bowl covered with plastic wrap. At room temperature.

FERMENTATION
FINAL PROOF

Understand

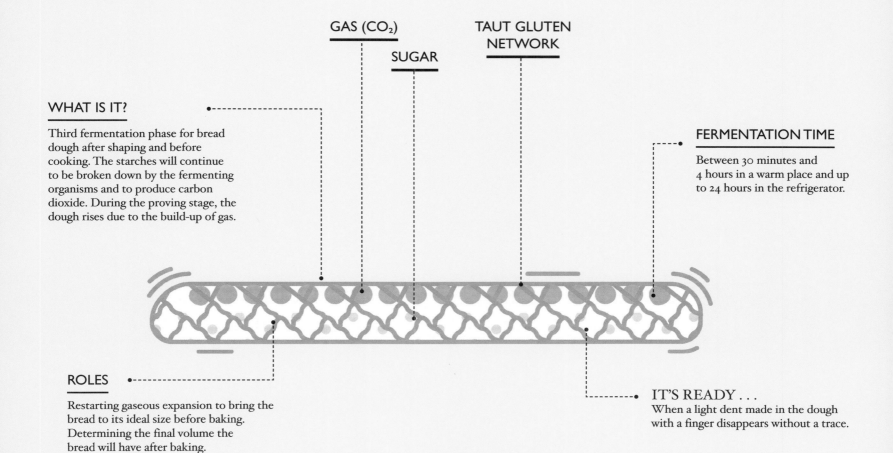

GAS (CO$_2$)

SUGAR

TAUT GLUTEN NETWORK

WHAT IS IT?

Third fermentation phase for bread dough after shaping and before cooking. The starches will continue to be broken down by the fermenting organisms and to produce carbon dioxide. During the proving stage, the dough rises due to the build-up of gas.

FERMENTATION TIME

Between 30 minutes and 4 hours in a warm place and up to 24 hours in the refrigerator.

ROLES

Restarting gaseous expansion to bring the bread to its ideal size before baking. Determining the final volume the bread will have after baking.

IT'S READY . . .
When a light dent made in the dough with a finger disappears without a trace.

WHY MUST PROVING HAPPEN IN A WARM PLACE?

During proving, part of the starch is broken down into simple sugars. These are then converted into ethanol and carbon dioxide by the enzymes of the fermenting microorganisms. For proving to be successful – and thus for the enzymes to work well – it must occur in a warm place, 25–28°C.

CONDITIONS FOR FERMENTATION

In a warm place (25–28°C) – on top of the refrigerator or over a central-heating radiator, for example. Cover with a clean tea towel to prevent a crust forming on the dough.

SHAPING

Understand

WHAT IS IT?

Manipulation of the dough
before cooking to give it its
final form. It follows pointage
and precedes proving.

TRICKY POINTS

Manipulating the dough without
crushing it or tearing it.
Making a neat shape.
Compressing the dough: adapt
the type of compression (more
or less accentuated) depending
on the consistency of the dough:
soft dough, strong compression;
firm dough, weak compression.

TIME TO ACHIEVE

Between 5 and 15 minutes,
depending on the difficulty
of the shape.

WHAT IS THE SEAM (OR KEY)?

*This is the place where the two edges of the dough come together during
shaping. In the fermentation stage, it is put underneath.*
*For baking, the seam is also on the bottom, except if we want it to burst
open during cooking; in this case it takes the place of slashing.*

Shaping consists of three basic stages (only two for balls of dough). For both types of shaping, both flattening and folding must be carried out. For elongated breads (baguettes, torpedo loaves, wheat-stalk bread), move on to elongation. For particular shaping methods, see pages 42–47.

1 FLATTENING

Once pre-shaping and resting are complete, turn the dough over, seam side up, and flatten gently to create a uniform surface and remove excess gas.

2 FOLDING

Bring the edges of the dough towards the centre in successive folds, while maintaining the shape and the integrity of the dough (the surface of the dough must be stretched for it to develop well during cooking). In this way we create the seam.

3 ELONGATION (EXCEPT FOR BALLS)

Create the desired length of dough by rolling the dough under the palms of your hands, from the middle to the edges.

Shaping into a ball

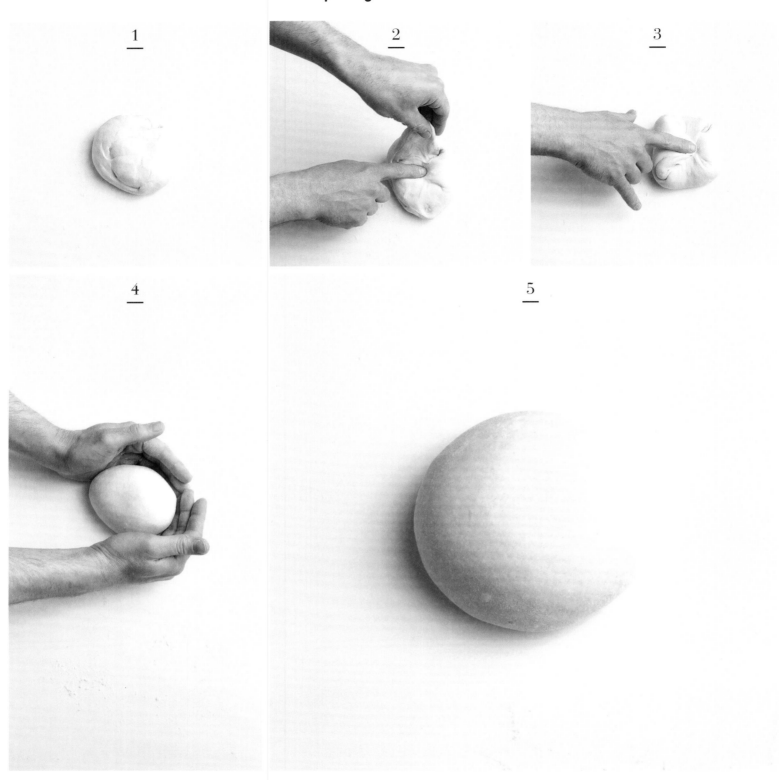

1   Place the dough, seam side down, on a lightly floured work surface.

2   Put your right index finger (left if you are left-handed) in the centre of the dough without pressing too hard. With your other hand, pull each side of the dough into the middle.

3   Hold the edges with your right (or left) index finger. Turn the dough ball over.

4   With your hands under the ball, pinch the dough to pull the top taut, then turn the ball a quarter turn.

5   Repeat the last step three times.

Shaping into a baguette

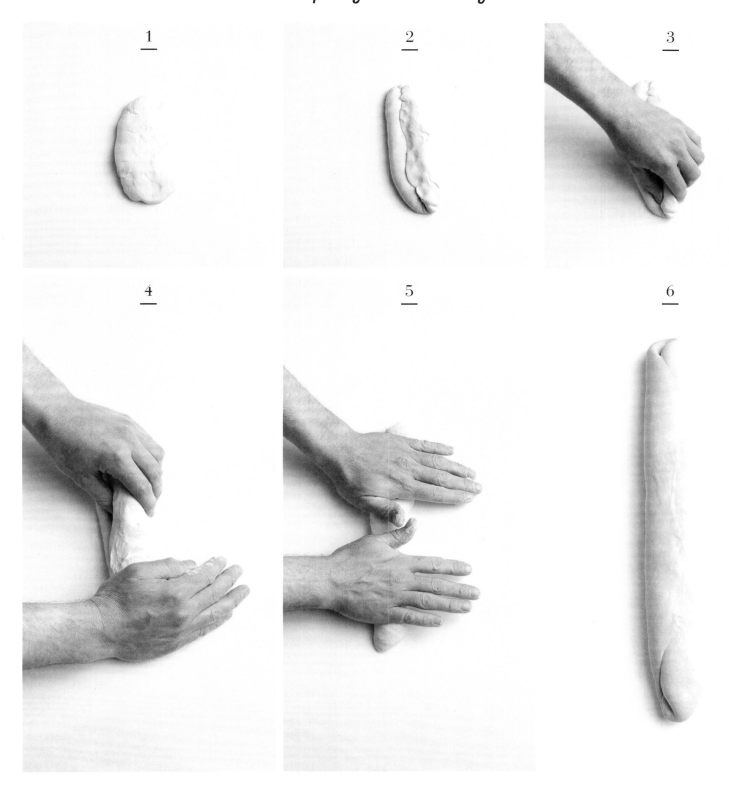

1   Place the dough, seam side up, on a lightly floured work surface. Push it into a rectangular shape.

2   Fold the dough in three lengthways.

3   Rest your left thumb (your right thumb if you are left-handed) at the right-hand (or left-hand) end of the dough and press lightly. Enclose your thumb in the dough using three fingers of the same hand.

4   Push your thumb along the dough and use the palm of your other hand to push the join together as you go.

5   Place both hands in the centre of the baguette. Elongate it by rolling it with two hands, working out towards the ends.

6   Continue to elongate to achieve the desired length.

Shaping into a French stick

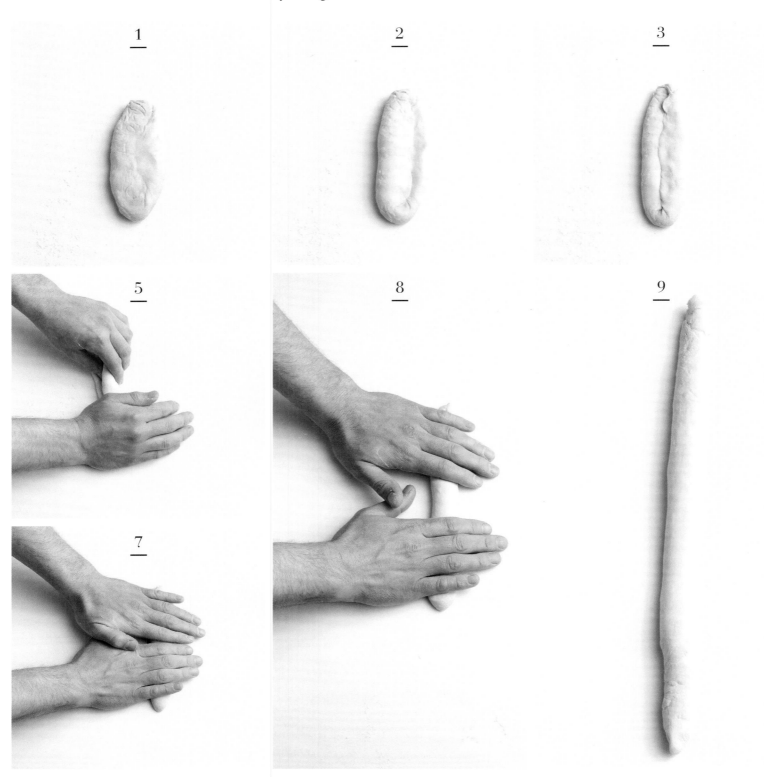

1 Place the dough, seam side up, on a lightly floured work surface. Push it into a rectangular shape.

2 Fold one side of the dough towards the middle.

3 Take the other side of the dough and fold into the middle, overlapping the other folded-in edge.

4 Place your left thumb (your right thumb if you are left-handed) at the right-hand (or left-hand) end of the dough and press lightly.

5 Enclose your thumb in the dough using three fingers of the same hand. Push your thumb along the dough and use your other palm to push the join together as you go.

6 Repeat the whole procedure once more to strengthen the loaf.

7 Place both hands in the middle of the bread stick.

8 Elongate it by rolling with both hands, working from the middle towards the ends.

9 Continue to elongate to achieve the desired length.

Shaping into a torpedo loaf

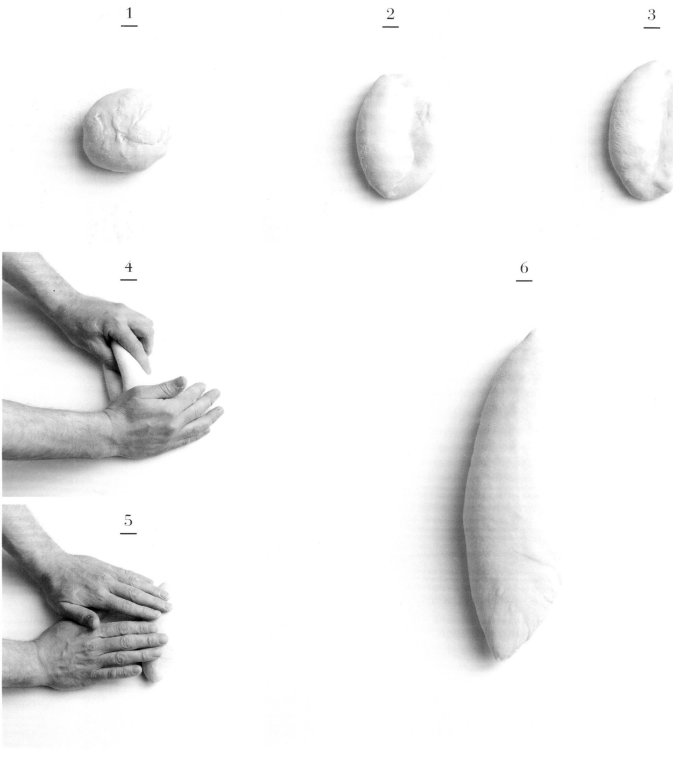

1 Place the dough, pre-formed into a ball, seam side up, on a lightly floured work surface.

2 Take one side of the dough and fold it into the middle.

3 Spin the dough around 180 degrees and repeat the last step.

4 Enclose your thumb in the dough using three fingers of the same hand. Push your thumb along the dough and use your other palm to push the top and bottom together as you go.

5 Place both hands in the middle of the dough and gently elongate the dough by rolling with both hands, working towards the ends.

6 Continue to elongate to achieve the desired length.

Shaping into a crown

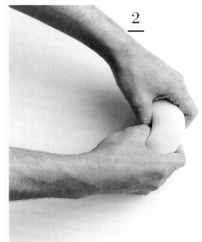

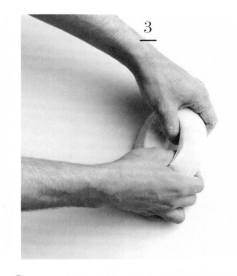

1 Place the dough, pre-formed into a ball, seam side down, on a lightly floured work surface. Lightly flour the centre of the dough, make a hole in the middle with your index finger, until it touches the work surface.

2 Dust your fingers with flour: hold the dough between the thumb and index finger of both hands.

3 With one hand, slide the dough around gently, slowly enlarging the hole in the middle and at the same time reducing the width of the dough ring. When the dough no longer stretches, leave it to rest for 5 minutes.

4 Start the last step again until the hole is 10 cm in diameter.

5 The central hole must be sufficiently large not to close up during proving and cooking.

Shaping into a plait

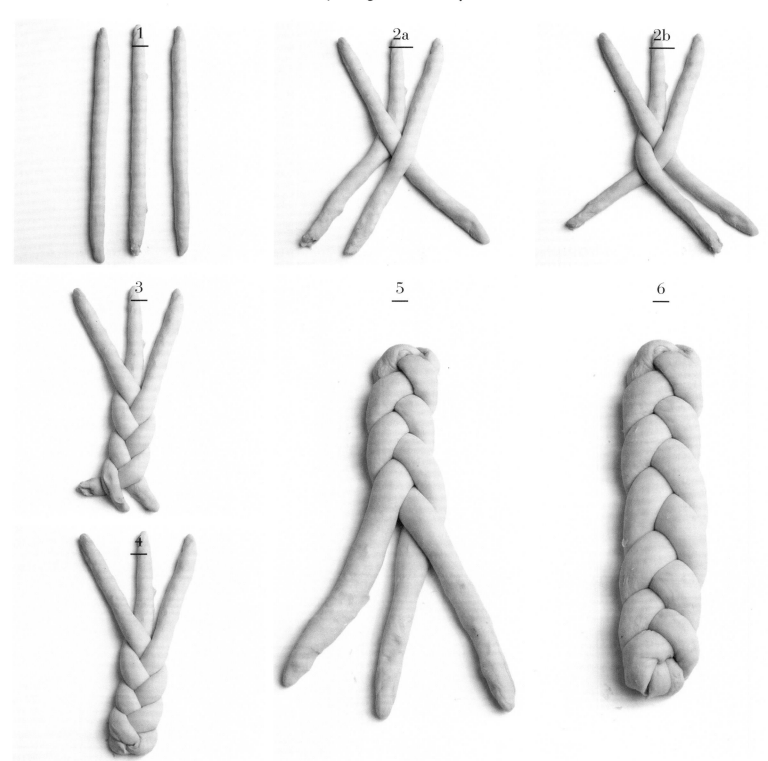

1   Make three sausages of the same length and place them parallel to each other. The left is number 1, the middle is number 2 and the right is number 3.

2   Start to plait in the middle of the three sausages: take strand 2 and put it in the place of strand 1; take strand 1 and put it in the place of 3; and take strand 3 and put it in the place of 2.

3   Repeat the last step until you reach the bottom end.

4   Join the three strands together at the end.

5   Turn the whole thing 180 degrees and complete the plait by placing the sausages under rather than over each other. Don't pull too tightly, to prevent the dough tearing during proving.

6   Join the three strands together at the end.

GLAZING

Understand

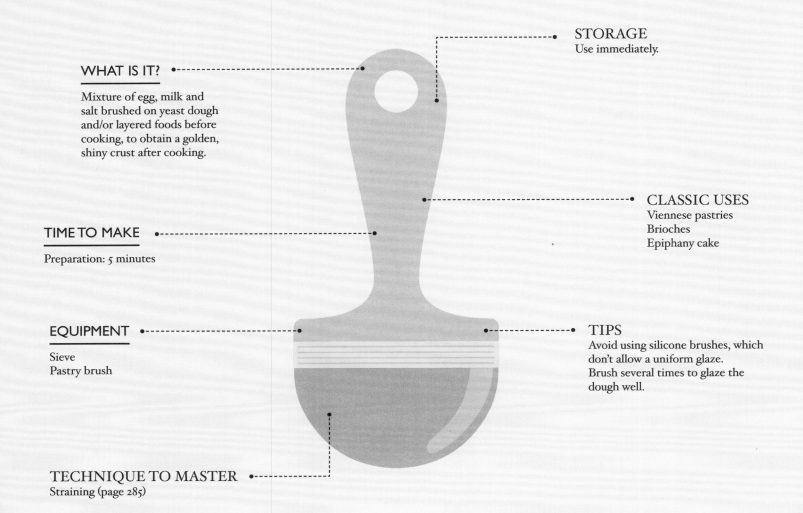

WHAT IS IT?

Mixture of egg, milk and salt brushed on yeast dough and/or layered foods before cooking, to obtain a golden, shiny crust after cooking.

TIME TO MAKE

Preparation: 5 minutes

EQUIPMENT

Sieve
Pastry brush

TECHNIQUE TO MASTER
Straining (page 285)

STORAGE
Use immediately.

CLASSIC USES
Viennese pastries
Brioches
Epiphany cake

TIPS
Avoid using silicone brushes, which don't allow a uniform glaze. Brush several times to glaze the dough well.

WHAT DOES THE GLAZE DO?

It plays an aesthetic role, giving shine and a lovely golden brown colour to the bread. It also provides a slight crunch.

WHY DO WE NEED TO ADD MILK TO THE EGG?

During cooking, the egg proteins and milk sugar react (Maillard reactions; see page 285). This allows the typical glazed colour to develop.

WHY MUST WE GLAZE BEFORE AND AFTER PROVING?

To glaze the areas that appear when the dough rises, and obtain a more even colouration during cooking.

GLAZES 1 BRIOCHE OR 6 CROISSANTS

1 egg
3 g (½ teaspoon) milk
pinch of salt

1 Beat the egg, milk and salt in a bowl with a whisk until smooth.

2 Strain (see page 285) to obtain a fluid mixture.

3 Apply the glaze using a pastry brush, brushing lightly and without pressing too hard, to avoid changing the surface of the dough.

SLASHING

Understand

WHAT IS IT?

Cut/s made in the dough with a
bread lame (razor) before cooking
to form blooms (notches).

TIME TO MAKE

5–10 minutes

EQUIPMENT

Bread lame, (clean) box
cutter or serrated knife.

ROLES

Allowing gas to escape and thus
the bread to develop evenly,
without bursting the crust.
Giving a visual identity
to finished products.

TRICKY ASPECT

Adjusting the cuts with the blade:
cut deeply with a poorly risen dough
and lightly with an over-risen dough.

TIPS

For breads: very lightly dusting the surface
of the dough with flour before slashing
gives a more aesthetically pleasing result.
Traditional slashing: to make a
straight and neat cut, keep an eye
on the other end of the lame.

**WHAT HAPPENS IF THE SLASH IS
TOO DEEP?**

*Sagging and loss of dough volume
during cooking. The blooms are too
thick. The bread goes stale faster.*

**WHAT HAPPENS IF THE SLASH
ISN'T DEEP ENOUGH?**

*Under the pressure of steam, the crust will
burst and deform. The blooms could close up
again, lack volume and look less appealing.*

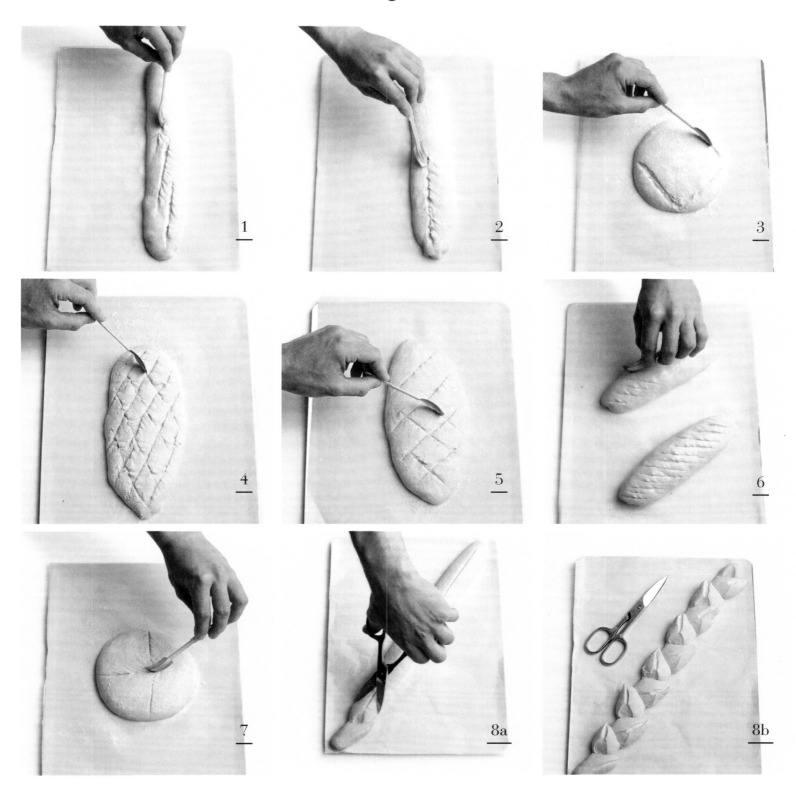

1 BAGUETTE

Hold the lame at a 30-degree angle. Make a diagonal cut 5 cm long. Make an identical cut, starting a third of the way from the end of the last. Cut five to seven times along the baguette.

2 TRADITIONAL

Hold the lame at a 30-degree angle. With a clean, continuous gesture, cut down the centre along the entire length of the dough.

3 DIAMOND

Holding the lame obliquely, cut a diamond shape with the corners touching the edge of the bread.

4 LATTICE (POLKA BREAD)

Make parallel diagonal cuts with the lame, not too deep, spaced 1–2 cm apart. Repeat on the opposite diagonal to make diamonds.

5 LARGE LATTICE

Make four parallel diagonal cuts with the lame. Repeat on the opposite diagonal: make one cut aiming for the start of the second cut. Make three more cuts to form three diamonds.

6 SAUSAGE

Hold the lame as close to the blade as possible. Cut deep oblique parallel lines, very close together.

7 CROSS

Flour the dough. Cut from top to bottom passing through the centre, then from left to right.

8 WHEAT STALK

Hold the lame at a 30-degree angle. Cut along the entire length of the baguette. Using scissors at a 45-degree angle, make parallel cuts across the dough, two-thirds of the way in and 10 cm apart. Push each dough 'piece' to one side then the other, along the baguette. Take care when removing from the oven – the baguette is very fragile.

BAKING

Understand

WHAT IS IT?

Last fermentation stage (the leavening agents die at 50°C). Transformation of the fermented dough into bread by the heat of the oven.

OVEN TEMPERATURE

Small pieces of bread: fast cooking at a high and constant temperature to keep the crumb moist.
Large pieces of bread (more than 400 g raw dough): oven preheated to a high temperature, then reduced when the bread goes in. At the end of cooking, open the oven door for 5–10 minutes to allow the crumb to dry out without burning the crust.

IT'S COOKED . . .
When the crust is very crunchy and slightly shiny, and the crumb is soft.

THE BURST OF STEAM
Creating steam in the oven at the moment you put in the bread.
Leave a bowl of water in the oven during preheating. When putting in the bread, spray the bottom of the oven with water to make as much steam as possible.

NOTE
Some breads, such as rye bread, are better once they have started to go stale.

WHY DOES THE BREAD STOP RISING WHEN IT REACHES 100°C?

Because at this temperature, the starch in the flour gelatinises and thickens the dough, and the gluten network sets. This stops the bread developing any further.

WHAT DOES THE STEAM DO?

It holds back the formation of the crust to give the dough time to finish rising. It gives a thinner and shinier crust. It helps the blooms develop (the slashes).

WHAT HAPPENS IF THERE ISN'T ENOUGH STEAM?

The blooms could tear, because the crust will form too quickly. The crust will be dull and thick.

WHAT HAPPENS IF THERE'S TOO MUCH STEAM?

The slashes don't open up into blooms. The bread is too shiny and silky: the crust won't be crisp and will have a rubbery texture.

CAN YOU EAT BREAD WHILE IT IS STILL HOT?

Hot bread has a strong smell but less taste. It's harder to digest because the gases haven't yet escaped.

Learn

1

2

THE STAGES DURING BAKING

Increase in volume of the dough: the strong heat of the oven inflates the gas within the dough, which gives the bread its final volume. Formation of the crust and the crumb.
Evaporation of water to make steam (the slashes aid in evaporation).
Once the bread reaches 100°C, it stops swelling. Solidification of the crust.
Final caramelisation of the sugars, which gives the crust its colour, taste and familiar bread aromas (Maillard reactions; see page 285).

THE STAGES AFTER BAKING

COOLING

What is it? Cooling down of the bread after removal from the oven.
Roles: The steam, carbon dioxide and ethanol in the crumb escape. The crumb takes on the humidity of the surrounding air and dries out. Fixation of the flavours.
Time and conditions: On a wire rack, until completely cool – from 30 minutes for small pieces to several hours for large loaves.

STALING

What is it? The bread dries out little by little, ageing from the moment it starts cooling.

Time: Fast for baguettes and buns. It accelerates over time for large loaves.

BAKING OUTCOMES

1 FAILED BAKING

Doughy and sticky centre. Dull and rubbery crust.

2 SUCCESSFUL BAKING

Caramelised crust (Maillard reactions; see page 285).
The underside of the bread is hard.
The dough is not too moist.

WHITE DOUGH

Understand

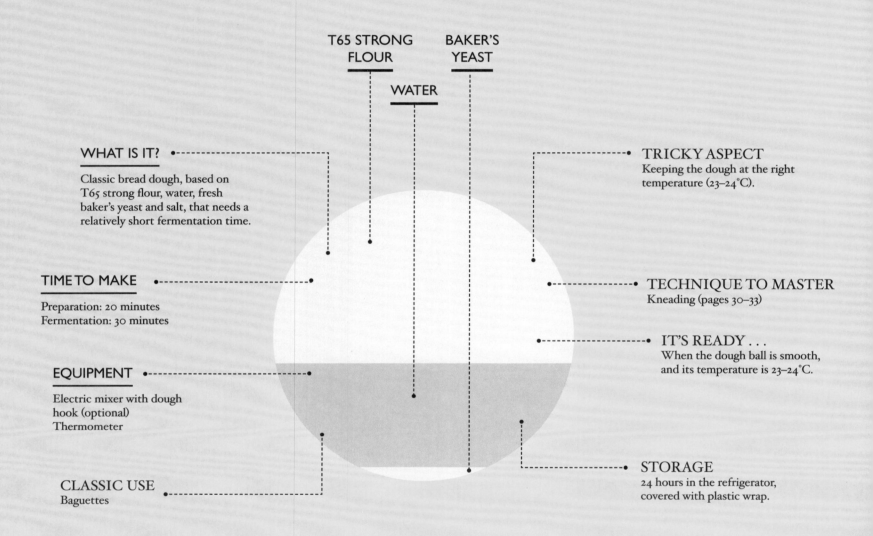

T65 STRONG FLOUR

WATER

BAKER'S YEAST

WHAT IS IT?
Classic bread dough, based on T65 strong flour, water, fresh baker's yeast and salt, that needs a relatively short fermentation time.

TIME TO MAKE
Preparation: 20 minutes
Fermentation: 30 minutes

EQUIPMENT
Electric mixer with dough hook (optional)
Thermometer

CLASSIC USE
Baguettes

TRICKY ASPECT
Keeping the dough at the right temperature (23–24°C).

TECHNIQUE TO MASTER
Kneading (pages 30–33)

IT'S READY . . .
When the dough ball is smooth, and its temperature is 23–24°C.

STORAGE
24 hours in the refrigerator, covered with plastic wrap.

WHY USE BAKER'S YEAST?
To obtain a dough with a neutral taste that can then be flavoured (with cheese, bacon, dried fruit, and so on). Baker's yeast also allows rapid rising. The crumb will thus be very airy.

DERIVATION: FERMENTED DOUGH
White dough that has been rested for 24 hours. This allows extra flavours to develop in the bread, without resorting to sourdough. It is used in the recipe for French sticks in particular.

1   **2**

3

5

4

MAKES 800 G

500 g T65 strong flour
300 g water
9 g salt
10 g fresh baker's yeast

1   Put the flour, water, salt and crumbled
yeast in the bowl of an electric mixer.

2   Knead (see pages 32–33) for
4 minutes at the lowest speed.

3   Knead for 6 minutes at medium speed. The
dough should pull away from the side of the
bowl. (For kneading by hand, see pages 30–31.)

4   Use a thermometer to check that the
temperature of the dough is 23–24°C.

5   Place the dough on a floured work surface,
cover with a clean tea towel and leave for
30 minutes to undergo pointage (see page 36).

TRADITIONAL DOUGH

Understand

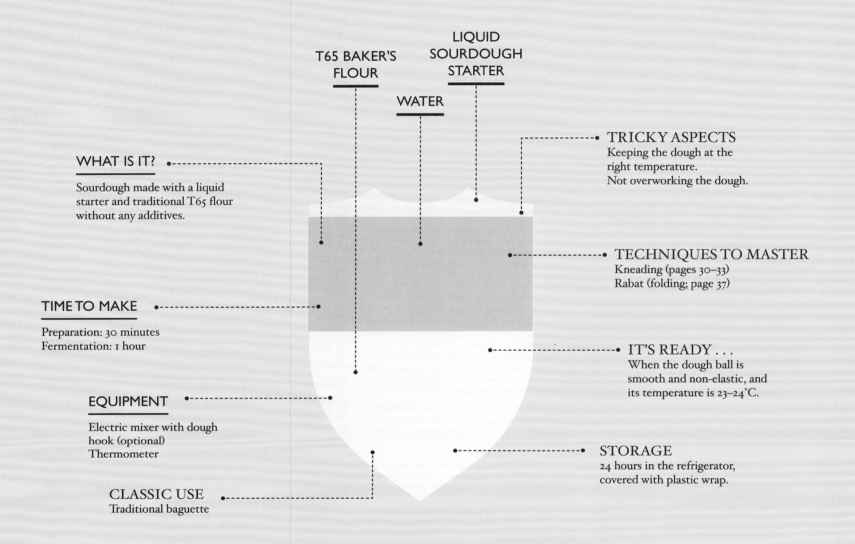

T65 BAKER'S FLOUR

LIQUID SOURDOUGH STARTER

WATER

WHAT IS IT?
Sourdough made with a liquid starter and traditional T65 flour without any additives.

TRICKY ASPECTS
Keeping the dough at the right temperature. Not overworking the dough.

TECHNIQUES TO MASTER
Kneading (pages 30–33)
Rabat (folding; page 37)

TIME TO MAKE
Preparation: 30 minutes
Fermentation: 1 hour

IT'S READY . . .
When the dough ball is smooth and non-elastic, and its temperature is 23–24°C.

EQUIPMENT
Electric mixer with dough hook (optional)
Thermometer

STORAGE
24 hours in the refrigerator, covered with plastic wrap.

CLASSIC USE
Traditional baguette

WHAT IS T65 BAKER'S FLOUR?

T65 baker's flour doesn't contain any additives, which makes the dough smoother. This absence of additives gives a 'rougher' crumb, more heterogeneous and tastier.

WHAT DOES THE SOURDOUGH STARTER DO?

Like yeast, sourdough starter is a fermenting agent: it makes the dough rise. It also adds aromatic notes and acidity, which gives the dough its characteristic taste and allows the formation of a more rustic crust.

HOW DOES IT DIFFER FROM WHITE DOUGH?

Traditional dough uses T65 baker's flour and often more water. Its kneading time is shorter and the pointage stage longer.

WHY IS RABAT (FOLDING) NECESSARY?

During pointage, the fermenting organisms break down the sugars in the flour and emit gas. This gas is imprisoned by the gluten network formed during kneading, which is what makes the dough rise. After a while,

the fermenting organisms exhaust the sugar supply and the gluten network relaxes. Less gas is being produced and we have a gluten network that retains less gas. The dough therefore sinks. Folding reactivates the microorganisms and tightens the gluten network, thus restrengthening the dough. It is necessary with traditional dough because T65 baker's flour contains more complex sugars (starch) than standard T65 strong flour. The fermenting organisms consume the simple sugars first, so it is necessary to reactivate fermentation to give the organisms time to break down the complex sugars.

MAKES 900 G

500 g T65 baker's flour
345 g water
10 g salt
50 g liquid sourdough starter
5 g fresh baker's yeast

1 Knead (see pages 32–33) the flour, water, salt, liquid starter and crumbled yeast using an electric mixer with the dough hook attachment for 4 minutes at the lowest speed.

2 Knead for a further 6 minutes at medium speed. The dough should pull away from the side of the bowl. (For kneading by hand, see pages 30–31.)

3 Use a thermometer to check that the temperature of the dough is 23–24°C.

4 Place the dough on a floured work surface, cover with a clean tea towel and leave for 30 minutes to undergo pointage (see page 36).

5 Fold the dough in half as for a rabat (folding; see page 37). Leave on the work surface under the tea towel for a further 30 minutes of pointage.

PIZZA DOUGH

Understand

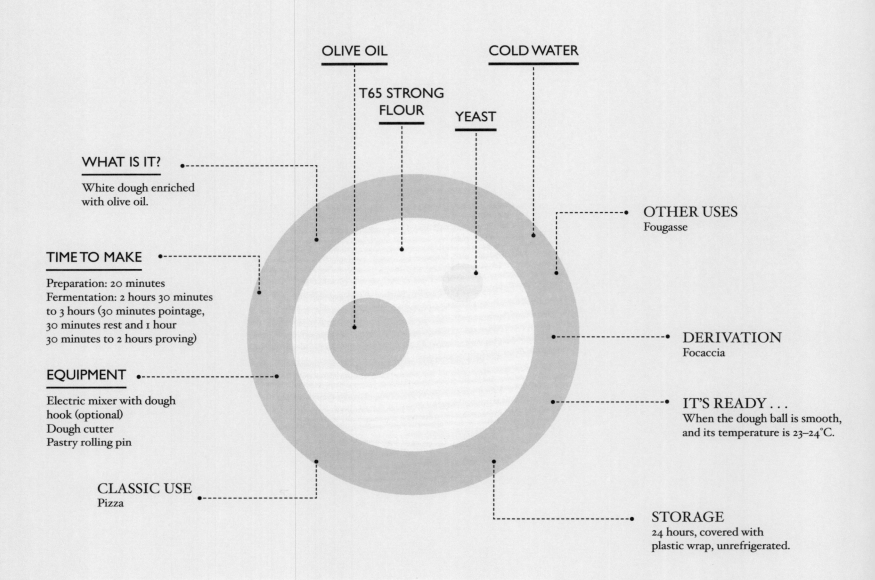

OLIVE OIL

COLD WATER

T65 STRONG
FLOUR

YEAST

WHAT IS IT?
White dough enriched
with olive oil.

TIME TO MAKE
Preparation: 20 minutes
Fermentation: 2 hours 30 minutes
to 3 hours (30 minutes pointage,
30 minutes rest and 1 hour
30 minutes to 2 hours proving)

EQUIPMENT
Electric mixer with dough
hook (optional)
Dough cutter
Pastry rolling pin

CLASSIC USE
Pizza

OTHER USES
Fougasse

DERIVATION
Focaccia

IT'S READY . . .
When the dough ball is smooth,
and its temperature is 23–24°C.

STORAGE
24 hours, covered with
plastic wrap, unrefrigerated.

HOW DOES IT DIFFER FROM WHITE DOUGH?
*Here, the olive oil is incorporated into the dough at the end of kneading.
The addition of this fat modifies the formation of the gluten network, which
limits honeycombing during cooking and keeps the bread moist.*

TRICKY ASPECT
The dough must be elastic
enough to be rolled thinly.

TECHNIQUES TO MASTER
Kneading (pages 30–33)
Pre-shaping into a ball (page 42)

TIP
Spread the dough out several
times so that it loosens and can be
rolled thinly without tearing.

Learn

MAKES TWO 40 CM × 30 CM BASES

500 g T65 strong flour
300 g cold water
10 g salt
15 g fresh baker's yeast
100 g olive oil

1 Knead (see pages 32–33) the flour, water, salt and crumbled baker's yeast using an electric mixer with the dough hook attachment for 5 minutes at the lowest speed. Increase the speed to medium and knead for another 6 minutes: the dough should pull away from the side of the bowl. (For kneading by hand, see pages 30–31.)

2 Gradually incorporate the oil while kneading at the lowest speed.

3 Cover the dough with plastic wrap and leave at room temperature for 30 minutes to undergo pointage (see page 36).

4 Divide the dough into two pieces, pre-shape them into balls (see page 42) and leave to rest for 30 minutes under a clean tea towel at room temperature.

5 Dust the dough ball all over with flour, then roll it out with a rolling pin from top to bottom and left to right, so that the dough has a uniform thickness.

6 Leave in a warm place to prove for 1 hour 30 minutes to 2 hours, covered with the tea towel.

VIENNA DOUGH

Understand

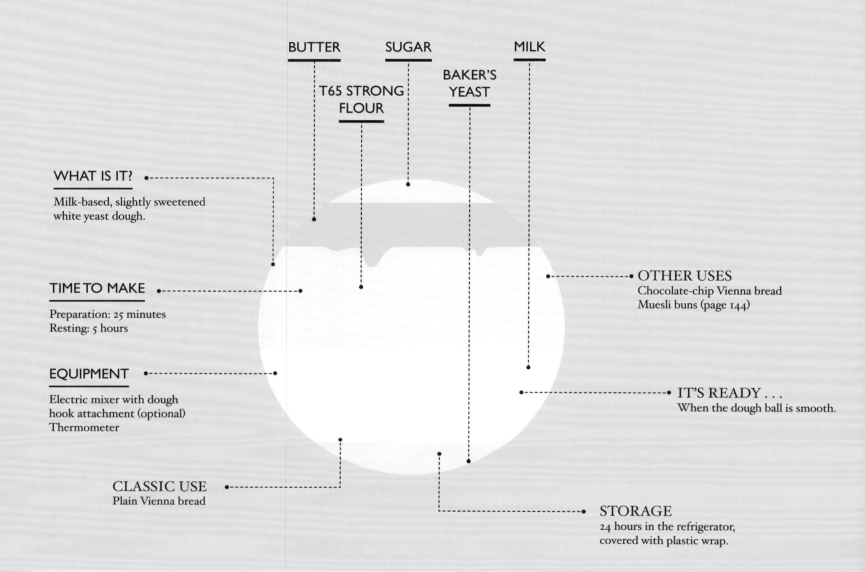

BUTTER   SUGAR   MILK

T65 STRONG FLOUR   BAKER'S YEAST

WHAT IS IT?

Milk-based, slightly sweetened white yeast dough.

TIME TO MAKE

Preparation: 25 minutes
Resting: 5 hours

EQUIPMENT

Electric mixer with dough hook attachment (optional)
Thermometer

OTHER USES

Chocolate-chip Vienna bread
Muesli buns (page 144)

IT'S READY . . .

When the dough ball is smooth.

CLASSIC USE

Plain Vienna bread

STORAGE

24 hours in the refrigerator, covered with plastic wrap.

WHAT'S SPECIAL ABOUT VIENNA DOUGH?

Compared with a brioche or a milk bread dough, Vienna dough contains less butter, less sugar and no egg. Its drier and less airy texture is explained by this difference in composition.

TRICKY ASPECT

Incorporating the butter without it melting, to retain a good consistency in the dough.

TECHNIQUE TO MASTER
Kneading (pages 30–33)

MAKES 450 G

250 g T65 strong flour
150 g milk
5 g salt
5 g fresh baker's yeast
20 g caster sugar
40 g unsalted butter, cut into small cubes

1 Put the flour, milk, salt, crumbled yeast and sugar in the bowl of an electric mixer fitted with a dough hook attachment.

2 Knead (see pages 32–33) for 4 minutes at the lowest speed. Knead for another 6 minutes at medium speed. The dough should pull away from the side of the bowl. (For kneading by hand, see pages 30–31.)

3 Add all the butter and knead at the lowest speed until completely incorporated.

4 Wrap the dough in plastic wrap and rest for 5 hours in the refrigerator.

LAYERED YEAST
DOUGH

Understand

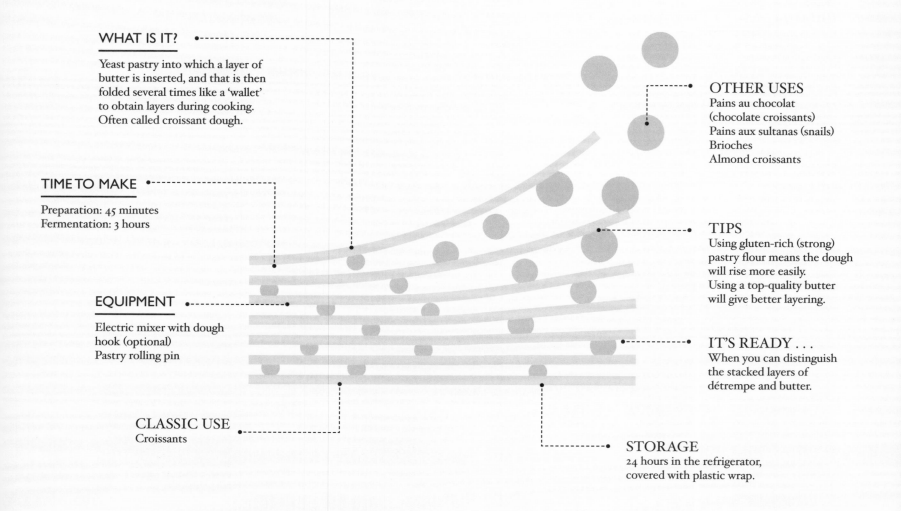

WHAT IS IT?

Yeast pastry into which a layer of butter is inserted, and that is then folded several times like a 'wallet' to obtain layers during cooking. Often called croissant dough.

TIME TO MAKE

Preparation: 45 minutes
Fermentation: 3 hours

EQUIPMENT

Electric mixer with dough hook (optional)
Pastry rolling pin

CLASSIC USE
Croissants

OTHER USES

Pains au chocolat (chocolate croissants)
Pains aux sultanas (snails)
Brioches
Almond croissants

TIPS

Using gluten-rich (strong) pastry flour means the dough will rise more easily.
Using a top-quality butter will give better layering.

IT'S READY . . .

When you can distinguish the stacked layers of détrempe and butter.

STORAGE

24 hours in the refrigerator, covered with plastic wrap.

HOW DO WE OBTAIN THE LAYERED TEXTURE?

Bread dough is folded with butter to form the layers. The butter layers prevent the dough layers from melding and thus they form leaves of dough. During cooking, the butter melts, and the steam and air lift the different layers and separate them from each other, creating the flaky pastry.

HOW IS IT DIFFERENT FROM CLASSIC PUFF PASTRY?

Layered yeast dough contains baker's yeast, which makes Viennese pastry rise during the proving stage. The number of turns is also less important for layered yeast dough, which will therefore be less flaky than classic puff pastry. Because it is based on bread dough, croissant dough is also moister and thus more melt-in-the-mouth than inverse puff pastry.

TRICKY ASPECTS

Folding into a 'wallet' and rolling the dough correctly to retain distinct layers of butter and dough. If they mix, the pastry won't flake.

TECHNIQUES TO MASTER

Kneading (pages 30–33)
Shaping into a ball (page 42)
Making a simple turn (page 283)

MAKES 370 G

<u>1</u> DÉTREMPE

110 g T65 strong flour
110 g T45 pastry flour
105 g cold milk
30 g caster sugar
4 g salt
7 g fresh baker's yeast

<u>2</u> LAYERING

120 g unsalted butter

Making layered yeast dough

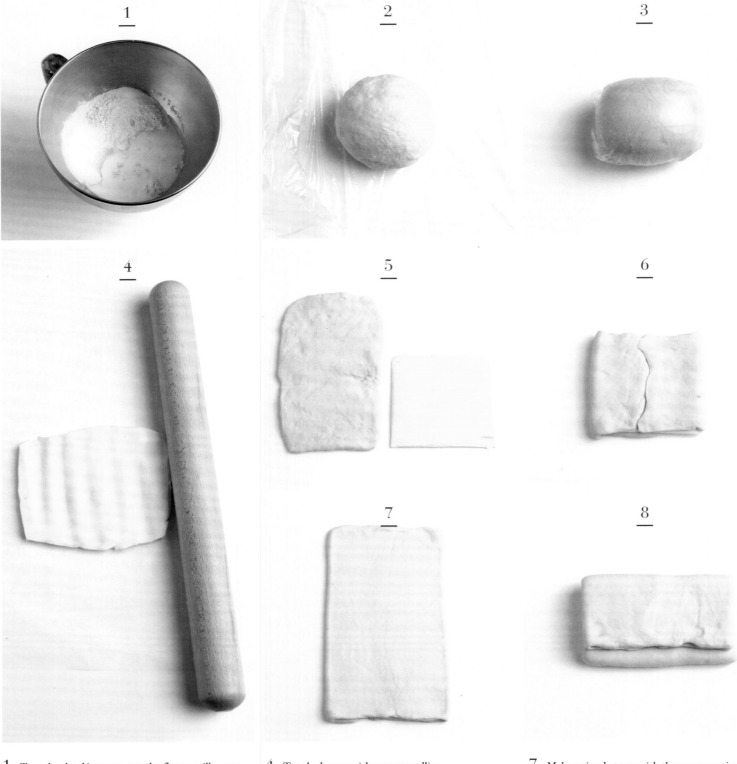

1   To make the détrempe, put the flours, milk, sugar, salt and crumbled yeast in the bowl of an electric mixer fitted with the dough hook attachement. Knead (see pages 32–33) for 5 minutes at the lowest speed, then a further 5 minutes at medium speed. (For kneading by hand, see pages 30–31.)

2   Shape into a ball (see page 42), pulling the dough very tight.

3   Cover with plastic wrap and rest in the refrigerator for 1 hour.

4   Tap the butter with a pastry rolling pin to soften it. Roll it out to a neat square 1 cm thick and 8 cm along the sides.

5   Roll the dough out to the same width as the butter and twice as long (16 cm). Place the square of butter in the centre of the dough.

6   Fold in the two sides of the dough, forming a seam in the middle. Make a quarter-turn with this pastry.

7   Make a simple turn: with the seam running vertical, roll the pastry out to 24 cm long.

8   Fold in three like a wallet or business letter to form a small rectangle of pastry. Wrap in plastic wrap and put in the freezer for 10 minutes, then the refrigerator for 30 minutes.

9   Repeat steps 7 and 8 twice. You will have made three simple turns.

BRIOCHE DOUGH

Understand

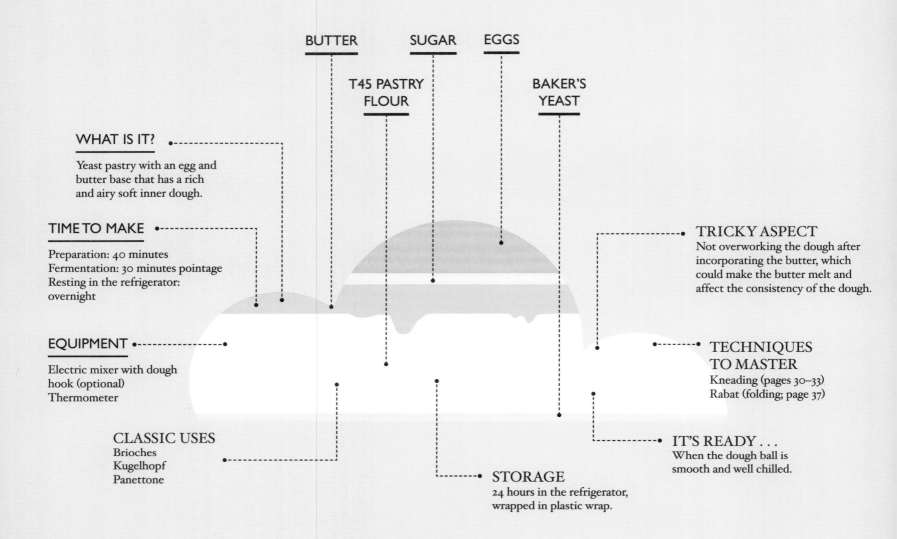

BUTTER SUGAR EGGS

T45 PASTRY FLOUR   BAKER'S YEAST

WHAT IS IT?
Yeast pastry with an egg and butter base that has a rich and airy soft inner dough.

TIME TO MAKE
Preparation: 40 minutes
Fermentation: 30 minutes pointage
Resting in the refrigerator: overnight

EQUIPMENT
Electric mixer with dough hook (optional)
Thermometer

CLASSIC USES
Brioches
Kugelhopf
Panettone

STORAGE
24 hours in the refrigerator, wrapped in plastic wrap.

TRICKY ASPECT
Not overworking the dough after incorporating the butter, which could make the butter melt and affect the consistency of the dough.

TECHNIQUES TO MASTER
Kneading (pages 30–33)
Rabat (folding; page 37)

IT'S READY . . .
When the dough ball is smooth and well chilled.

WHY ADD THE BUTTER ONLY AFTER THE END OF KNEADING?

Because it envelops the gluten proteins and thus limits the development of the gluten network. But to obtain an airy, moist texture, the gluten network must be well developed. The two first kneading stages without butter ensure its formation. The addition of butter then gives the dough its characteristic moistness.

WHY INCORPORATE THE BUTTER AT ROOM TEMPERATURE?

So that it mixes easily into the dough. The temperature of the butter, and therefore its consistency, influences the texture of the crumb of the brioche. Butter at room temperature allows a moist, soft centre (if the butter is too cold or too warm, the brioche will be dry).

WHY USE PASTRY FLOUR?

It is gluten-rich, so it assists in the development of a strong gluten network. This means the network retains the gases formed during fermentation well and the crumb will be well honeycombed.

WHY DO THE FIRST RISING IN THE REFRIGERATOR?

The cold slows the rising of the dough and thus avoids too strong a rise, which wouldn't allow the necessary development of the gluten network.

MAKES 580 G

250 g T45 pastry flour

3 eggs

5 g salt

35 g caster sugar

8 g fresh baker's yeast

125 g unsalted butter at room
    temperature, cut into small cubes

1 Keep all the ingredients in the refrigerator overnight before making. Put the flour, eggs, salt, sugar and crumbled yeast in the bowl of an electric mixer. Knead (see pages 32–33) for 4 minutes at the lowest speed.

2 Knead for 6 minutes at medium speed. The dough should pull away from the side of the bowl. (For kneading by hand, see pages 30–31.)

3 With the mixer at the lowest speed, add all the butter, then continue to knead until it is completely incorporated into the dough.

4 Transfer the dough to a round-bottomed bowl.

5 Cover with a clean tea towel and leave to rest for 30 minutes.

6 Make a rabat (fold; see page 37).

7 Return the dough to the round-bottomed bowl, cover with plastic wrap, with the wrap touching the dough (see page 285), and leave to rest in the refrigerator until the next day.

INVERSE PUFF PASTRY

Understand

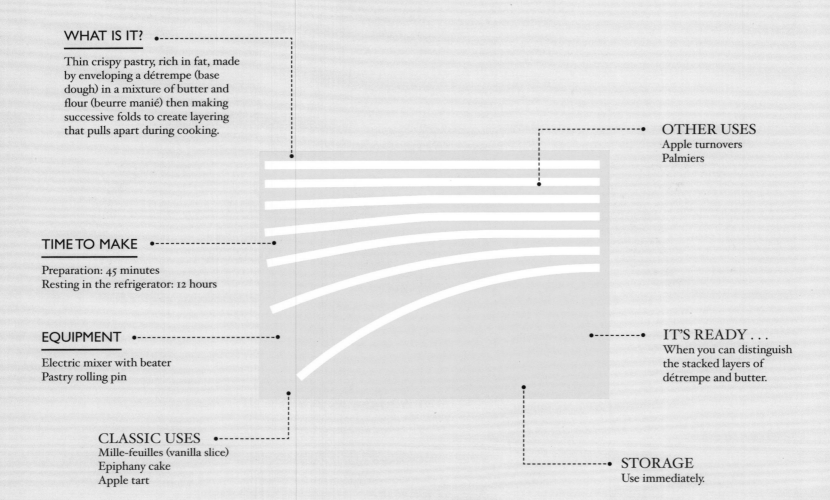

WHAT IS IT?

Thin crispy pastry, rich in fat, made by enveloping a détrempe (base dough) in a mixture of butter and flour (beurre manié) then making successive folds to create layering that pulls apart during cooking.

TIME TO MAKE

Preparation: 45 minutes
Resting in the refrigerator: 12 hours

EQUIPMENT

Electric mixer with beater
Pastry rolling pin

CLASSIC USES
Mille-feuilles (vanilla slice)
Epiphany cake
Apple tart

OTHER USES
Apple turnovers
Palmiers

IT'S READY . . .
When you can distinguish the stacked layers of détrempe and butter.

STORAGE
Use immediately.

HOW DOES IT DIFFER FROM CLASSIC PUFF PASTRY?

Its taste: the layering butter is enriched with flour, which adds taste during cooking, like a roux.
The method: the layering butter is wrapped around the détrempe during the first fold, whereas in classic puff pastry the butter is placed in the détrempe before folding.
The quantity of butter: one and a half times the butter of a classic puff pastry.

TRICKY ASPECT
Don't roll the dough too vigorously, to ensure the layers of détrempe and butter don't mix.

TECHNIQUES TO MASTER
Kneading (pags 30–33)
Making a simple turn (page 283)
Making a double turn (page 283)
Softening butter (page 284)

TIP
Always roll out away from you, to make it easier and to obtain neater layers.

MAKES 600 G

1 DÉTREMPE

180 g T65 strong flour
80 g cold water
8 g salt
60 g softened unsalted butter (page 284)
2 g white vinegar

2 BEURRE MANIÉ (KNEADED BUTTER)

200 g softened unsalted butter
   (page 284), cut into cubes
80 g T65 strong flour

Making inverse puff pastry

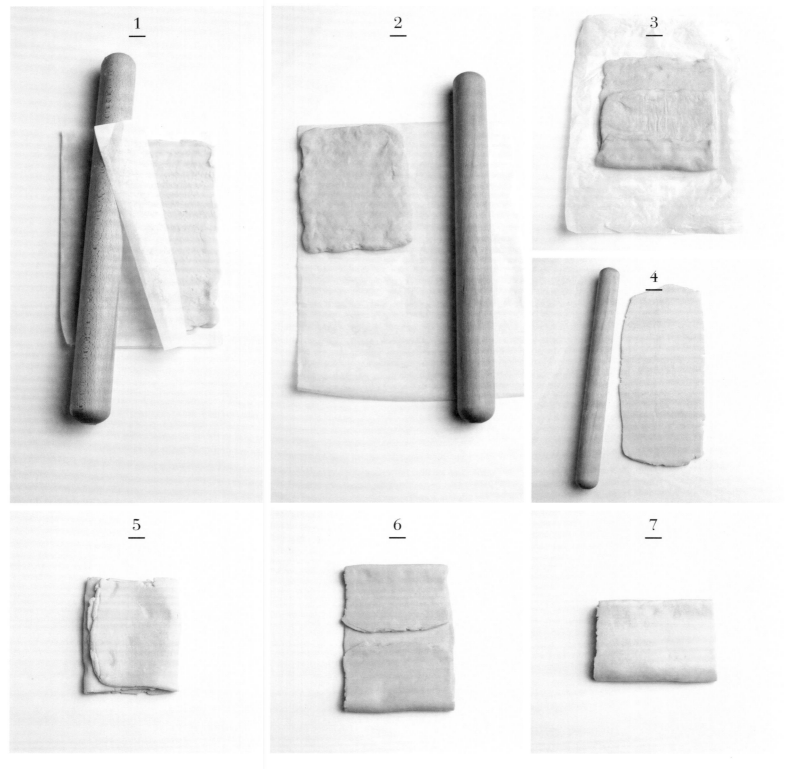

1   To make the beurre manié, mix the butter and the flour using an electric mixer with the beater attachment for 5 minutes. Turn out onto a floured work surface, or between two sheets of baking paper, and use a pastry rolling pin to shape into a 20 cm × 30 cm rectangle. Cover with plastic wrap and refrigerate for 2 hours.

2   To make the détrempe, mix the flour, water, salt, butter and vinegar in the bowl of an electric mixer with the beater attachment for 7 minutes at the lowest speed. Turn the dough out onto a floured work surface, or between two sheets of baking paper, and use a pastry rolling pin to shape into a 15 cm × 20 cm rectangle. Cover with plastic wrap and refrigerate for 2 hours.

3   Place the détrempe in the centre of the beurre manié and fold the two sides of the butter over the top to enclose it.

4   Make a simple turn: roll the dough out until it is three times longer than wide (60 cm × 20 cm).

5   Fold the dough in three like a business letter or wallet. Cover with plastic wrap and leave to rest in the refrigerator for 2 hours.

6   Place on the work surface with the seam running vertical and make a double turn (see page 283): roll the dough out until it is three times longer than wide (60 cm × 20 cm). Fold a quarter of the pastry from each end in towards the centre.

7   Fold in half at the middle. Cover with plastic wrap and refrigerate for 2 hours.

8   Place on the work surface with the seam running vertical and make another double turn: roll the dough out until it is three times longer than wide. Fold a quarter of the pastry from each end in towards the centre. Fold in half at the middle. Cover with plastic wrap and refrigerate for 2 hours.

9   Place on the work surface with the seam running vertical and make a simple turn (see page 283): roll the dough out until it is three times longer than wide, fold the pastry in three, cover with plastic wrap and leave to rest in the refrigerator for 2 hours.

CHOUX PASTRY

Understand

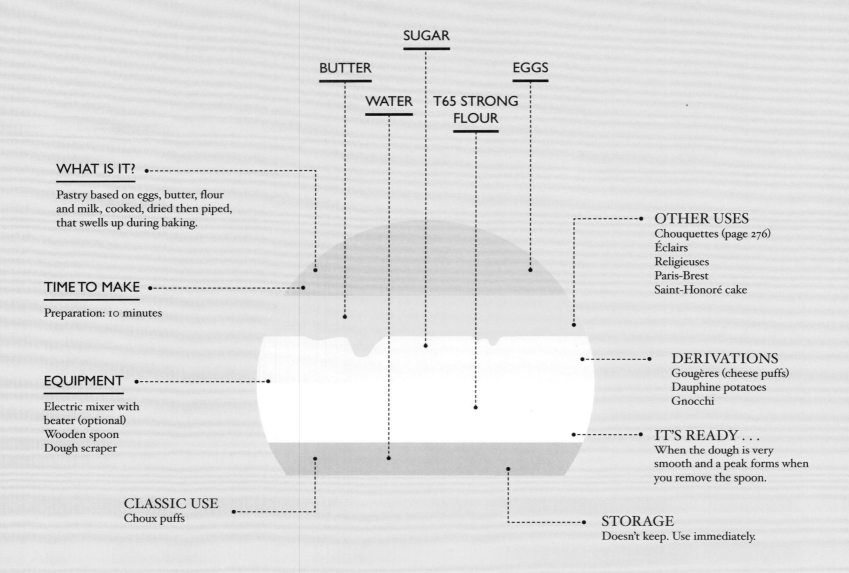

SUGAR

BUTTER

EGGS

WATER

T65 STRONG
FLOUR

WHAT IS IT?
Pastry based on eggs, butter, flour
and milk, cooked, dried then piped,
that swells up during baking.

TIME TO MAKE
Preparation: 10 minutes

EQUIPMENT
Electric mixer with
beater (optional)
Wooden spoon
Dough scraper

CLASSIC USE
Choux puffs

OTHER USES
Chouquettes (page 276)
Éclairs
Religieuses
Paris-Brest
Saint-Honoré cake

DERIVATIONS
Gougères (cheese puffs)
Dauphine potatoes
Gnocchi

IT'S READY . . .
When the dough is very
smooth and a peak forms when
you remove the spoon.

STORAGE
Doesn't keep. Use immediately.

**WHAT MAKES THE CHOUX
PASTRY RISE?**

*During baking at 180°C, the water
in the pastry will evaporate as steam.
Because the pastry is viscous after being
first cooked in the saucepan, it will
retain the steam and thus swell up.*

**WHY DOES IT SINK AGAIN IF THE
OVEN IS OPENED TOO SOON?**

*Because the temperature of the oven
drops and the steam condenses back into
water. As the volume of liquid water is
less than that of steam, the choux sinks.*

TRICKY ASPECT
Drying the dough well without burning it.

TECHNIQUE TO MASTER
Scraping out (page 282)

TIP
Drying the dough well means the choux
will develop better during baking.

Learn

1

2a   2b

3

4

5

MAKES 700 G

165 g milk
90 g water
110 g unsalted butter
2 g caster sugar
2 g salt
150 g T65 strong flour
4 eggs

1 Combine the milk, water, butter, sugar and salt in a saucepan and heat until melted and dissolved together, then bring to the boil.

2 Add all the flour at once. Stir the mixture constantly with a wooden spoon for 1 minute to dry the dough, until it pulls away from the side of the saucepan. This mixture is called the 'panade'.

3 Transfer the panade to the bowl of an electric mixer and stir with the beater attachment at the lowest speed for 1–2 minutes (or stir with a wooden spoon).

4 Incorporate the eggs one at a time, mixing constantly.

5 Scrape down the sides of the bowl and the beater using a dough scraper, then mix one last time for 1 minute until the mixture is very smooth, with no lumps.

SWEET SABLÉ
PASTRY

Understand

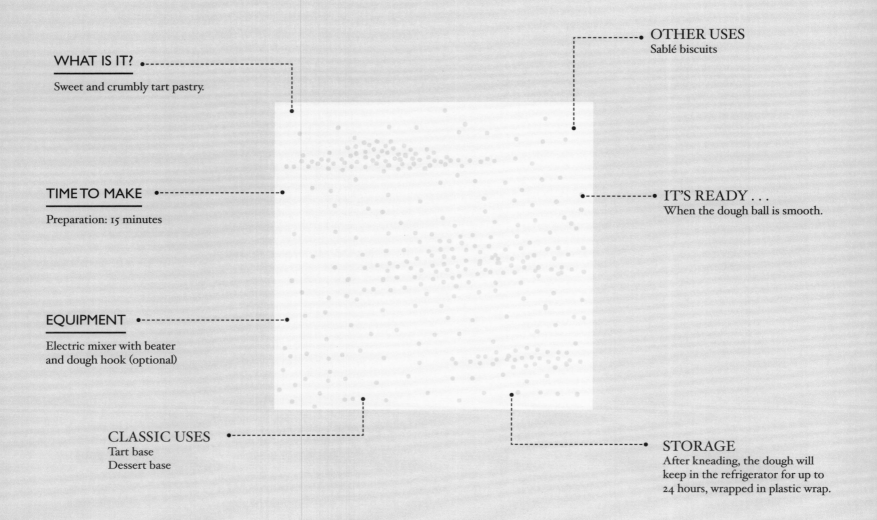

OTHER USES
Sablé biscuits

WHAT IS IT?
Sweet and crumbly tart pastry.

TIME TO MAKE
Preparation: 15 minutes

IT'S READY . . .
When the dough ball is smooth.

EQUIPMENT
Electric mixer with beater
and dough hook (optional)

CLASSIC USES
Tart base
Dessert base

STORAGE
After kneading, the dough will
keep in the refrigerator for up to
24 hours, wrapped in plastic wrap.

HOW DO YOU OBTAIN A CRUMBLY, SANDY PASTRY?

By the butter stopping too many linkages forming between the ingredients. With this technique, no gluten network develops and the pastry doesn't become too elastic. In addition, the sugar doesn't dissolve in the fat, which means a certain amount of the sugar remains as crystals. This adds to the sandy texture of the pastry.

TRICKY ASPECT
Not overworking the pastry, so
that the butter doesn't melt and
make the dough too elastic.

TECHNIQUE TO MASTER
Kneading (pages 30–33)

TIP
To make without an electric mixer, combine
the icing sugar, ground almonds, salt and
flour in a round-bottomed bowl. Make a
well in the centre and add the cubed butter
and the egg. Mix everything quickly then
flatten the dough (frasage; see page 282)
once or twice with the heel of your hand.

Learn

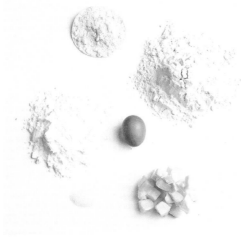

5

1

2

3

4

MAKES ONE 24–26 CM BASE

155 g unsalted butter, cut into cubes
100 g icing sugar
30 g ground almonds
1 g salt
260 g T65 strong flour
1 egg

1   Put the butter in the bowl of an electric mixer with the beater attachment. Beat for 2 minutes at the lowest speed to soften it.

2   Sift the icing sugar and ground almonds, and add them to the bowl. Mix for 2 minutes at the lowest speed.

3   Add the salt and the sifted flour; replace the beater attachment with the dough hook and mix at the lowest speed until the pastry is smooth.

4   Add the egg and mix for 5 minutes at the lowest speed.

5   Shape the dough into a rectangle, wrap in plastic wrap and refrigerate until ready to use.

PASTRY CREAM

Understand

WHAT IS IT?

Custard-like cream prepared over heat, based on milk and egg yolk, with a thick texture. Also known by its French name, crème pâtissière.

TRICKY ASPECT

Cooking: don't burn the cream.

TIME TO MAKE

Preparation: 20 minutes
Resting in the refrigerator: 1 hour

TECHNIQUE TO MASTER

Blanching egg yolks (page 284)

CLASSIC USES

Pain suisse
Pains aux sultanas (snails)
Éclairs
Mille-feuilles

IT'S READY . . .

When the cream is thick, the whisk leaves furrows or large bubbles come to the surface.

DERIVATIONS

Chiboust cream = pastry cream + Italian meringue
Diplomat cream = pastry cream + whipped cream + gelatine
Frangipane cream = pastry cream + almond cream
German buttercream (crème mousseline) = pastry cream + butter

STORAGE

Use on the same day.

HOW DO WE GO FROM A LIQUID MIXTURE TO A CREAM?

When cornflour is mixed with the other ingredients, the starch it contains absorbs water (from the eggs and the milk). During cooking, the eggs will coagulate and the starch will gelatinise, breaking down into its components, amylose and amylopectin, which will thicken the mixture. The texture will evolve further while resting in the refrigerator because bonds will form between the water-swollen starch molecules.

WHY CAN A 'SKIN' FORM ON THE SURFACE OF THE CREAM AFTER COOLING?

It is due to the coagulation of the proteins during heating (like the skin that forms when milk is heated) and dehydration at the surface.

HOW DOES A PASTRY CREAM MADE WITH FLOUR DIFFER FROM ONE MADE WITH CORNFLOUR?

By changing the thickening ingredient, we change the starch source, and therefore the texture of the cream. Each starch source has different properties. A pastry cream made with cornflour will be lighter than one made with an equal quantity of wheat flour.

MAKES 600 G

500 g milk
100 g caster sugar
½ vanilla bean
45 g cornflour
2 eggs

1 Pour the milk and half the sugar into a saucepan.

2 Flatten the vanilla bean with the back of a utility knife. Split it in half lengthways and scrape out the seeds. Add the seeds to the saucepan then gently bring to the boil. Remove from the heat.

3 Mix the cornflour with the remaining sugar. Add the eggs and whisk until slightly paler.

4 Pour some of the milk mixture into the egg mixture. Whisk together until smooth. Pour back into the saucepan with the rest of the milk mixture. Whisk again and return to the heat. When the mixture boils, cook for a further 1 minute, whisking constantly.

5 Pour the cream into a baking tin and cover with plastic wrap, with the plastic touching the cream, to prevent a skin forming (see page 285). Refrigerate for at least 1 hour.

6 Whisk before using to return it to a smooth consistency.

ALMOND CREAM

Understand

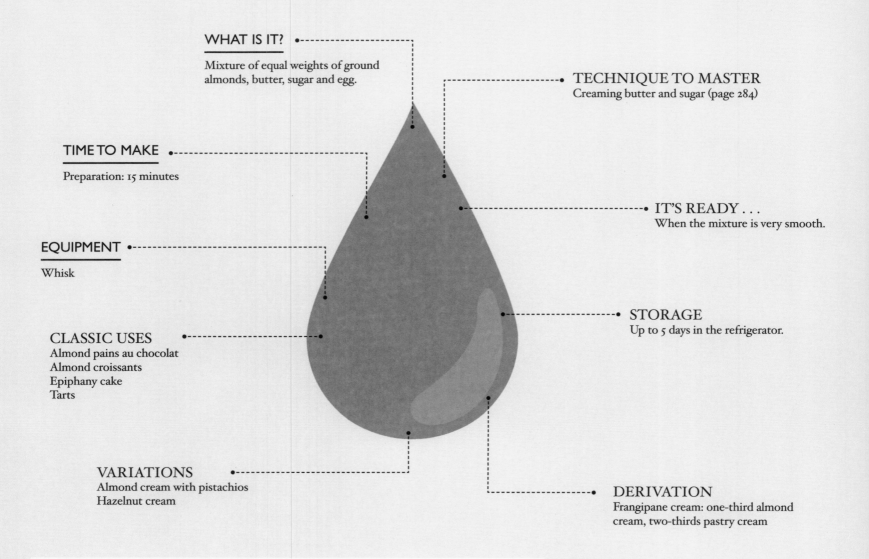

WHAT IS IT?
Mixture of equal weights of ground almonds, butter, sugar and egg.

TECHNIQUE TO MASTER
Creaming butter and sugar (page 284)

TIME TO MAKE
Preparation: 15 minutes

IT'S READY . . .
When the mixture is very smooth.

EQUIPMENT
Whisk

STORAGE
Up to 5 days in the refrigerator.

CLASSIC USES
Almond pains au chocolat
Almond croissants
Epiphany cake
Tarts

VARIATIONS
Almond cream with pistachios
Hazelnut cream

DERIVATION
Frangipane cream: one-third almond cream, two-thirds pastry cream

---

WHY CREAM THE BUTTER AND SUGAR?

This allows the sugar to dissolve in the water that the butter contains, to prevent the formation of sugar crystals in the almond cream.

HOW DOES IT SWELL UP DURING COOKING?

During cooking, the air bubbles incorporated into the different mixtures will inflate and make the cream swell, giving it a mousse-like consistency.

MAKES 400 G

100 g softened unsalted butter (see page 284)
100 g caster sugar
100 g ground almonds
10 g cornflour (or plain flour)
2 eggs

1   Cream the butter and sugar by whisking together in a round-bottomed bowl.

2   Add the ground almonds and cornflour, and mix.

3   Add the eggs. Whisk until smooth and creamy. Cover with plastic wrap, with the plastic (see page 285), and refrigerate until ready to use.

STEWED APPLE

Understand

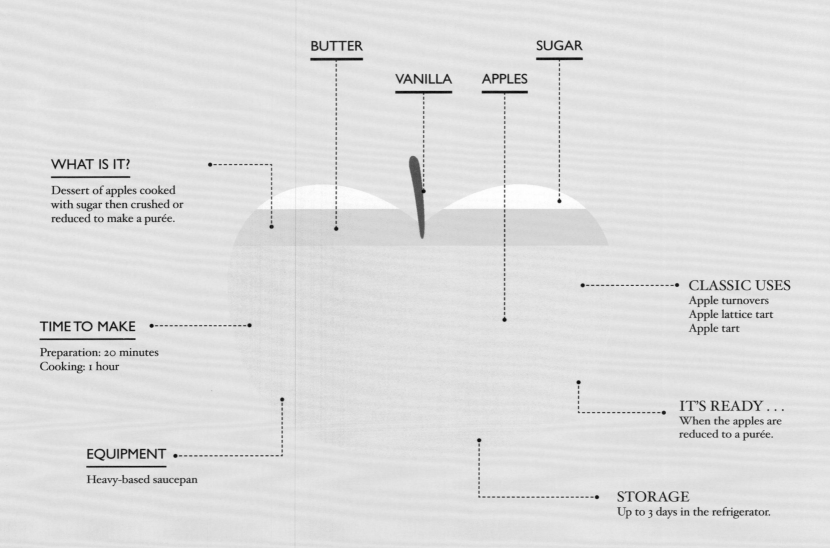

BUTTER

VANILLA   APPLES

SUGAR

WHAT IS IT?

Dessert of apples cooked
with sugar then crushed or
reduced to make a purée.

CLASSIC USES

Apple turnovers
Apple lattice tart
Apple tart

TIME TO MAKE

Preparation: 20 minutes
Cooking: 1 hour

IT'S READY . . .

When the apples are
reduced to a purée.

EQUIPMENT

Heavy-based saucepan

STORAGE

Up to 3 days in the refrigerator.

WHAT DOES THE BUTTER DO?

*Adds aromatic notes and moistness to the eating experience. In fact,
the butter will melt and coat the palate, bringing a depth to the taste
that the stewed apple would lack without some fat added.*

TIP

For a completely smooth purée, pass the
apple through a food mill after cooking
and don't add the raw diced apple.

MAKES 1 KG

880 g apples
50 g caster sugar
70 g unsalted butter
½ vanilla bean

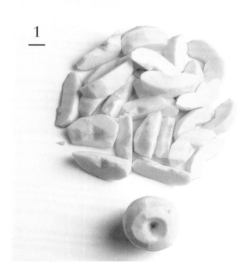

1 Peel the apples. Cut all but one into quarters and remove the core.

2 Put the apple quarters in a large heavy-based saucepan with the sugar and butter. Split the vanilla bean lengthways, scrape out the seeds and add the bean and seeds to the pan. Cover and cook for 1 hour over a medium heat. Stir regularly.

3 Remove from the heat and allow to cool. Dice the remaining apple and stir into the stewed apple.

CHAPTER 2
RECIPES

BAGUETTES

Understand

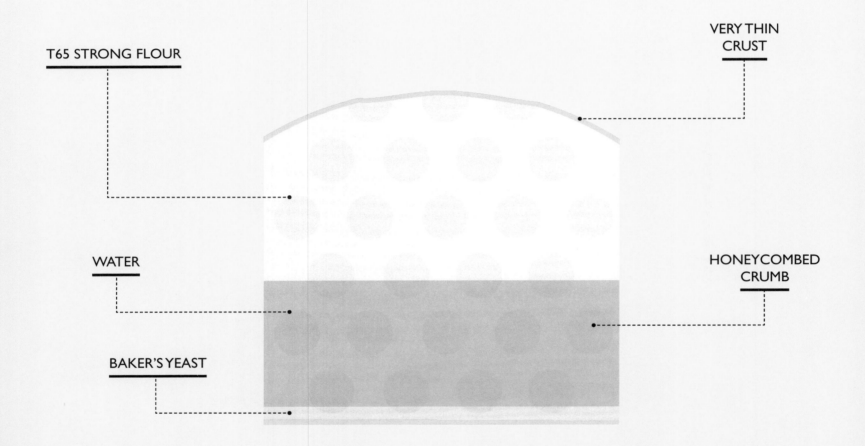

T65 STRONG FLOUR

WATER

BAKER'S YEAST

VERY THIN CRUST

HONEYCOMBED CRUMB

WHAT ARE THEY?

Long loaves made with white dough and shaped into batons.

CHARACTERISTICS

Weight: 250 g
Size: 60 cm
Crumb: honeycombed, even
Crust: very thin
Taste: neutral

EQUIPMENT

Electric mixer with dough hook (optional)
Dough cutter
Bread lame (razor)

TIME TO MAKE

Preparation: 35 minutes
Fermentation: 2 hours 30 minutes
(30 minutes resting, 2 hours proving)
Baking: 20–25 minutes

TECHNIQUES TO MASTER

Kneading (pages 30–33)
Shaping into a baguette (page 43)
Slashing (page 50)

THEY'RE READY . . .

When the crusts are lightly golden.

WHAT MAKES THE CRUMB SO SOFT?

The high quantity of yeast allows the dough to rise very quickly. We obtain, in very little time (only 2 hours for rising), a very soft crumb.

WHAT EXPLAINS THE THIN CRUST?

The dough contains lots of water, which means it only starts to dry out quite late during its time in the oven, and so the crust has little time to form.

MAKES 2

390 g T65 strong flour
240 g water at 20–25°C
7 g salt
6 g fresh baker's yeast

Making baguettes

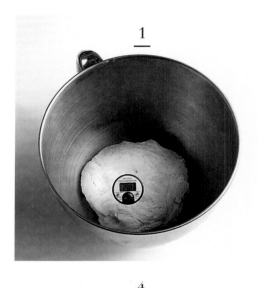

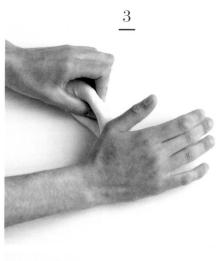

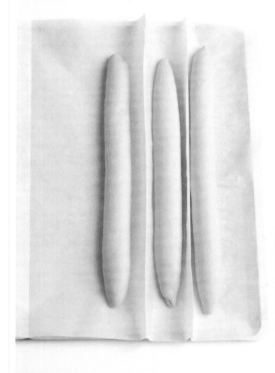

1 Knead the flour, water, salt and crumbled yeast using an electric mixer (see pages 32–33) for 4 minutes at the lowest speed, then 6 minutes at medium speed. The dough should pull away from the side of the bowl. (For kneading by hand, see pages 30–31.)

2 Divide the dough into two 320 g pieces using a dough cutter. Dust a work surface lightly with flour. Take a piece of dough and lay it smooth side down on the work surface. Flatten it into a rectangular shape. Repeat with the other piece of dough. Cover with a clean tea towel and leave to rest for 30 minutes at room temperature.

3 Shape each dough piece into a baguette (see page 43): fold the upper and lower sides into the centre so they overlap. Place your left thumb (right if you are left-handed) at the right (or left) of the dough, pressing lightly on the seam with the opposite palm. Gradually turn down the dough like this along the whole dough piece, sliding your thumb along and pressing down as you go. Flatten the dough again and repeat the folding and pressing once more.

4 Rest your hands on the middle of a baguette and roll it to elongate it, moving each hand towards the ends. Repeat with the other baguette.

5 Place them on a clean tea towel, seam side down, and cover with a second towel to prevent a crust forming on the dough. Leave the dough to prove for 2 hours in a warm place (25–28°C). The dough is risen when a light push with a finger leaves no trace.

6 Place a baking sheet and a heatproof bowl filled with water in the oven and preheat to 260°C (conventional oven). Remove the warmed baking sheet from the oven, line it with baking paper and place the baguettes on it, seam side down. Make three slashes in each baguette (see page 50). Spray the bottom of the oven with water and bake the baguettes for 20–25 minutes (keeping the bowl of water in the oven).

TRADITIONAL
BAGUETTES

Understand

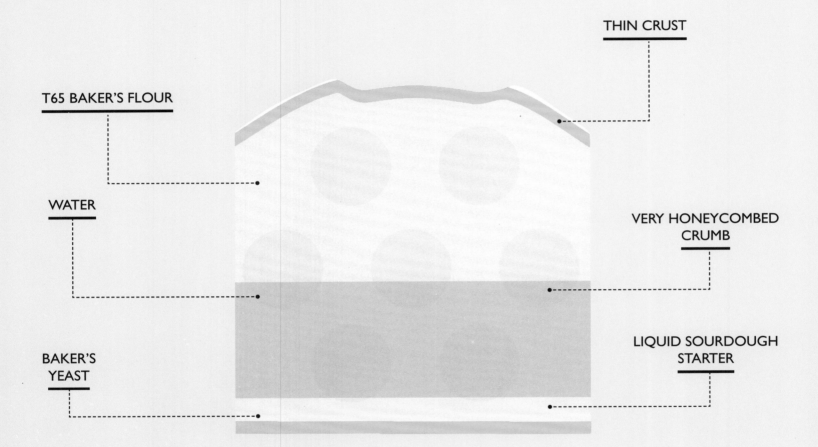

THIN CRUST

T65 BAKER'S FLOUR

WATER

VERY HONEYCOMBED
CRUMB

BAKER'S
YEAST

LIQUID SOURDOUGH
STARTER

WHAT ARE THEY?

Long loaves made with dough from T65 baker's flour and sourdough starter, with a long rising time and shaped into baguettes. 'La baguette de tradition française' (traditional French baguette) is a label defined by the *Bread Decree* of 13 September 1993.

CHARACTERISTICS

Weight: 270 g
Size: 45 cm
Crumb: very honeycombed, rustic
Crust: thin
Taste: slightly acidic

TIME TO MAKE

Preparation: 15 minutes
Fermentation: 3 hours 30 minutes (1 hour of pointage, 30 minutes resting, 2 hours proving)
Baking: 20–25 minutes

EQUIPMENT

Electric mixer with dough hook (optional)
Bread lame (razor)
Dough cutter

TECHNIQUES TO MASTER

Kneading (pages 30–33)
Pre-shaping into a log (page 41)
Shaping into a baguette (page 43)
Slashing (page 50)
Rabat (folding; page 37)

THEY'RE READY . . .

When the crusts are golden and crisp and the bread sounds hollow when you tap on it.

WHAT MAKES THE CRUMB SO HONEYCOMBED?

The fermentation in two stages (pointage and proving) allows the dough to rise well. In addition, the sourdough starter gives a more honeycombed crumb than baker's yeast alone.

MAKES 4

700 g T65 baker's flour, plus 20 g
   extra (for dusting baguettes)
490 g water at room temperature
14 g salt
70 g liquid sourdough starter (page 20)
5 g fresh baker's yeast

Making traditional baguettes

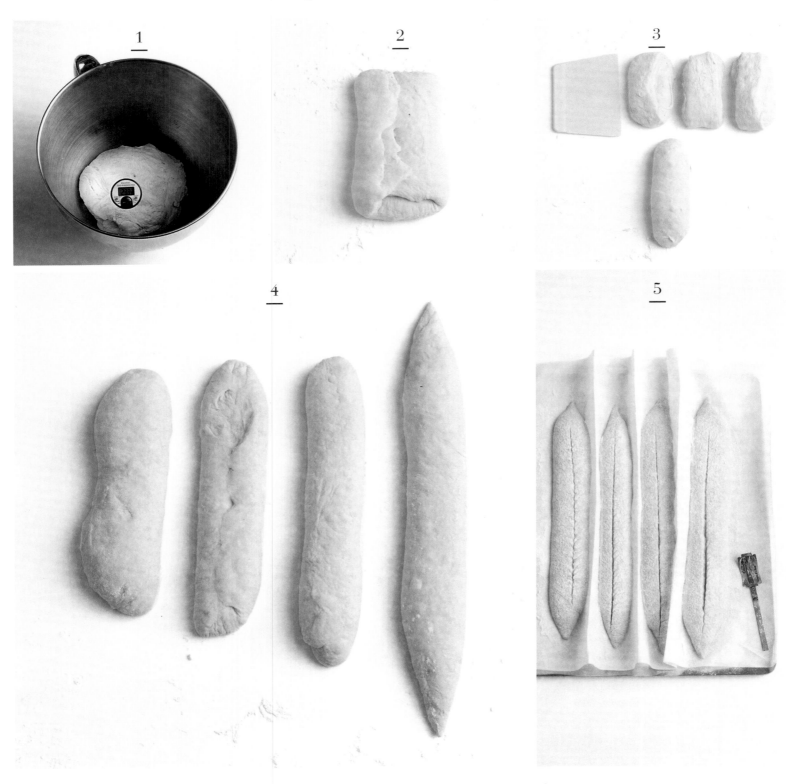

1 Knead the flour, water, salt, liquid starter and crumbled baker's yeast using an electric mixer (see pages 32–33) for 4 minutes at the lowest speed, then 6 minutes at medium speed: the dough should pull away from the side of the bowl. (For kneading by hand, see pages 30–31.)

2 Leave the dough on a floured work surface, covered with a clean tea towel, for 30 minutes to undergo pointage. Make a rabat (fold; see page 37). Leave again on the floured work surface under the tea towel to undergo pointage for a further 30 minutes.

3 Divide the dough into four 330 g pieces using a dough cutter. Make each into a slightly elongated shape (see page 41). Leave on the floured work surface under the tea towel to rest for another 30 minutes.

4 Shape the dough pieces into baguettes (see page 43), place on a clean tea towel, seam side down, and cover with a second tea towel to prevent a crust forming on the dough. Leave to prove for 2 hours in a warm place (25–28°C). The dough is risen when a light push with a finger leaves no trace.

5 Place a baking sheet and a heatproof bowl filled with water in the oven and preheat to 260°C (conventional oven). Remove the warmed baking sheet from the oven, line it with baking paper and place the baguettes on it, seam side down. Sift the extra flour over the baguettes. Make a single slash the length of each baguette (see page 50), holding the bread lame blade at an angle of 45 degrees.

6 Spray the bottom of the oven with water and bake the baguettes for 20–25 minutes (keeping the bowl of water in the oven).

TRADITIONAL SEED
BAGUETTES

Understand

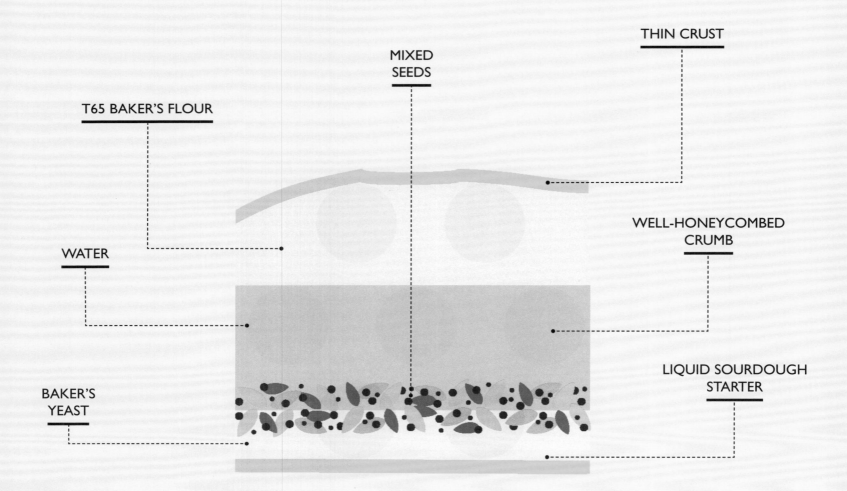

THIN CRUST

MIXED
SEEDS

T65 BAKER'S FLOUR

WELL-HONEYCOMBED
CRUMB

WATER

LIQUID SOURDOUGH
STARTER

BAKER'S
YEAST

WHAT ARE THEY?

Long loaves made with traditional dough enriched with toasted seeds and shaped into wheat-stalk baguettes.

CHARACTERISTICS

Weight: 270 g
Size: 45 cm
Crumb: very honeycombed, rustic
Crust: thin
Taste: slightly acidic

TIME TO MAKE

Soaking: overnight
Preparation: 25 minutes
Fermentation: 3 hours 30 minutes (1 hour of pointage, 30 minutes resting, 2 hours proving)
Baking: 20–25 minutes

EQUIPMENT

Electric mixer with dough hook (optional)
Bread lame (razor)
Scissors

TECHNIQUES TO MASTER

Kneading (pages 30–33)
Pre-shaping into a log (page 41)
Shaping into a baguette (page 43)
Slashing into a wheat stalk (page 51)
Rabat (folding; page 37)

TIP

The dough is risen when a light push with a finger leaves no trace.

THEY'RE READY . . .

When the baguettes are golden.

MAKES 2

1 DOUGH

350 g T65 baker's flour
245 g water at 20–25°C
5 g salt
35 g liquid sourdough starter (see page 20)
2 g fresh baker's yeast

2 SEEDS

60 g mixed organic seeds (linseeds,
   poppy seeds, sesame seeds)
60 g water

Making traditional seed baguettes

THE DAY BEFORE

1 Toast the seeds on a baking sheet lined with baking paper for 10–15 minutes in a 180°C oven. Place them in a round-bottomed bowl with the water. Set aside at room temperature and leave overnight. The seeds will absorb all the water; if not, drain them.

ON THE DAY

2 Knead the flour, water, salt, liquid starter, crumbled yeast and seeds using an electric mixer (see pages 32–33) for 4 minutes at the lowest speed, then 6 minutes at medium speed. The dough should pull away from the side of the bowl. (For kneading by hand, see pages 30–31.)

3 Leave on a floured work surface under a clean tea towel to undergo pointage for 30 minutes.

4 Make a rabat (fold; see page 37). Leave again on the floured work surface under the tea towel to undergo pointage for a further 30 minutes.

5 Divide the dough into two pieces, form them into logs (see page 41) and leave on the floured work surface under the tea towel to rest for another 30 minutes at room temperature. Shape into baguettes (see page 43).

6 Place them on a sheet of baking paper, seam side down, and cover with a clean tea towel to prevent a crust forming on the dough. Leave to prove for 1 hour 30 minutes to 2 hours in a warm place (25–28°C). Slash into wheat stalks (see page 51).

7 Place a baking sheet and a heatproof bowl filled with water in the oven and preheat to 260°C (conventional oven). Remove the warmed baking sheet from the oven and place the baguettes and baking paper on it. Spray the bottom of the oven with water and bake the baguettes for 20–25 minutes (keeping the bowl of water in the oven).

PAIN MAISON

Understand

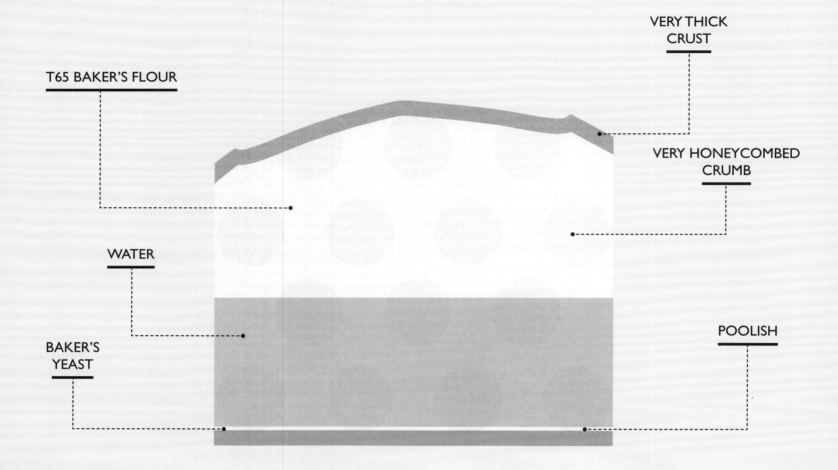

VERY THICK CRUST

T65 BAKER'S FLOUR

VERY HONEYCOMBED CRUMB

WATER

POOLISH

BAKER'S YEAST

WHAT IS IT?

Traditional home-made dough prepared using a base of poolish, and shaped into small torpedo loaves.

CHARACTERISTICS

Weight: 250 g
Size: 20 cm
Crumb: very honeycombed, rustic
Crust: thick
Taste: mild, slightly acidic

TIME TO MAKE

Preparation: 40 minutes
Fermentation: 17 hours 45 minutes

(16 hours for the poolish, 1 hour of pointage, 45 minutes proving)
Baking: 20–25 minutes

EQUIPMENT

Electric mixer with dough hook (optional)
Dough cutter

TRICKY ASPECT

Making the poolish.

TECHNIQUES TO MASTER

Kneading (pages 30–33)
Rabat (folding; page 37)

TIP

When making the poolish, use a large enough container for it to double in volume.

THEY'RE READY . . .

When the bread is golden.

STORAGE

4–5 days

WHAT DOES THE POOLISH DO?

It is a fermenting agent that is easy to get underway, which can replace sourdough while bringing a particular taste (stronger than baker's yeast).

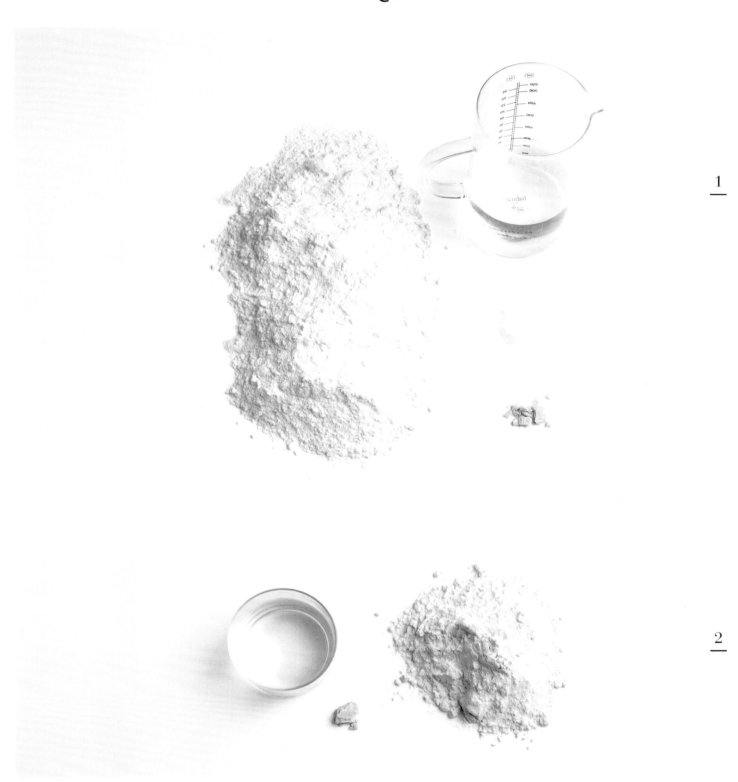

MAKES 4 LOAVES

1 POOLISH

1 g fresh baker's yeast
175 g water at 20°C
175 g T65 baker's flour

2 DOUGH

500 g T65 baker's flour
325 g water at 20–25°C
11 g salt
1 g fresh baker's yeast

Making pain maison

OVERNIGHT

1 Make the poolish (see page 24).

ON THE DAY

2 Knead the flour, water, salt, crumbled baker's yeast and poolish using an electric mixer (see pages 32–33) for 10–15 minutes at the lowest speed. The dough should pull away from the side of the bowl. (For kneading by hand, see pages 30–31.)

3 Place the dough in a round-bottomed bowl, cover with plastic wrap and leave to undergo pointage for 1 hour.

4 Make a rabat (fold; see page 37) at the end of 20 minutes, returning the dough to the bowl, then again at the 40-minute mark.

5 Divide the dough into four 250 g pieces using a dough cutter. Shape each dough piece into a rough rectangle by gently folding the two long sides underneath.

6 Place the dough pieces, seam side down, on a well-floured clean tea towel.

7 Leave the dough to prove for 45 minutes in a warm place (25–28°C).

8 Place a baking sheet and a heatproof bowl filled with water in the oven and preheat to 260°C (conventional oven). Remove the warmed baking sheet from the oven, line it with baking paper and place the turned-over baguettes on it, seam side up. Spray the bottom of the oven with water and bake the baguettes for 20–25 minutes (keeping the bowl of water in the oven).

COUNTRY BREAD

Understand

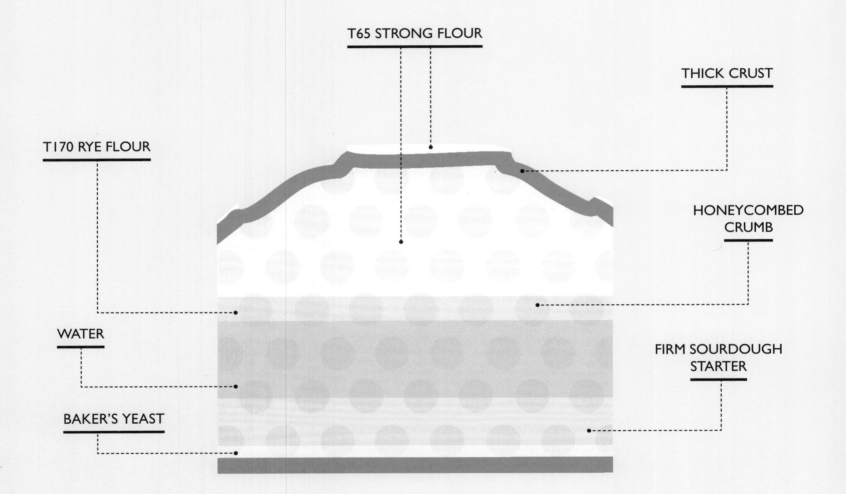

T65 STRONG FLOUR

THICK CRUST

T170 RYE FLOUR

HONEYCOMBED CRUMB

WATER

FIRM SOURDOUGH STARTER

BAKER'S YEAST

WHAT IS IT?

Torpedo loaf made with wheat and rye flours and firm sourdough starter.

CHARACTERISTICS

Weight: 200 g
Size: 20 cm
Crumb: honeycombed
Crust: thick
Taste: complex and acidic

TIME TO MAKE

Preparation: 30 minutes
Fermentation: 3 hours to 3 hours 30 minutes (1 hour of pointage, 30 minutes resting, 1 hour 30 minutes to 2 hours proving)
Baking: 25–30 minutes

EQUIPMENT

Electric mixer with dough hook (optional)
Dough cutter, bread lame (razor)

TECHNIQUES TO MASTER

Kneading (pages 30–33)
Rabat (folding; page 37)
Shaping into a torpedo loaf (page 45)
Slashing into a lattice (polka; page 51)

TRICKY ASPECT

Bassinage (page 32): enough to make the dough supple, but not so much it becomes sticky.

THEY'RE READY . . .

When the diamonds of the crust are spread out, and the bread is golden and sounds hollow.

STORAGE

5 days well wrapped uncut; 2–3 days once cut.

WHAT EXPLAINS THE LIGHT TEXTURE OF THE CRUMB?

There is enough wheat flour to provide a sufficient quantity of gluten to form the gluten network. The fermentation gases are retained, the bread rises and it is airy while still tasting of rye.

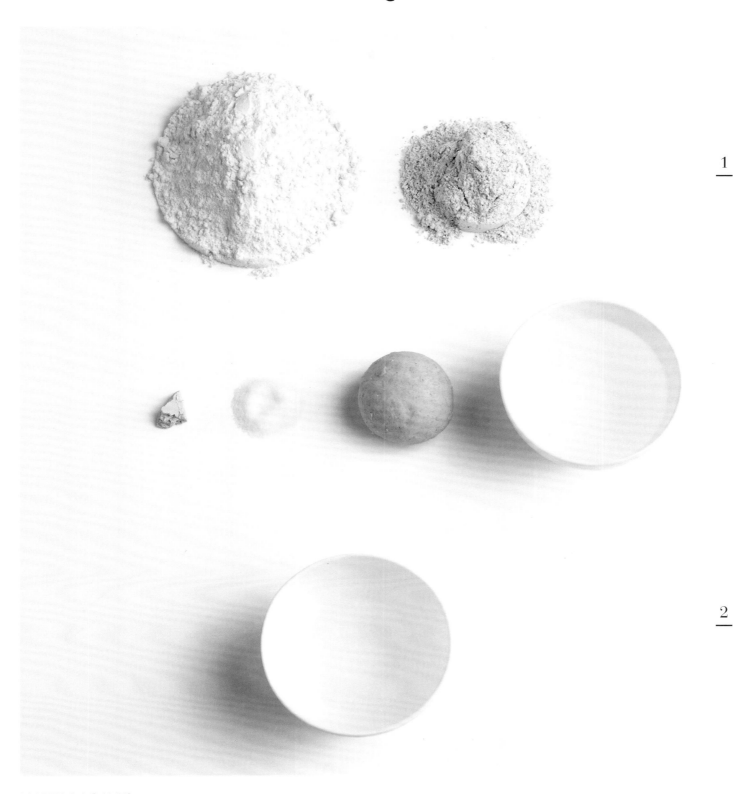

1

2

MAKES 2 LOAVES

1 DOUGH

155 g T65 stong flour
60 g T170 rye flour
150 g water
100 g firm sourdough starter (page 22)
2 g fresh baker's yeast
6 g salt

2 BASSINAGE

30 g water

Making country bread

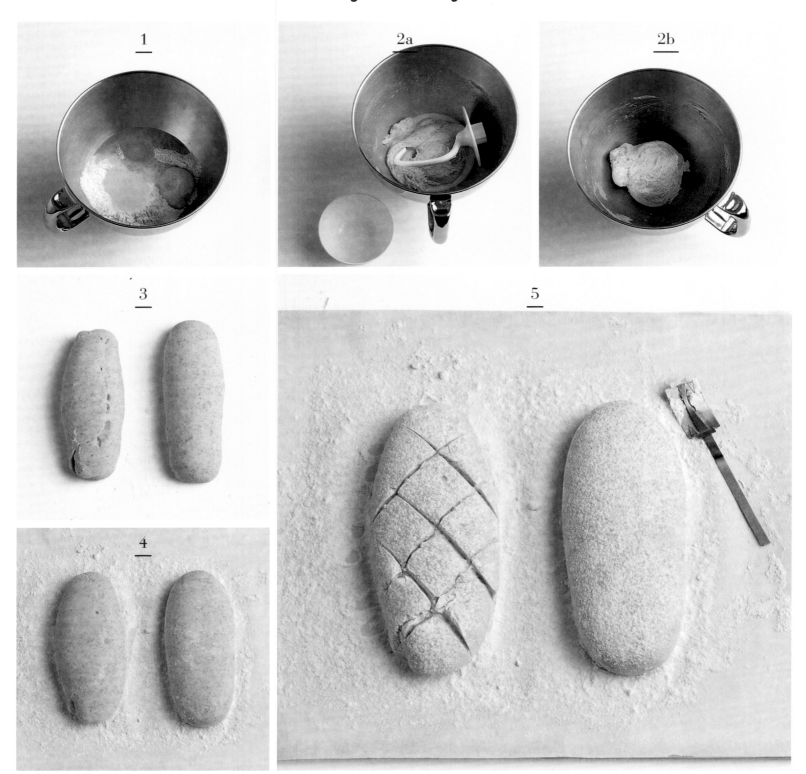

1   Knead the flours, water, firm starter, crumbled baker's yeast and salt using an electric mixer (see pages 32–33) for 4 minutes at the lowest speed, then 6 minutes at medium speed. The dough should pull away from the side of the bowl. (For kneading by hand, see pages 30–31.)

2   Add the bassinage at the end of kneading to adjust the consistency of the dough. Mix until the water is completely incorporated. Leave the dough on a floured work surface under a tea towel to undergo pointage for 1 hour. Make a rabat (fold; see page 37) after 30 minutes.

3   Using a dough cutter, cut the dough into two pieces of 250 g each. Pre-shape each into a log (see page 41), cover with a clean tea towel and leave to rest for 30 minutes at room temperature. Shape into torpedo loaves (see page 45).

4   With the seam side up, place both on a baking sheet lined with baking paper and cover with the tea towel to prevent a crust forming on the dough. Leave to prove for 1 hour 30 minutes to 2 hours in a warm place (25–28°C). The dough is risen when a light push with a finger leaves no trace.

5   Place a baking sheet and a heatproof bowl filled with water in the oven and preheat to 260°C (conventional oven). Remove the warmed baking sheet from the oven and line it with baking paper. Turn the loaves over and brush the undersides with your hand to remove any excess flour. Place the loaves, seam side down, on the warmed baking sheet. Slash the loaves in a lattice (polka; see page 51) using a bread lame (razor) held at a 45-degree angle. Spray the bottom of the oven with water and bake the bread for 25–30 minutes (keeping the bowl of water in the oven).

OLD-FASHIONED BREAD

Understand

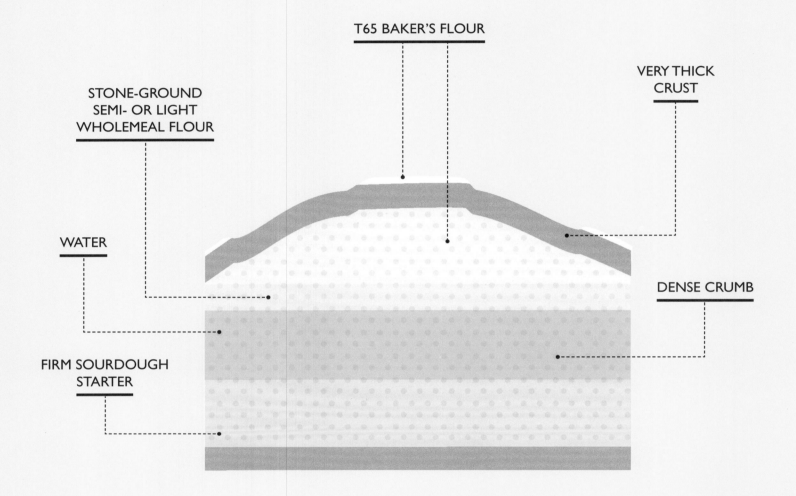

STONE-GROUND
SEMI- OR LIGHT
WHOLEMEAL FLOUR

T65 BAKER'S FLOUR

VERY THICK
CRUST

WATER

DENSE CRUMB

FIRM SOURDOUGH
STARTER

WHAT IS IT?

Bread made using firm sourdough
starter and a mixture of baker's flour and
stone-ground flour (which retains the
bran), shaped into a large long loaf.

CHARACTERISTICS

Weight: 500 g
Size: torpedo loaf 50–55 cm long
Crumb: dense
Crust: very thick
Taste: acidic, distinctive

TIME TO MAKE

Preparation: 40 minutes
Fermentation: 4 hours 30 minutes (2 hours of
pointage, 30 minutes resting, 2 hours proving)
Baking: 40 minutes

EQUIPMENT

Electric mixer with dough hook (optional)
Bread lame (razor)
Sieve

TECHNIQUES TO MASTER
Kneading (pages 30–33)
Rabat (folding; page 37)
Pre-shaping into a log (page 41)
Shaping into a torpedo loaf (page 45)
Slashing in a lattice (polka; page 51)

IT'S READY . . .
When the bread is golden and it sounds
hollow when tapped on the bottom.

STORAGE
4–5 days protected from the air.

MAKES I LOAF

130 g stone-ground T80 semi-wholemeal
or T110 light wholemeal flour
60 g T65 baker's flour
160 g water
150 g firm sourdough starter (page 22)
6 g salt

1 Knead the flours, water, crumbled firm starter and salt using an electric mixer (see pages 32–33) for 4 minutes at the lowest speed, then 6 minutes at medium speed. The dough should pull away from the side of the bowl. (For kneading by hand, see pages 30–31.)

2 Transfer the dough to a round-bottomed bowl, cover with plastic wrap and leave to undergo pointage for 1 hour at room temperature.

3 Make a rabat (fold; see page 37), then return the dough to the round-bottomed bowl, cover with plastic wrap and leave once more to undergo pointage for 1 hour at room temperature.

4 Form into a log (see page 41) and leave to rest for 30 minutes at room temperature.

5 Shape into a long torpedo loaf (see page 45).

6 Place the loaf, seam side down, on a sheet of baking paper, then cover with a clean tea towel and leave to prove for 2 hours in a warm place (25–28°C).

7 Place a baking sheet and a heatproof bowl filled with water in the oven and preheat to 260°C (conventional oven). Remove the warmed baking sheet from the oven and place the baking paper and the bread on it. Sift extra flour (see page 285) over the loaf and slash in a lattice (polka; see page 51) using a bread lame (razor).

8 Spray the bottom of the oven with water and bake the bread for 40 minutes (keeping the bowl of water in the oven). Open the oven 5–10 minutes before the end of cooking.

TOURTE DE MEULE

Understand

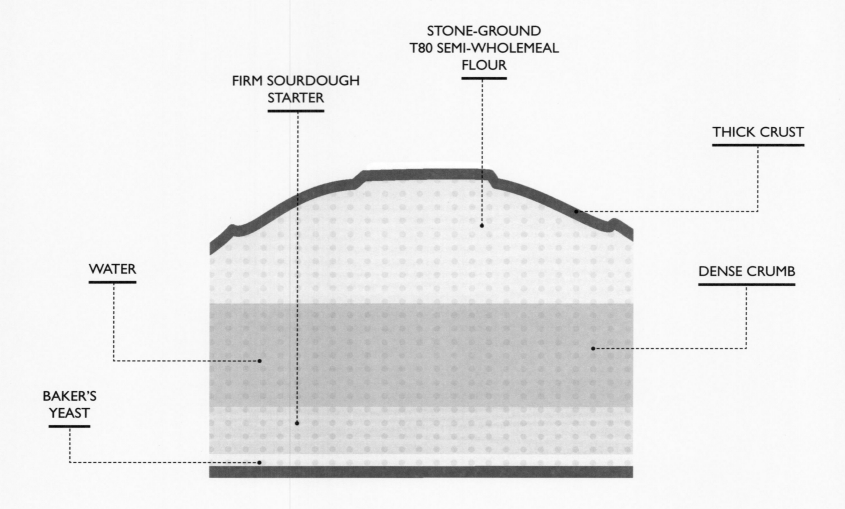

STONE-GROUND
T80 SEMI-WHOLEMEAL
FLOUR

FIRM SOURDOUGH
STARTER

THICK CRUST

WATER

DENSE CRUMB

BAKER'S
YEAST

WHAT IS IT?

Bread made with stone-ground
semi-wholemeal flour (which retains
the bran) and firm sourdough starter,
shaped into a large round.

CHARACTERISTICS

Weight: 550 g
Size: 20 cm diameter
Crumb: dense
Crust: thick
Taste: slightly acidic

TIME TO MAKE

Preparation: 30 minutes
Fermentation: 5 hours to 5 hours 30 minutes
(3 hours of pointage, 2 hours to
2 hours 30 minutes proving)
Baking: 35–40 minutes

EQUIPMENT

Electric mixer with dough hook (optional)
Bread lame (razor)

TECHNIQUES TO MASTER
Kneading (pages 30–33)
Rabat (folding; page 37)
Shaping into a ball (page 42)
Slashing a diamond (page 51)

TIP
Open the oven at the end of
baking and leave the door open for
10–15 minutes to dry out the crumb.

IT'S READY . . .
When the crust is nice and dark.

STORAGE
4–5 days protected from the air.

Learn

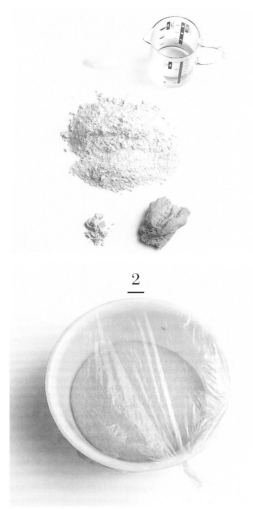

MAKES I LOAF

220 g stone-ground semi-wholemeal T80 flour
110 g firm sourdough starter (page 22)
4 g fresh baker's yeast
200 g water at 25°C
6 g salt

1   Knead the flour, firm starter, crumbled baker's yeast, water and salt using an electric mixer (see pages 32–33) for 4 minutes at the lowest speed, then 6 minutes at medium speed. The dough should pull away from the side of the bowl. (For kneading by hand, see pages 30–31.)

2   Transfer the dough to a round-bottomed bowl, cover with plastic wrap and leave to undergo pointage for 1 hour in a warm place (25–28°C).

3   Make a first rabat (fold; see page 37). Leave to undergo pointage for another 1 hour.

4   Make a second rabat (fold) then leave to undergo pointage for another 1 hour.

5   Shape into a ball (see page 42). Place seam side up on a clean, well-floured tea towel in a round-bottomed bowl and cover with another clean tea towel.

6   Leave to prove for 2 hours to 2 hours 30 minutes in a warm place (25–28°C).

7   Place a baking sheet and a heatproof bowl filled with water in the oven and preheat to 260°C (conventional oven). Remove the warmed baking sheet from the oven and line with baking paper. Place the bread seam side down on the lined sheet. Sift extra flour and slash in a diamond (see page 51) using a bread lame (razor).

8   Spray the bottom of the oven with water and bake for 35–40 minutes (keeping the bowl of water in the oven). Open the oven 5–10 minutes before the end of cooking.

SEED BREAD

Understand

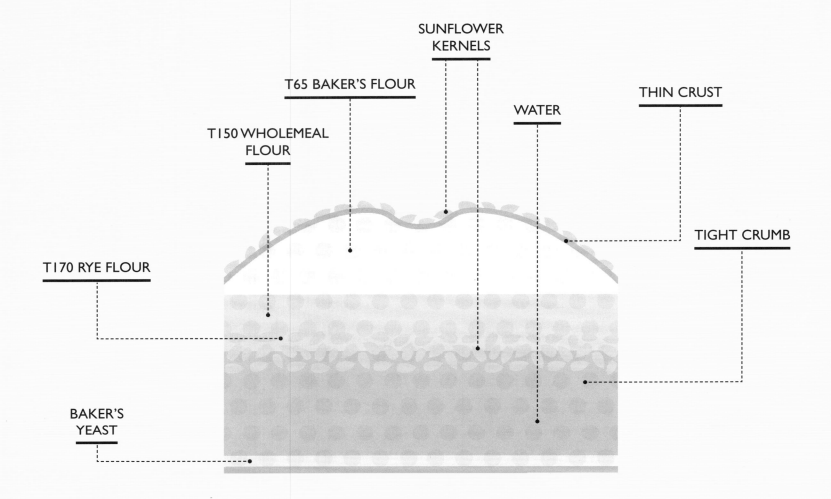

T150 WHOLEMEAL FLOUR

T65 BAKER'S FLOUR

SUNFLOWER KERNELS

WATER

THIN CRUST

TIGHT CRUMB

T170 RYE FLOUR

BAKER'S YEAST

WHAT IS IT?

Bread made with a mixture of baker's, wholemeal and rye flours, enriched and topped with sunflower kernels.

CHARACTERISTICS

Weight: 400 g
Size: 15 cm diameter
Crumb: tight
Crust: thin
Taste: grains and seeds

TIME TO MAKE

Preparation: 30 minutes
Fermentation: 3 hours (1 hour of pointage, 30 minutes resting, 1 hour 30 minutes proving)
Baking: 25–30 minutes

EQUIPMENT

Electric mixer with dough hook (optional)
Bread lame (razor)
Pastry brush

TECHNIQUES TO MASTER

Kneading (pages 30–33)
Pre-shaping into a ball (page 41)
Rabat (folding; page 37)

Shaping into a ball (page 42)
Slashing in a cross (page 51)

IT'S READY . . .

When the crust is brown and the bread sounds hollow when tapped on the bottom.

STORAGE

3–4 days wrapped in a tea towel to protect it from the air.

WHY IS THE CRUST THIN?

Compared with other large wholemeal loaves such as that on page 112, this seed bread contains no sourdough starter (which makes thick crusts) but baker's yeast instead (which makes thinner crusts).

MAKES 1 LOAF

1 DOUGH

100 g T65 baker's flour
50 g T150 wholemeal flour
50 g T170 rye flour
150 g water
4 g fresh baker's yeast
4 g salt
25 g sunflower kernels

2 TOPPING

10 g sunflower kernels

Making seed bread

1   Knead the flours, water, crumbled baker's yeast and salt using an electric mixer (see pages 32–33) for 4 minutes at the lowest speed, then 6 minutes at medium speed. The dough should pull away from the side of the bowl. (For kneading by hand, see pages 30–31.)

2   Add the sunflower kernels and knead at the lowest speed until incorporated.

3   Transfer the dough to a round-bottomed bowl.

4   Cover with plastic wrap and leave to undergo pointage for 30 minutes at room temperature.

5   Make a rabat (fold; page 37).

6   Return the dough to the round-bottomed bowl, cover with plastic wrap and leave for another 30 minutes of pointage.

7   Pre-shape into a ball (see page 41). Leave to rest under a clean tea towel at room temperature for 30 minutes. Shape into a ball (see page 42) then place seam side down on a sheet of baking paper. Use a pastry brush to brush the top of the bread with cold water, then scatter the topping sunflower kernels over.

8   Cover with the tea towel and leave to prove for 1 hour 30 minutes in a warm place (25–28°C).

9   Place a baking sheet and a heatproof bowl filled with water in the oven and preheat to 260°C (conventional oven). Slash a cross in the loaf (see page 51).

10   Remove the warmed baking sheet from the oven and place the bread and baking paper on it. Spray the bottom of the oven with water and bake the bread for 25–30 minutes (keeping the bowl of water in the oven). Open the oven 5–10 minutes before the end of cooking.

WHOLEMEAL BREAD

Understand

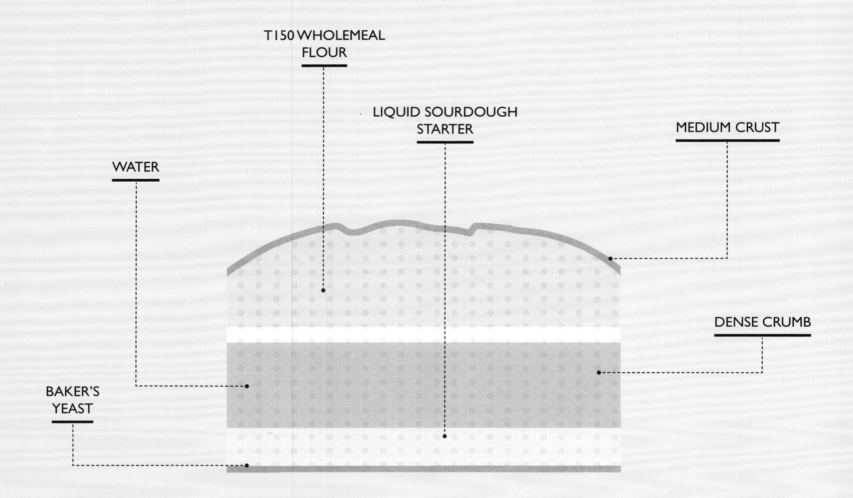

T150 WHOLEMEAL FLOUR

LIQUID SOURDOUGH STARTER

MEDIUM CRUST

WATER

DENSE CRUMB

BAKER'S YEAST

WHAT IS IT?

Bread made with liquid sourdough starter and wholemeal flour, shaped into a torpedo loaf.

CHARACTERISTICS

Weight: 360 g
Size: 25 cm
Crumb: dense
Crust: medium
Taste: rustic

TIME TO MAKE

Preparation: 15 minutes
Fermentation: 3 hours to 3 hours 30 minutes
(1 hour of pointage, 30 minutes resting,
1 hour 30 minutes to 2 hours proving)
Baking: 25–30 minutes

EQUIPMENT

Electric mixer with dough hook (optional)
Bread lame (razor)
Sieve

TECHNIQUES TO MASTER

Kneading (pages 30–33)
Pre-shaping into a ball (page 41)
Shaping into a torpedo loaf (page 45)
Slashing in sausage style (page 51)

TIP

At the end of proving, the dough
is risen when a light push with
a finger leaves no trace.

IT'S READY . . .

When the bread is golden and it
sounds hollow when tapped.

STORAGE

2 days

MAKES 1 LOAF

DOUGH

180 g T150 wholemeal flour
130 g water
45 g liquid sourdough starter (page 20)
4 g salt
3 g fresh baker's yeast

DUSTING

15 g T65 strong flour

1   Knead the wholemeal flour, water, liquid starter, salt and crumbled baker's yeast using an electric mixer (see pages 32–33) for 4 minutes at the lowest speed, then 6 minutes at medium speed. The dough should pull away from the side of the bowl. (For kneading by hand, see pages 30–31.)

2   Transfer the dough to a round-bottomed bowl, cover with a clean tea towel and leave to undergo pointage for 1 hour in a warm place (25–28°C).

3   Pre-shape the dough into a ball (see page 41). Place on a floured work surface, cover with the tea towel and leave to rest for 30 minutes.

4   Shape into a torpedo loaf (see page 45). Place the loaf seam side down on a sheet of baking paper. Sift the dusting flour over the loaf (see page 285).

5   Slash the loaf in sausage style (see page 51).

6   Cover with the tea towel and leave to prove for 1 hour 30 minutes to 2 hours in a warm place (25–28°C).

7   Place a baking sheet and a heatproof bowl filled with water in the oven and preheat to 260°C (conventional oven). Remove the warmed baking sheet from the oven and place the bread and baking paper on it. Spray the bottom of the oven with water and bake the bread for 25–30 minutes (keeping the bowl in the oven). Open the oven 5 minutes before the end of cooking.

RYE BREAD

Understand

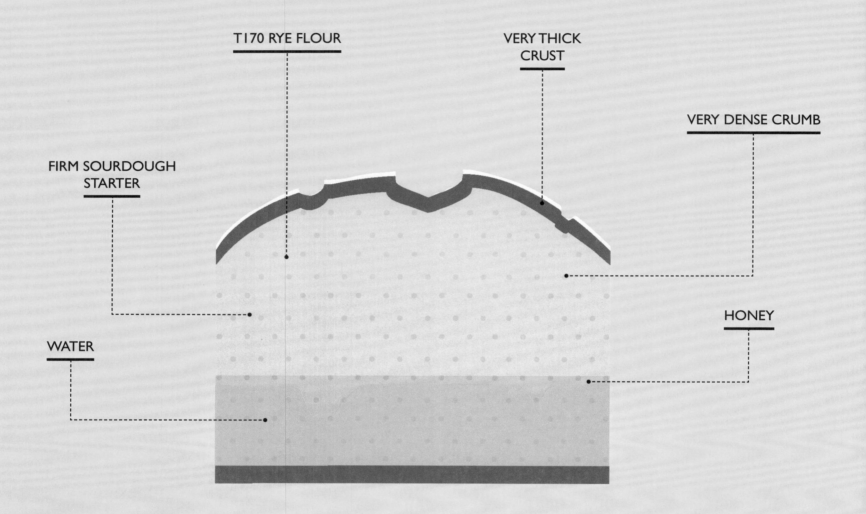

T170 RYE FLOUR

VERY THICK CRUST

VERY DENSE CRUMB

FIRM SOURDOUGH STARTER

WATER

HONEY

WHAT IS IT?

Bread made with rye flour as the only flour and firm sourdough starter, flavoured with honey and shaped into a large round.

CHARACTERISTICS

Weight: 500 g
Size: 20 cm diameter
Crumb: very dense
Crust: very thick, cracked and dusted with flour
Taste: strong, acidic, with a slight taste of caramel

TIME TO MAKE

Preparation: 30 minutes
Fermentation: 3 hours 30 minutes (2 hours of pointage, 1 hour 30 minutes proving)
Baking: 40–45 minutes

EQUIPMENT

Electric mixer with dough hook (optional)

TECHNIQUES TO MASTER

Kneading (pages 30–33)
Shaping into a ball (page 42)

IT'S READY . . .

When the bread is well browned. If you tap on it, it should sound hollow.

STORAGE

4–5 days wrapped in a clean tea towel.

WHY IS THE CRUMB SO DENSE?

The acidity of the dough (from the firm sourdough starter) and small proportion of gluten (rye flour contains very little) makes the formation of a gluten network difficult. The gases from fermentation escape and the crumb is therefore denser and less honeycombed.

MAKES 1 LOAF

170 g T170 rye flour
165 g water at 60°C
170 g firm sourdough starter (page 22)
5 g salt
7 g honey

Making rye bread

1   Knead the flour, water, crumbled firm starter, salt and honey using an electric mixer (see pages 32–33) for 4 minutes at the lowest speed, then 6 minutes at medium speed. (For kneading by hand, see pages 30–31.)

2   Cover the bottom of a round-bottomed bowl with flour and place the dough on top.

3   Cover the bowl with plastic wrap and leave to undergo pointage for 2 hours.

4   Shape into a ball (see page 42). Don't hesitate to dust your hands and the work surface with flour.

5   Line the bottom of the round-bottomed bowl with a floured tea towel and place the ball of dough on top, seam side down.

6   Cover with another clean tea towel and leave to prove for 1 hour 30 minutes in a warm place (25–28°C).

7   Place a baking sheet and a heatproof bowl filled with water in the oven and preheat to 260°C (conventional oven). Remove the warmed baking sheet from the oven and line it with baking paper. Turn the dough over so the seam is on top, remove any excess flour with your hand and place on the lined baking sheet. Spray the bottom of the oven with water and bake the bread for 40–45 minutes (keeping the bowl in the oven). Open the oven 5–10 minutes before the end of cooking.

RYE BREAD
WITH LEMON

Understand

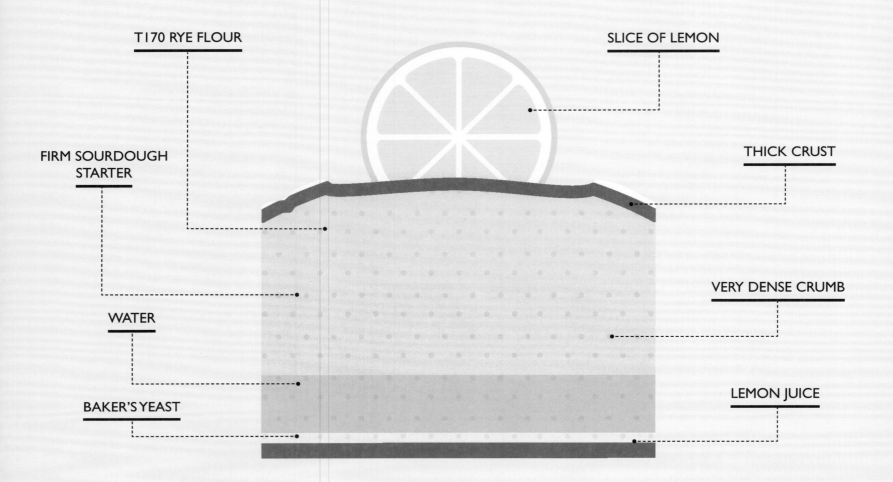

T170 RYE FLOUR

SLICE OF LEMON

FIRM SOURDOUGH STARTER

THICK CRUST

VERY DENSE CRUMB

WATER

BAKER'S YEAST

LEMON JUICE

WHAT IS IT?

Bread made using rye flour as the only flour and sourdough starter, flavoured with lemon (juice and zest).

CHARACTERISTICS

Weight: 250 g
Size: 15 cm diameter
Crumb: very dense
Crust: thick
Taste: acidic and lemony

TIME TO MAKE

Preparation: 30 minutes
Fermentation: 1 hour 45 minutes
(45 minutes of pointage, 1 hour proving)
Baking: 35 minutes

EQUIPMENT

Electric mixer with dough hook (optional)
Dough cutter

TECHNIQUES TO MASTER

Kneading (pages 30–33)
Shaping into a ball (page 42)

TIP

Add a few drops of lemon essence to reinforce the taste.

THEY'RE READY . . .

When the crusts are well browned. If you tap on them, they should sound hollow.

STORAGE

2 days

WHY IS THE CRUMB SO DENSE?

Rye flour contains very little gluten. The gluten network is therefore weaker. The gases from fermentation escape, the crumb isn't honeycombed and it is very dense after baking.

Learn

MAKES 2 LOAVES

160 g T170 rye flour
140 g water
160 g firm sourdough starter (page 22)
2 g fresh baker's yeast
5 g salt
15 g organic lemon juice
10 g organic lemon zest

TOPPING

15 g T65 strong flour
water
2 slices organic lemon

1 Knead the flour, water, firm starter, crumbled baker's yeast, salt, and lemon juice and zest using an electric mixer (see pages 32–33) for 4 minutes at the lowest speed, then 6 minutes at medium speed. The dough should pull away from the side of the bowl. (For kneading by hand, see pages 30–31.)

2 Transfer the dough to a round-bottomed bowl dusted with flour.

3 Cover with a clean tea towel and leave to undergo pointage for 45 minutes.

4 Divide the dough into two 250 g pieces using a dough cutter. Shape each into a ball (see page 42).

5 Place the pieces of dough on a sheet of baking paper, seam side down. Cover with a tea towel and leave to prove for 1 hour in a warm place (25–28°C).

6 Preheat the oven to 240°C (conventional oven) with a baking sheet inside. For the topping, sift the flour over the loaves (see page 285). Dampen the centre of the loaves slightly using a pastry brush and place a lemon slice on each one, pressing lightly. Place the loaves and the baking paper on the warmed baking sheet. Spray the bottom of the oven with water and bake the loaves for 35 minutes. Open the oven door 5 minutes before the end of cooking to dry out the crumb.

BLACK BREAD

Understand

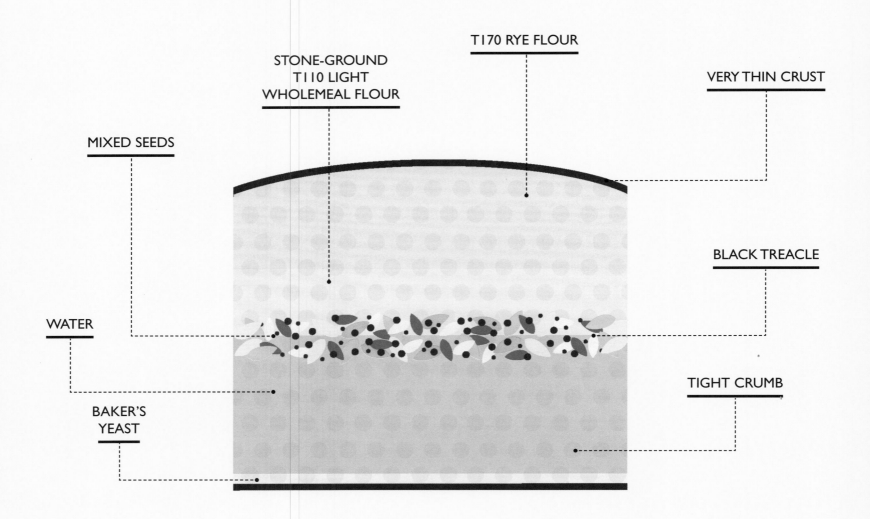

MIXED SEEDS

STONE-GROUND
T110 LIGHT
WHOLEMEAL FLOUR

T170 RYE FLOUR

VERY THIN CRUST

BLACK TREACLE

WATER

TIGHT CRUMB

BAKER'S
YEAST

WHAT IS IT?

Bread made using rye flour and
stone-ground wheat flour, enriched
with black treacle and seeds.

CHARACTERISTICS

Weight: 750 g
Size: 20 cm
Crumb: tight
Crust: very thin, soft
Taste: rustic, pronounced

TIME TO MAKE

Soaking: overnight
Preparation: 30 minutes
Fermentation: 1 hour (proving)
Baking: 45 minutes

EQUIPMENT

Electric mixer with dough hook (optional)
20 cm long loaf tin
Pastry brush

TECHNIQUES TO MASTER

Kneading (pages 30–33)

IT'S READY . . .
When the blade of a knife inserted
to the bottom comes out dry. If not,
return to the oven for a few minutes.

STORAGE
4–5 days protected from the air.

WHY ISN'T THE CRUST
CRUNCHY?

*Baking in a tin limits the development of
the crust because the dough cooks in a
moist environment and can't dry out.*

2

3

5

4

MAKES 1 LOAF

DOUGH

250 g T170 rye flour
150 g stone-ground T110 light wholemeal flour
320 g water at 20–25°C
10 g fresh baker's yeast
10 g salt
20 g black treacle

FLAVOURING

50 g mixed seeds (poppy, brown linseeds, sesame, sunflower)
40 g water

GREASING

olive oil

THE DAY BEFORE

1 Soak the seeds in the water overnight. The seeds will absorb all the water; if not, drain them.

ON THE DAY

2 Knead the flours, water, crumbled yeast, salt and treacle using an electric mixer (see pages 32–33) for 4 minutes at the lowest speed, then 6 minutes at medium speed. The dough should pull away from the side of the bowl. (For kneading by hand, see pages 30–31.)

3 Add the seeds and knead for a few moments at the lowest speed until well incorporated.

4 Use a pastry brush to grease a 20 cm long loaf tin with olive oil, then add the dough.

5 Cover with a clean tea towel and leave to prove for 1 hour in a warm place (25–28°C).

6 Place a baking sheet and a heatproof bowl filled with water in the oven and preheat to 230°C (conventional oven). Place the loaf tin on the warmed baking sheet. Spray the bottom of the oven with water and bake the bread for 45 minutes (keeping the bowl of water in the oven). Open the oven 5–10 minutes before the end of cooking.

CHESTNUT FLOUR
BREAD

Understand

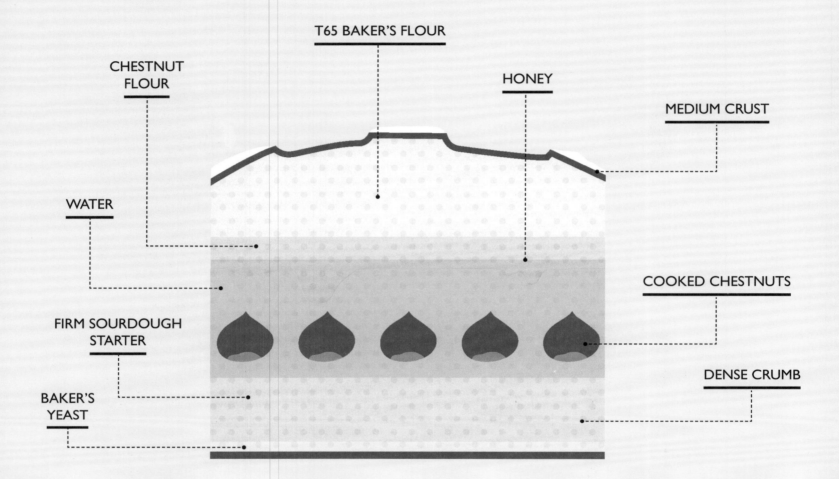

T65 BAKER'S FLOUR

CHESTNUT FLOUR

HONEY

MEDIUM CRUST

WATER

COOKED CHESTNUTS

FIRM SOURDOUGH STARTER

DENSE CRUMB

BAKER'S YEAST

WHAT IS IT?

Bread made with baker's flour (T65, without additives) and chestnut flour, enriched with whole chestnuts cooked in butter.

CHARACTERISTICS

Weight: 300 g
Size: 16–18 cm diameter
Crumb: dense
Crust: medium
Taste: strongly of chestnut

TIME TO MAKE

Preparation: 40 minutes
Fermentation: 2 hours 35 minutes
(45 minutes of pointage, 20 minutes resting, 1 hour 30 minutes proving)
Baking: 30 minutes

EQUIPMENT

Electric mixer with dough hook (optional)
Dough cutter
Bread lame (razor)

TECHNIQUES TO MASTER

Kneading (pages 30–33)
Pre-shaping into a ball (page 41)
Shaping into a ball (page 42)
Slashing in a lattice (polka; page 51)

THEY'RE READY . . .

When the crusts are golden and the diamonds created by slashing have separated slightly.

STORAGE

Up to 1 week uncut if protected from the air and 2–3 days once cut.

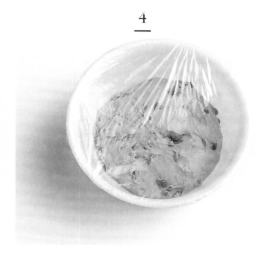

MAKES 2 LOAVES

DOUGH

200 g T65 baker's flour
25 g chestnut flour
160 g water
90 g firm sourdough starter (page 22)
3 g fresh baker's yeast
6 g salt
10 g honey

CHESTNUTS

100 g cooked chestnuts (in a
    jar or vacuum-packed)
10 g unsalted butter

DUSTING

15 g T65 strong flour

1   Put the chestnuts in a saucepan with the butter and leave over a low heat for 10 minutes. Remove from the heat and allow to cool for 5 minutes. Cut them in half, or quarters if they are large.

2   Knead the flours, water, firm starter, crumbled baker's yeast and salt using an electric mixer (see pages 32–33) for 4 minutes at the lowest speed, then 6 minutes at medium speed. The dough should pull away from the side of the bowl. (For kneading by hand, see pages 30–31.)

3   Preheat the oven to 180°C. Add the chestnuts and honey to the dough and knead to distribute them well.

4   Transfer the dough to a round-bottomed bowl, cover with plastic wrap and leave to undergo pointage for 45 minutes at room temperature.

5   Using a dough cutter, divide the dough into two 300 g pieces. Pre-shape into balls (see page 41) and leave to rest for 20 minutes. Shape into balls (see page 42). Place the loaves on a sheet of baking paper, seam side down. Cover with a clean tea towel and leave to prove for 1 hour 30 minutes in a warm place (25–28°C).

6   Preheat the oven to 260°C (conventional oven) with a baking sheet inside. Remove the warmed baking sheet from the oven and slide the baking paper with the loaves onto it. Dust the loaves with the flour then slash in a lattice (polka; see page 51). Spray the bottom of the oven with water and bake the loaves for 30 minutes.

BREAD WITH
CORNFLOUR

Understand

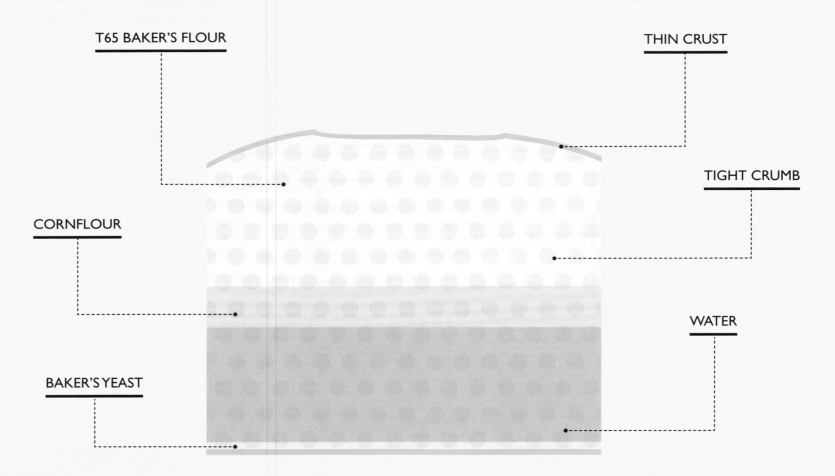

T65 BAKER'S FLOUR

THIN CRUST

TIGHT CRUMB

CORNFLOUR

WATER

BAKER'S YEAST

WHAT IS IT?

Bread made using baker's flour and cornflour, shaped into a torpedo loaf. In Australia, cornflour is sometimes made from wheat, so make sure you are using genuine cornflour.

CHARACTERISTICS

Weight: 250 g
Size: 20 cm
Crumb: tight
Crust: thin
Taste: slightly sweet

TIME TO MAKE

Preparation: 30 minutes
Fermentation: 2 hours 5 minutes
(30 minutes of pointage, 20 minutes resting, 1 hour 15 minutes proving)
Baking: 25 minutes

EQUIPMENT

Electric mixer with dough hook (optional)
Dough cutter
Bread lame (razor)

TECHNIQUES TO MASTER

Kneading (pages 30–33)
Pre-shaping into a ball (page 41)
Shaping into a torpedo loaf (page 45)
Traditional slashing (page 51)

TIP

At the end of proving, the dough is risen if a light push with a finger leaves no trace.

THEY'RE READY . . .

When the bread is golden and sounds hollow when tapped.

STORAGE

2–3 days

Learn

2a

2b

4

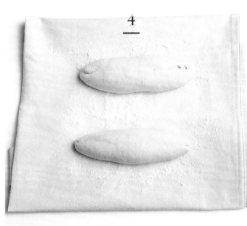

5

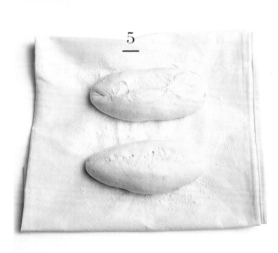

6

MAKES 2 LOAVES

285 g T65 baker's flour
70 g cornflour
225 g water at 20–25°C
11 g fresh baker's yeast
8 g salt

DUSTING

15 g cornflour

1   Knead the baker's flour, cornflour, water, crumbled yeast and salt using an electric mixer (see pages 32–33) for 4 minutes at the lowest speed, then 6 minutes at medium speed. The dough should pull away from the side of the bowl. (For kneading by hand, see pages 30–31.)

2   Transfer the dough to a round-bottomed bowl, cover with plastic wrap and leave to undergo pointage for 30 minutes at room temperature.

3   Divide the dough into two 300 g pieces using a dough cutter and pre-shape them into balls (see page 41). Cover and leave on a floured work surface to rest for 20 minutes.

4   Shape into torpedo loaves (see page 45). Place the loaves, seam side up, on a clean tea towel dusted with the cornflour.

5   Cover with another clean tea towel and leave to prove for 1 hour 15 minutes in a warm place (25–28°C).

6   Place a baking sheet and a heatproof bowl filled with water in the oven and preheat to 260°C (conventional oven). Remove the warmed baking sheet from the oven, line it with baking paper, then turn the loaves over and place them on the lined sheet, seam side down. Slash the loaves in the traditional pattern (see page 51), along their length.

7   Spray the bottom of the oven with water and bake the loaves for 25 minutes (keeping the bowl of water in the oven).

GLUTEN-FREE BREAD

Understand

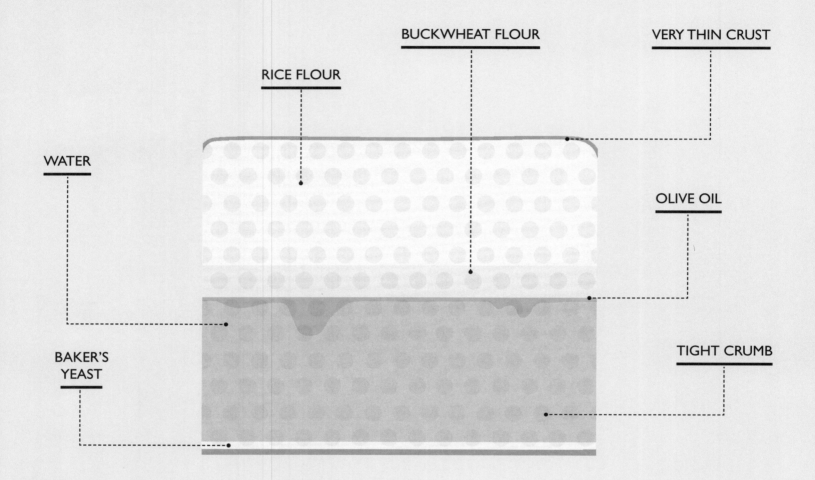

BUCKWHEAT FLOUR

VERY THIN CRUST

RICE FLOUR

WATER

OLIVE OIL

BAKER'S YEAST

TIGHT CRUMB

WHAT IS IT?

Bread without gluten made from rice flour and buckwheat flour, which requires a lot of water and a single rising.

CHARACTERISTICS

Weight: 300 g
Size: 15–20 cm depending on the tin
Crumb: tight
Crust: very thin, soft
Taste: quite neutral

TIME TO MAKE

Preparation: 15 minutes
Fermentation: 1 hour 15 minutes (proving)
Baking: 45 minutes

EQUIPMENT

Electric mixer with beater, or flexible spatula
Pastry brush
500 ml loaf tin

TIP

The dough is risen when a light push with a finger leaves no trace.

IT'S READY . . .

When the bread is golden and it sounds hollow when tapped.

STORAGE

2–3 days protected from the air.

WHY IS LOTS OF WATER
NEEDED?

The gluten-free flours contain more starch than flours with gluten. The starch requires water to swell and gelatinise during baking. For the loaf to form, it therefore needs lots of water.

MAKES I LOAF

DOUGH

260 g rice flour
60 g buckwheat flour
300 g water
5 g salt
6 g fresh baker's yeast
10 g olive oil

GREASING

15 g softened unsalted butter (page 284)

1 Using an electric mixer with the beater attachment, mix the flours, water, salt, crumbled yeast and olive oil for 5 minutes at the lowest speed.

2 Using a pastry brush, grease the tin with the butter, then pour in the dough.

3 Cover with a clean tea towel and leave the dough to prove for 1 hour 15 minutes at room temperature.

4 Preheat the oven to 220°C (fan-forced) with a baking sheet inside. Place the tin on the baking sheet and bake for 45 minutes.

BEER BREAD

Understand

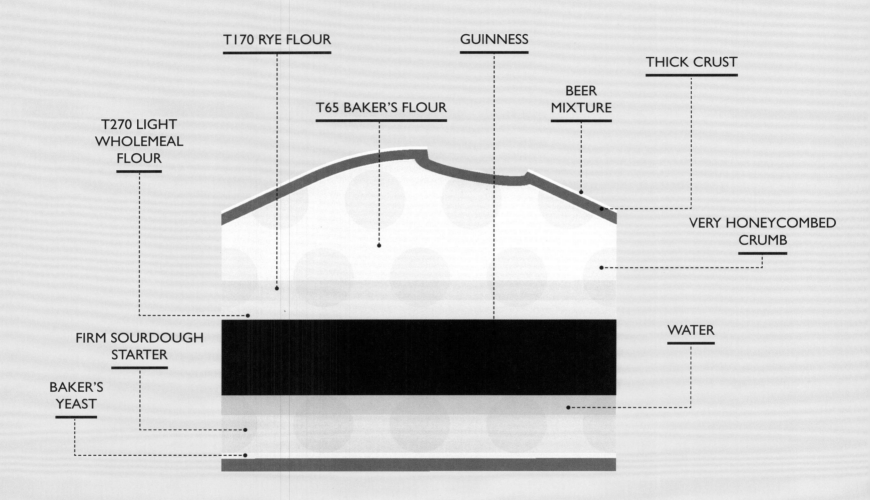

T170 RYE FLOUR

GUINNESS

THICK CRUST

T65 BAKER'S FLOUR

BEER MIXTURE

T270 LIGHT WHOLEMEAL FLOUR

VERY HONEYCOMBED CRUMB

FIRM SOURDOUGH STARTER

WATER

BAKER'S YEAST

WHAT IS IT?

Bread made with three flours – baker's (wheat flour without additives), rye and light wholemeal (page 15) – and dark beer, shaped into a triangle and covered with a beer mixture that makes the crust crackly.

CHARACTERISTICS

Weight: 300 g
Size: about 15 cm
Crumb: very honeycombed, rough
Crust: thick
Taste: malty

TIME TO MAKE

Preparation: 30 minutes
Fermentation: 2 hours 30 minutes (1 hour of pointage, 1 hour 30 minutes proving)
Resting: 1 hour 30 minutes (beer mixture)
Baking: 25 minutes

EQUIPMENT

Electric mixer with dough hook (optional)
Bent palette knife, or silicone spatula

TRICKY ASPECT

The beer mixture: it must be very smooth and spread uniformly over the bread to obtain a good cracked crust.

TECHNIQUES TO MASTER

Kneading (pages 30–33)
Rabat (folding; page 37)

THEY'RE READY . . .

When the crusts are well cooked and cracked.

STORAGE

3 days after cutting.

WHAT CREATES THE TEXTURE OF THE CRUMB?

The acidity provided by the beer mixture limits the formation of bonds in the gluten network. This is thus less well formed and the crumb is very fragile.

MAKES 2 LOAVES

1 BREAD DOUGH

200 g T65 baker's flour
40 g T170 rye flour
40 g T110 light wholemeal flour
180 g Guinness
80 g firm sourdough starter (page 22)
2 g fresh baker's yeast
6 g salt

2 BASSINAGE

40 g water

3 BEER MIXTURE

1 g fresh baker's yeast
10 g water
30 g rice flour
5 g melted unsalted butter
5 g caster sugar
1 g salt

4 DUSTING

15 g T65 strong flour

Making beer bread

1 Knead the flours, Guinness, firm starter, crumbled yeast and salt using an electric mixer (see pages 32–33) for 4 minutes at the lowest speed, then 6 minutes at medium speed. (For kneading by hand, see pages 30–31.)

2 Add the bassinage (see page 32) at the end of kneading to adjust the consistency of the dough. Knead until the water is completely incorporated. Transfer the dough to a round-bottomed bowl, cover with a clean tea towel and leave to undergo pointage for 30 minutes.

3 Make a rabat (fold; see page 37).

4 Return the dough to the round-bottomed bowl, cover again with the tea towel, and leave at room temperature to undergo further pointage for another 30 minutes.

5 Cut the dough in half and shape each half into a triangle using the flat of your hands.

6 Place the loaves on a sheet of baking paper, seam side down.

7 Cover with a clean tea towel and leave to prove for 1 hour 30 minutes in a warm place (25–28°C).

8 Prepare the beer mixture: dilute the crumbled yeast in the water, then add the remaining ingredients. Whisk until the mixture is smooth. Leave to rest for 1 hour 30 minutes.

9 Preheat the oven to 260°C (conventional oven) with a baking sheet inside. Spread the beer mixture on the loaves using a bent palette knife or a spatula.

10 Remove the warmed baking sheet from the oven and place the loaves and baking paper on it. Dust the tops of the loaves with the dusting flour. Spray the bottom of the oven with water and bake the loaves for 25 minutes.

MULTIGRAIN BREAD

Understand

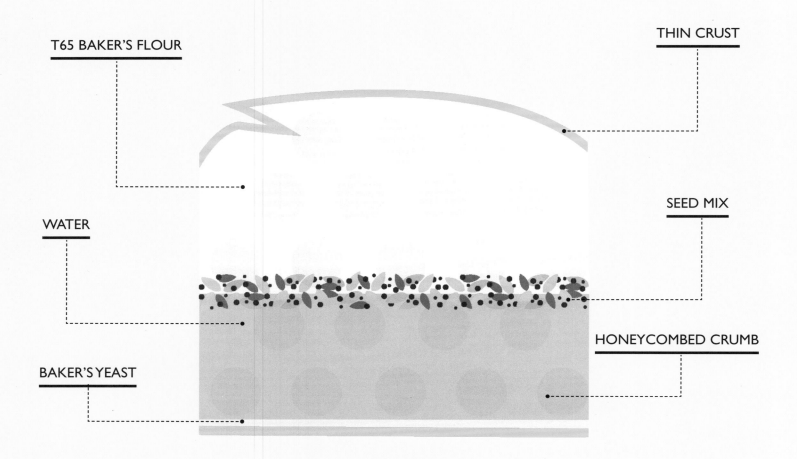

T65 BAKER'S FLOUR

THIN CRUST

WATER

SEED MIX

BAKER'S YEAST

HONEYCOMBED CRUMB

WHAT IS IT?

White bread enriched with seeds
and shaped into a crown.

CHARACTERISTICS

Weight: 150 g
Size: 18 cm diameter
Crumb: honeycombed, rough
Crust: thin
Taste: neutral plus the taste of the seeds

EQUIPMENT

Electric mixer with dough hook (optional)
Dough cutter, bread lame
(razor), sieve, scissors

TIME TO MAKE

Soaking: overnight
Preparation: 30 minutes
Fermentation: 3 hours 30 minutes (1 hour of
pointage, 30 minutes resting , 2 hours proving)
Baking: 20 minutes

TRICKY ASPECT

Shaping into a crown.

TECHNIQUES TO MASTER

Kneading (pages 30–33)
Pre-shaping into a ball (page 41)
Shaping into a crown (page 46)
Slashing into a wheat stalk (page 51)

THEY'RE READY . . .

When the bread is golden and
sounds hollow when tapped.

STORAGE

2–3 days

WHY IS IT NECESSARY TO REST
THE DOUGH DURING SHAPING
INTO A CROWN?

*To allow time for the gluten network to
relax. The dough should be supple enough
for the crown to be even and the same
all around before and after baking.*

<u>1</u>

<u>2</u>

MAKES 2 CROWNS

<u>1</u> DOUGH

220 g T65 baker's flour
145 g water at 20–25°C
4 g salt
4 g fresh baker's yeast

<u>2</u> SEEDS

30 g mixed seeds (sesame,
   linseeds, millet, poppy)
30 g water

<u>3</u> DUSTING

15 g T65 strong flour

Making multigrain bread

<u>3</u>

<u>5</u>

<u>6</u>

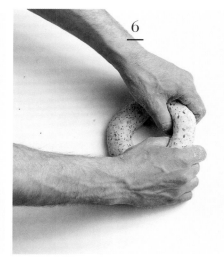

<u>7</u>

<u>8</u>

<u>9</u>

THE DAY BEFORE

1 Preheat the oven to 180°C and toast the seeds for 10–15 minutes in the oven. Allow them to cool then put them with the water in a round-bottomed bowl. Set aside at room temperature and leave overnight. The seeds will absorb all the water; if not, drain them.

ON THE DAY

2 Knead the flour, water, salt and crumbled yeast using an electric mixer (see pages 32–33) for 4 minutes at the lowest speed, then 6 minutes at medium speed. (For kneading by hand, see pages 30–31.)

3 Add the seed mixture and knead at the lowest speed until the seeds are well incorporated into the dough. Cover with plastic wrap and leave at room temperature to undergo pointage for 1 hour.

4 Divide the pastry into two 200 g pieces using a dough cutter, and pre-shape into balls (see page 41). Cover and leave on a floured work surface to rest for 30 minutes.

5 Shape both pieces into a crown (see page 46): dip an index finger in flour and pierce the centre of the dough ball until you feel the work surface.

6 Place both thumbs inside the hole and spread the dough in a circular movement. When the dough no longer stretches, leave it to rest for 5 minutes. Repeat the procedure until the interior diameter of the crown is 10 cm.

7 Place the crowns, seam side down, on a baking sheet lined with baking paper, cover with a clean tea towel and leave to prove for 2 hours in a warm place (25–28°C).

8 Dust the tops of the crowns with the dusting flour.

9 Preheat the oven to 260°C (conventional oven) with a heatproof bowl filled with water in it. Slash the crowns into wheat stalks (see page 51): make cuts with scissors held at a 45-degree angle, following the curve of the crown, and slightly detach the 'sheaves' towards the exterior.

10 Spray the bottom of the oven with water and bake the crowns for 20 minutes (keeping the bowl of water in the oven).

WALNUT BREAD

Understand

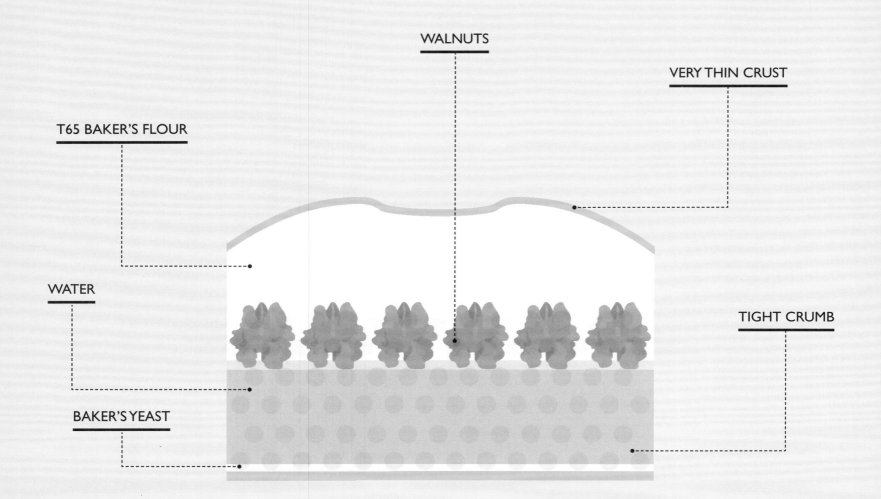

WALNUTS

VERY THIN CRUST

T65 BAKER'S FLOUR

WATER

TIGHT CRUMB

BAKER'S YEAST

WHAT IS IT?

Traditional dough enriched with
walnuts and shaped into a ball.

CHARACTERISTICS

Weight: 550 g
Size: 15 cm diameter
Crumb: tight
Crust: thin and supple

TIME TO MAKE

Preparation: 45 minutes
Fermentation: 3 hours (1 hour of pointage,
30 minutes resting, 1 hour 30 minutes proving)
Baking: 20–25 minutes

EQUIPMENT

Electric mixer with dough hook (optional)
Dough cutter
Bread lame (razor)

DERIVATIONS

Walnuts and hazelnuts
Walnuts, hazelnuts and sultanas

TECHNIQUES TO MASTER

Kneading (pages 30–33)
Pre-shaping into a ball (page 41)
Shaping into a ball (page 42)
Slashing in a cross (page 51)

IT'S READY . . .

When the bread sounds hollow when tapped
on the bottom.

STORAGE

2 days in a clean dry tea towel
protected from the air.

MAKES 1 LOAF

TRADITIONAL DOUGH (500 G)

270 g T65 baker's flour
190 g water at 20–25°C
5 g salt
30 g liquid sourdough starter (page 20)
3 g fresh baker's yeast

FLAVOURING

100 g walnuts, chopped

1 Knead the flour, water, salt, liquid starter and crumbled yeast using an electric mixer (see pages 32–33) for 4 minutes at the lowest speed, then 6 minutes at medium speed. The dough should pull away from the side of the bowl. (For kneading by hand, see pages 30–31.)

2 Add the walnuts. Knead at the lowest speed until they are well incorporated.

3 Transfer the dough to a round-bottomed bowl, cover with plastic wrap and leave to undergo pointage for 1 hour in a warm place (25–28°C). Make a rabat (fold; see page 37) after the first 30 minutes.

4 Pre-shape into a ball (see page 41) on a floured work surface. Cover with a clean tea towel and leave to rest for 30 minutes in a warm place (25–28°C).

5 Shape the dough into a ball (see page 42).

6 Place the dough seam side down, cover with a clean tea towel and leave to prove for 1 hour 30 minutes in a warm place (25–28°C).

7 Place a baking sheet and a heatproof bowl filled with water in the oven and preheat to 240°C (conventional oven). Remove the warmed sheet from the oven, line it with baking paper, then place the dough on the lined sheet, seam side down. Slash the dough in a cross (see page 51) using a bread lame (razor).

8 Spray the bottom of the oven with water and bake the loaf for 20–25 minutes (keeping the bowl of water in the oven).

CHOCOLATE BREAD

Understand

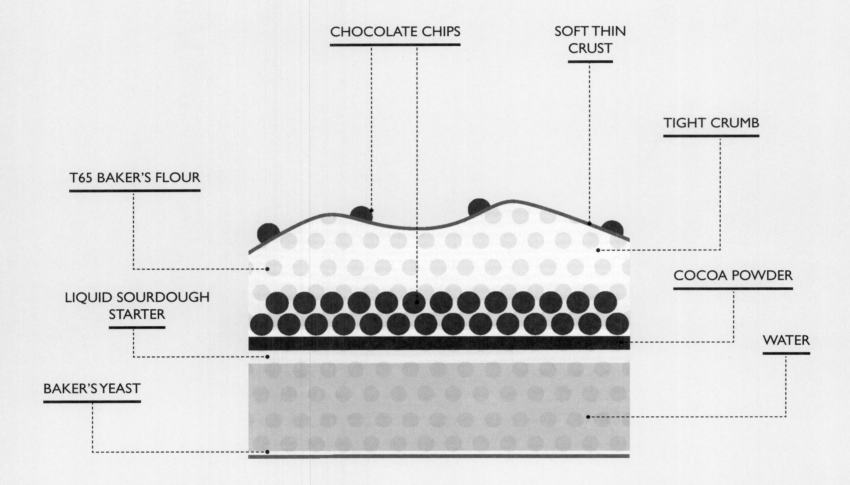

CHOCOLATE CHIPS

SOFT THIN CRUST

TIGHT CRUMB

T65 BAKER'S FLOUR

COCOA POWDER

LIQUID SOURDOUGH STARTER

WATER

BAKER'S YEAST

WHAT IS IT?

Traditional dough enriched with unsweetened cocoa powder and large dark chocolate chips, shaped into torpedo loaves.

CHARACTERISTICS

Weight: 150 g
Size: 12 cm
Crumb: tight
Crust: thin and supple

EQUIPMENT

Electric mixer with dough hook (optional)
Dough cutter, bread lame (razor)

TIME TO MAKE

Preparation: 45 minutes
Fermentation: 3 hours 30 minutes to 4 hours
(2 hours of pointage, 30 minutes resting,
1 hour to 1 hour 30 minutes proving)
Baking: 15 minutes

TRICKY ASPECT

The chocolate chips: stop kneading as soon as they are incorporated into the dough, to prevent them from melting.

TECHNIQUES TO MASTER

Kneading (pages 30–33)
Pre-shaping into a ball (page 41)
Rabat (folding; page 37)

Shaping into a torpedo loaf (page 45)
Slashing in traditional style (page 51)

THEY'RE READY . . .

When the crusts just start to harden.

STORAGE

3–4 days

WHAT DOES THE BASSINAGE DO?

*It softens the dough, which will be
very firm after the cocoa is added.
Incorporated after kneading, it prevents
adding too much water in one go.*

MAKES 3 LOAVES

1 TRADITIONAL DOUGH (310 G)

170 g T65 baker's flour
115 g water at 20–25°C
4 g salt
20 g liquid sourdough starter (page 20)
2 g fresh baker's yeast

2 FLAVOURING

10 g caster sugar
20 g cocoa powder
15 g water
70 g chocolate chips

3 BASSINAGE

15 g water at 20–25°C

<u>1</u>

<u>2</u>

<u>4</u>

<u>10</u>

<u>12</u>

1 Knead the flour, water, salt, liquid starter and crumbled yeast using an electric mixer (see pages 32–33) for 4 minutes at the lowest speed, then 6 minutes at medium speed. The dough should pull away from the side of the bowl. (For kneading by hand, see pages 30–31.)

2 Add the sugar, cocoa powder and water. Knead at the lowest speed until the dough is evenly coloured.

3 Add the bassinage (see page 32) and continue to knead slowly until the water is completely incorporated.

4 Add the chocolate chips and knead at the lowest speed until they are well incorporated.

5 Transfer the dough to a round-bottomed bowl, cover with plastic wrap and leave to undergo pointage for 30 minutes in a warm place (25–28°C).

6 Make a first rabat (fold; see page 37). Return the dough to the round-bottomed bowl, cover with plastic wrap and leave to undergo further pointage for 30 minutes in a warm place (25–28°C).

7 Make a second rabat (fold). Return the dough to the bowl, cover with plastic wrap and leave again to undergo pointage for another 1 hour in a warm place (25–28°C).

8 Using a dough cutter, divide the dough into three pieces, about 150 g each. Pre-shape each into a ball (see page 41) on a floured work surface.

9 Cover with a clean tea towel and leave to rest for 30 minutes in a warm place (25–28°C).

10 Shape each dough piece into a torpedo loaf (see page 45).

11 Place the loaves on a sheet of baking paper, seam side down. Cover with the tea towel and leave to prove for 1 hour to 1 hour 30 minutes in a warm place (25–28°C).

12 Place a baking sheet and a heatproof bowl filled with water in the oven and preheat to 240°C (conventional oven). Remove the warmed sheet from the oven, then place the loaves and the baking paper on it. Slash in the traditional style (see page 51).

13 Spray the bottom of the oven with water and bake the loaves for 15 minutes (keeping the bowl of water in the oven).

HAZELNUT AND FIG
BUNS

Understand

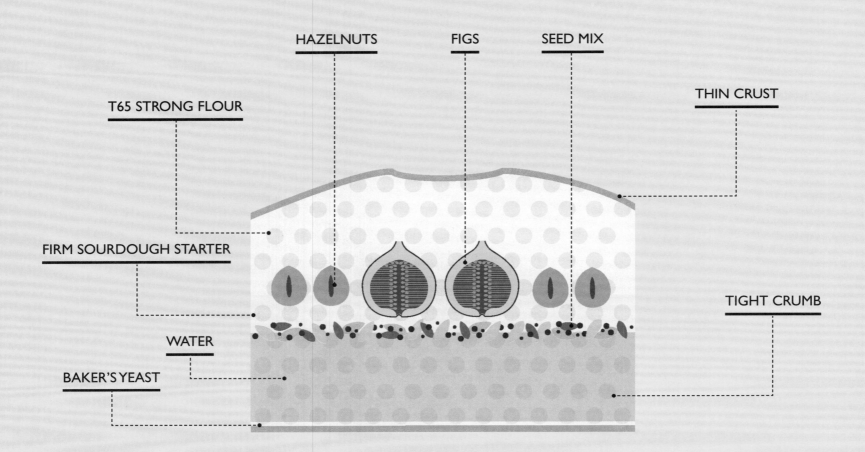

HAZELNUTS
FIGS
SEED MIX

T65 STRONG FLOUR

THIN CRUST

FIRM SOURDOUGH STARTER

TIGHT CRUMB

WATER

BAKER'S YEAST

WHAT ARE THEY?

Bread dough made with T65 strong flour and firm sourdough starter, enriched with toasted seeds, figs and hazelnuts, and shaped into buns.

CHARACTERISTICS

Weight: 75 g
Size: 10 cm diameter
Crumb: tight
Crust: thin

TIME TO MAKE

Soaking: overnight
Preparation: 25 minutes
Fermentation: 3 hours to 3 hours 30 minutes
(1 hour of pointage, 30 minutes resting,
1 hour 30 minutes to 2 hours proving)
Baking: 15 minutes

EQUIPMENT

Electric mixer with dough hook (optional)
Dough cutter
Bread lame (razor)

TECHNIQUES TO MASTER

Kneading (pages 30–33)
Pre-shaping into a ball (page 41)
Shaping into a ball (page 42)
Rabat (folding; page 37)
Slashing in a cross (page 51)

TIPS

If the seeds have not absorbed all the water, drain them before adding to the dough.

THEY'RE READY . . .

When the rolls are golden and they sound hollow when tapped.

STORAGE

3 days

MAKES 6

DOUGH

190 g T65 strong flour
60 g firm sourdough starter (page 22)
2 g fresh baker's yeast
130 g water
4 g salt

FLAVOURING

30 g mixed seeds (sesame, yellow linseeds,
   brown linseeds, millet, poppy)
30 g water
15 g hazelnuts
15 g dried figs, cut into quarters

THE DAY BEFORE

1 Preheat the oven to 180°C and toast the seeds for 10 minutes. Cool then put with the water in a round-bottomed bowl. Set aside at room temperature and leave overnight. The seeds will absorb all the water; if not, drain them.

ON THE DAY

2 Knead the dough ingredients using an electric mixer (see pages 32–33) for 4 minutes at the lowest speed, then 6 minutes at medium speed. The dough should pull away from the side of the bowl. Add the hazelnuts, figs and seeds, then knead at the lowest speed until well incorporated. (For kneading by hand, see pages 30–31.)

3 Transfer to a round-bottomed bowl. Cover with plastic wrap and leave to undergo pointage for 30 minutes at room temperature. Make a rabat (fold; see page 37), return the dough to the bowl and leave for another 30 minutes of pointage.

4 Divide into six 75 g pieces using a dough cutter. Pre-shape each piece into a ball (see page 41) and leave to rest on a floured work surface, covered with a clean tea towel, for 30 minutes.

5 Shape into balls (see page 42). Place on a sheet of baking paper, seam side down, cover with the tea towel and leave to prove for 1 hour 30 minutes to 2 hours in a warm place (25–28°C).

6 Slash in a cross (see page 51). Place a baking sheet and a heatproof bowl filled with water in the oven and preheat to 240°C (conventional oven). Slide the baking paper with the rolls onto the warmed sheet. Spray the bottom of the oven with water and bake for 15 minutes (keeping the bowl of water in the oven).

MUESLI
BUNS

Understand

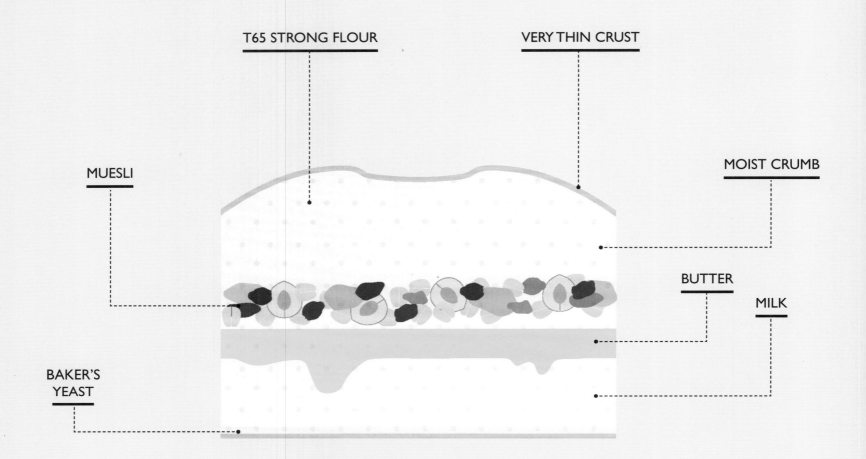

MUESLI

T65 STRONG FLOUR

VERY THIN CRUST

MOIST CRUMB

BUTTER

MILK

BAKER'S YEAST

WHAT ARE THEY?

Vienna dough enriched with muesli and shaped into buns.

CHARACTERISTICS

Weight: 80 g
Size: 10 cm diameter
Crumb: soft and moist
Crust: very thin, supple

TIME TO MAKE

Preparation: 30 minutes
Fermentation: 8 hours (30 minutes of pointage, 5 hours pointage in the refrigerator, 30 minutes resting, 2 hours proving)
Baking: 15 minutes

EQUIPMENT

Electric mixer with dough hook (optional)
Dough cutter
Bread lame (razor)
Pastry brush

TECHNIQUES TO MASTER

Kneading (pages 30–33)
Rabat (folding; page 37)
Pre-shaping into a ball (page 41)
Shaping into a ball (page 42)
Glazing (page 49)
Slashing in a lattice (polka; page 51)

TIPS

Use a muesli with rolled oats.
Avoid fresh fruits, which will add too much moisture to the dough.

THEY'RE READY . . .

When the crusts are golden.

STORAGE

No more than 1–2 days.

2

4

5

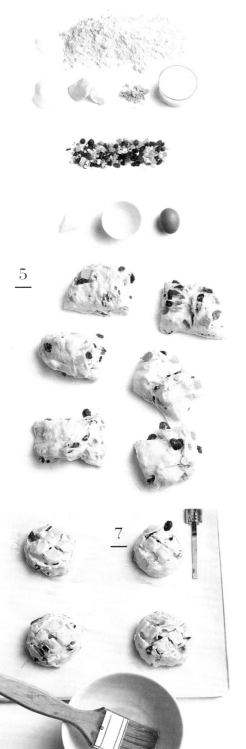

7

MAKES 6

VIENNA DOUGH

240 g T65 strong flour
150 g milk
5 g salt
5 g fresh baker's yeast
20 g caster sugar
40 g unsalted butter, cut into small cubes

FLAVOURING

60 g muesli (rolled oats, hazelnuts, sultanas, dried tropical fruits)

GLAZE

1 egg
3 g (½ teaspoon) milk
pinch of salt

1   Make the Vienna dough (see page 60).

2   Add the muesli and knead at low speed to spread it evenly through the dough.

3   Transfer the dough to a round-bottomed bowl, cover with plastic wrap and leave for 30 minutes to undergo pointage.

4   Make a rabat (fold; see page 37), return to the bowl, cover with plastic wrap touching the dough (see page 285) and refrigerate for another 5 hours of pointage.

5   Using a dough cutter, divide the dough into six pieces of about 80 g each. Pre-shape each piece into a ball (see page 43). Cover with a clean tea towel and leave for 30 minutes on a floured work surface to rest.

6   Shape each dough piece into a ball (see page 42). Place them on a sheet of baking paper, seam side down.

7   Make the glaze (see page 49). Glaze the rolls using a pastry brush. Slash in a lattice (polka; see page 51). Cover with the tea towel and leave to prove for 2 hours in a warm place (25–28°C).

8   Preheat the oven to 200°C with a baking sheet inside. Remove the warmed sheet from the oven and slide the baking paper with the rolls onto it. Re-glaze if necessary and bake for 15 minutes.

CHEESE
BREAD

Understand

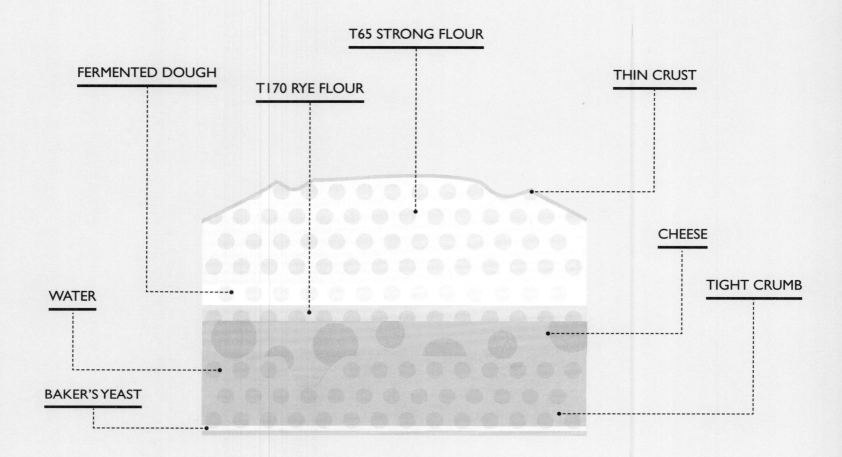

FERMENTED DOUGH

T170 RYE FLOUR

T65 STRONG FLOUR

THIN CRUST

CHEESE

WATER

TIGHT CRUMB

BAKER'S YEAST

WHAT IS IT?

Yeast dough enriched with wheat and rye flours, filled with cheese and shaped into three torpedo loaves.

CHARACTERISTICS

Weight: 200 g
Size: 15 cm
Crumb: tight
Crust: thin

TIME TO MAKE

Preparation: 30 minutes
Fermentation: 2 hours 30 minutes (1 hour of pointage, 30 minutes resting, 1 hour proving)
Baking: 20–25 minutes

EQUIPMENT

Electric mixer with dough hook (optional)
Dough cutter
Bread lame (razor)

TRICKY ASPECT

Baking: the bread must be cooked but stay moist.

TECHNIQUES TO MASTER

Kneading (pages 30–33)
Pre-shaping into a ball (page 41)
Shaping into a torpedo loaf (page 45)
Slashing in sausage style (page 51)

TIP

At the end of proving, the dough is risen when a light push with a finger leaves no trace.

THEY'RE READY . . .

When the bread is golden and sounds hollow when tapped.

STORAGE

2–3 days

2

5

6a

6b

7

MAKES 3 LOAVES

DOUGH

250 g T65 strong flour
30 g rye flour
200 g water at 20–25°C
3 g fresh baker's yeast
60 g fermented dough (page 56)
5 g salt

FLAVOURING

120 g comté or cantal cheese

1 Knead the flours, water, crumbled yeast, fermented dough and salt using an electric mixer (see pages 32–33) for 4 minutes at the lowest speed, then 6 minutes at medium speed. The dough should pull away from the side of the bowl. (For kneading by hand, see pages 30–31.)

2 Cut the cheese into 1 cm cubes. Knead into the dough to spread them evenly.

3 Transfer the dough to a round-bottomed bowl.

4 Cover with a clean tea towel and leave to undergo pointage for 1 hour in a warm place (25–28°C).

5 Divide the dough into three 200 g pieces using a dough cutter, and pre-shape each into a ball (see page 41). Leave on a floured work surface, covered with the tea towel, for 30 minutes to rest.

6 Shape each dough piece into a torpedo (see page 45).

7 Slash the loaves in sausage style (see page 51).

8 Place the loaves on a sheet of baking paper, seam side down. Cover with the tea towel and leave to prove for 1 hour in a warm place (25–28°C).

9 Place a baking sheet and a heatproof bowl filled with water in the oven and preheat to 250°C (conventional oven). Remove the warmed baking sheet from the oven and slide the baking paper with the loaves onto it. Spray the bottom of the oven with water and bake the bread for 20–25 minutes (keeping the bowl in the oven).

ITALIAN ROLLS

Understand

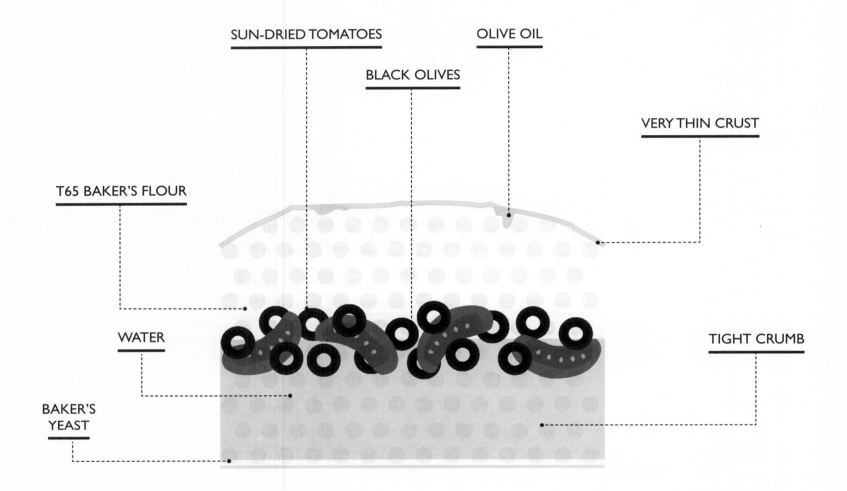

SUN-DRIED TOMATOES

BLACK OLIVES

OLIVE OIL

VERY THIN CRUST

T65 BAKER'S FLOUR

WATER

TIGHT CRUMB

BAKER'S YEAST

WHAT ARE THEY?

Traditional bread enriched with olives, sun-dried tomatoes and mixed herbs, shaped into rolls.

CHARACTERISTICS

Weight: 85 g
Size: 20 cm
Crumb: tight
Crust: very thin, soft

TIME TO MAKE

Preparation: 25 minutes
Fermentation: 3 hours 30 minutes
(1 hour 30 minutes of pointage, 30 minutes resting, 1 hour 30 minutes proving)
Baking: 10 minutes

EQUIPMENT

Electric mixer with dough hook (optional)
Dough cutter
Pastry brush

TECHNIQUES TO MASTER
Kneading (pages 30–33)
Rabat (folding; page 37)
Pre-shaping into a log (page 41)
Shaping into French sticks (page 44)

THEY'RE READY . . .
When the crusts have just started to brown.

STORAGE
1 day

Learn

MAKES 6

TRADITIONAL DOUGH (410 G)

245 g T65 baker's flour
160 g water
4 g salt
4 g fresh baker's yeast

FLAVOURING

60 g pitted black olives
40 g sun-dried tomatoes
pinch of mixed herbs (herbes de Provence)
olive oil, for brushing

1 Drain the olives and sun-dried tomatoes well. Make the traditional dough (see page 56). Add the olives, sun-dried tomatoes and herbs, and knead using an electric mixer (see pages 32–33) at the lowest speed until well incorporated. (To knead by hand, see pages 30–31.)

2 Transfer the dough to a round-bottomed bowl, cover with plastic wrap and leave to undergo pointage for 30 minutes at room temperature.

3 Make a rabat (fold; see page 37). Return the dough to the bowl, cover with plastic wrap and leave for another 1 hour of pointage at room temperature.

4 Using a dough cutter, divide the dough into six pieces of about 85 g each. Pre-shape the dough pieces into short logs (see page 41).

5 Leave the dough to rest on a floured work surface, covered with a clean tea towel for 30 minutes.

6 Shape the dough pieces into French sticks (see page 44). Place on a sheet of baking paper, seam side down, cover with the tea towel and leave to prove for 1 hour 30 minutes in a warm place (25–28°C).

7 Place a baking sheet and a heatproof bowl filled with water in the oven and preheat to 240°C (conventional oven). Remove the warmed baking sheet from the oven and slide the baking paper with the French sticks onto it. Spray the bottom of the oven with water and bake the bread for 10 minutes (keeping the bowl in the oven).

8 Use a pastry brush to brush the rolls with a little olive oil when they come out of the oven.

FRENCH STICKS
WITH CHEESE

Understand

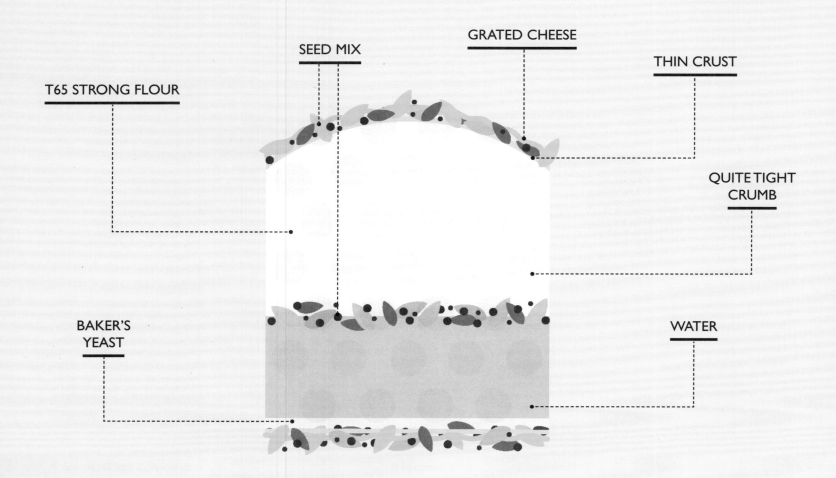

SEED MIX

GRATED CHEESE

THIN CRUST

T65 STRONG FLOUR

QUITE TIGHT
CRUMB

BAKER'S
YEAST

WATER

WHAT ARE THEY?

White dough enriched with cream, shaped into thin French sticks, and rolled in a mixture of grated cheese, fleur de sel (a type of salt) and seeds before baking.

CHARACTERISTICS

Weight: 120 g
Size: 25 cm
Crumb: quite tight, even
Crust: thin

TIME TO MAKE

Preparation: 40 minutes over 2 days
(20 minutes per day)
Fermentation: 1 hour 20 minutes
(20 minutes of pointage, 1 hour proving)
Baking: 15–20 minutes

EQUIPMENT

Electric mixer with dough hook (optional)
Dough cutter
Pastry brush

TRICKY ASPECT

Coating the rolls in the mixture of seeds and cheese.

TECHNIQUES TO MASTER

Kneading (pages 30–33)
Shaping into a French stick (page 44)

THEY'RE READY . . .

When the rolls are lightly golden.

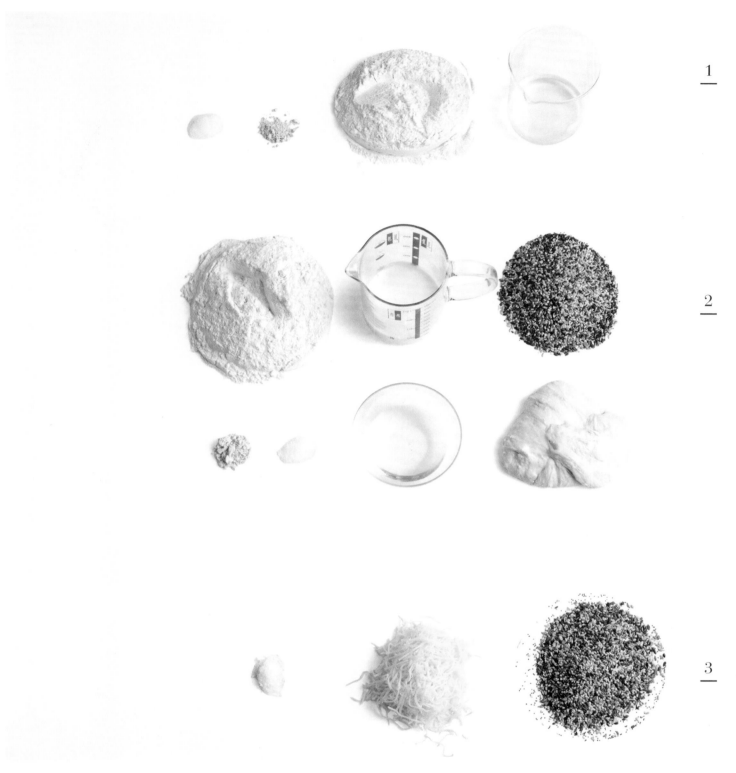

MAKES 4

1 FERMENTED WHITE DOUGH

125 g T65 strong flour
65 g water
2 g salt
1 g fresh baker's yeast

2 BREAD DOUGH

190 g T65 strong flour
40 g water
190 g fermented dough
100 g pouring (single) cream
4 g salt
3 g fresh baker's yeast
70 g mixed seeds (linseeds, poppy, sesame)

3 TO FINISH

60 g mixed seeds (linseeds, poppy, sesame)
50 g finely grated cheese
2 g fleur de sel

Making French sticks with cheese

1

3

4

5

6

7

THE DAY BEFORE

1   Make the white dough base (see page 54) and leave to rest for at least 24 hours, to make fermented dough.

ON THE DAY

2   Knead the flour, water, fermented dough, cream, salt and crumbled yeast using an electric mixer (see pages 32–33) for 4 minutes at the lowest speed, then 6 minutes at medium speed. (For kneading by hand, see pages 30–31.)

3   Add the seeds and continue to knead at the lowest speed to spread them evenly through the dough.

4   Transfer the dough to a round-bottomed bowl. Cover with a clean tea towel and leave to undergo pointage for 20 minutes.

5   Divide the dough into four 145 g pieces using a dough cutter. Shape each piece into a French stick (see page 44).

6   Moisten the seam side of the sticks with water using a pastry brush. Cover a plate with the mixed seeds, cheese and salt and lay the moistened side of each roll in this mixture to coat.

7   Place the sticks on a sheet of baking paper, seam and coating side up. Cover with the tea towel and leave to prove for 1 hour in a warm place (25–28°C).

8   Place a baking sheet and a heatproof bowl filled with water in the oven and preheat to 240°C (conventional oven). Remove the warmed baking sheet from the oven and slide the baking paper with the sticks onto it. Spray the bottom of the oven with water and bake the bread for 15–20 minutes (keeping the bowl in the oven).

SURPRISE BREAD

Understand

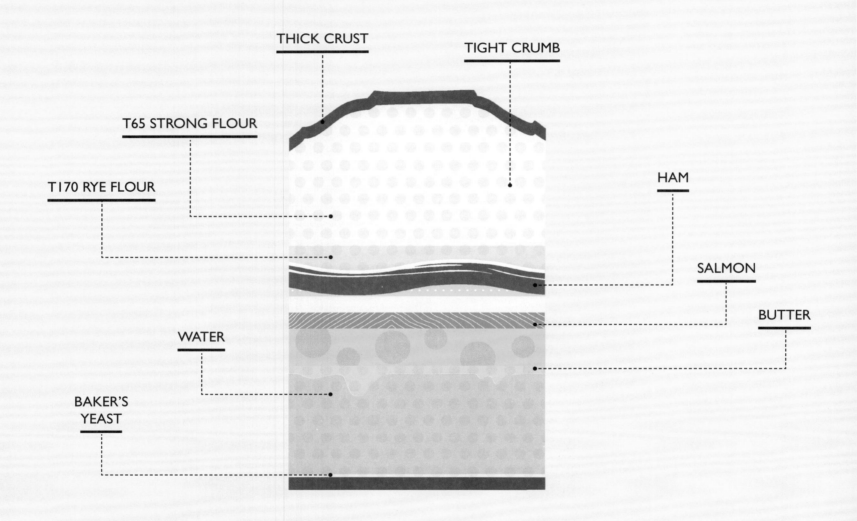

THICK CRUST

TIGHT CRUMB

T65 STRONG FLOUR

T170 RYE FLOUR

HAM

SALMON

BUTTER

WATER

BAKER'S YEAST

WHAT IS IT?

Bread based on a mixture of wheat and rye flours, baked in a high round cooking ring. After baking, the centre of the bread is filled and cut into sandwiches.

CHARACTERISTICS

Size: 35 cm high
Weight: 2 kg
Crumb: tight
Crust: thick

TIME TO MAKE

Preparation: 40 minutes
Fermentation: 2 hours (30 minutes of pointage, 1 hour 30 minutes proving)
Baking: 1 hour 20 minutes

EQUIPMENT

Electric mixer with dough hook (optional)
Sieve
Bread lame (razor) and bread knife
Tart ring 16 cm diameter and 12 cm high
Pastry brush

TRICKY ASPECT

Cleanly removing the centre of the bread.

TECHNIQUES TO MASTER

Kneading (pages 30–33)
Rabat (folding; page 37)
Shaping into a ball (page 42)
Slashing in a lattice (polka; page 51)

TIP

Cover the bread with a sheet of baking paper after 30 minutes in the oven, to prevent the top burning.

IT'S READY . . .

When the top is well browned and the blooms have separated.

STORAGE

4–5 days protected from the air.

1

2–3

4

FOR I SURPRISE BREAD:
60–70 SANDWICHES

1 BREAD DOUGH

725 g T65 strong flour
80 g T170 rye flour
525 g cold water
12 g fresh baker's yeast
15 g salt

2 DUSTING

20 g T65 strong flour

3 GREASING

40 g softened unsalted butter (page 284)

4 FILLING

25 g softened unsalted butter (page 284)
6 slices Bayonne ham (or proscuitto)
25 g softened butter (page 284)
150 g comté cheese, sliced
100 g fromage frais (or sour cream)
4 slices smoked salmon

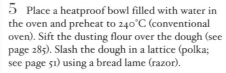

1   Knead the flours, water, crumbled yeast and salt using an electric mixer (see pages 32–33) for 4 minutes at the lowest speed, then 6 minutes at medium speed. The dough should pull away from the side of the bowl. (For kneading by hand, see pages 30–31.)

2   Transfer to a floured work surface, cover with a clean tea towel and leave to undergo pointage for 30 minutes at room temperature. Make a rabat (fold; see page 37) after 15 minutes, folding the dough in half.

3   Grease the pastry ring with the butter using a pastry brush. Shape the dough into a ball (see page 42) and put it in the ring on a baking sheet lined with baking paper.

4   Leave the dough to prove under the tea towel for 1 hour 30 minutes in a warm place (25–28°C): the dough should emerge from the top of the ring slightly.

5   Place a heatproof bowl filled with water in the oven and preheat to 240°C (conventional oven). Sift the dusting flour over the dough (see page 285). Slash the dough in a lattice (polka; see page 51) using a bread lame (razor).

6   Spray the bottom of the oven with water and bake for 40 minutes (keeping the bowl in the oven), then reduce the temperature to 180°C and bake for a further 40 minutes. Open the oven door 5–10 minutes before the end of cooking. Remove the ring from the bread and leave to cool on a wire rack.

7   Cut the top off the bread with a large bread knife. Cut 1 cm off the bottom of the bread. Insert the point of a knife vertically, at the border between the crust and the crumb. Cut all around the bread with top-to-bottom movements to separate the crust. Carefully remove the crust while

pressing lightly on the inner block of bread. Set aside the crust tower and the top of the bread.

8   Rest the crumbless bread on its side and cut into 20 slices about 5 mm thick.

9   Butter four slices and lay ham on them. Spread three more slices of bread with butter and lay slices of cheese on them. Spread three more slices with fromage frais and lay the smoked salmon slices on them.

10   Cover each topped slice with another slice of buttered bread to make a large sandwich, then cut each into six wedge-shaped sandwiches.

11   Place the crust ring on a serving plate. Place the sandwiches inside, alternating the flavours to reform the centre of the bread. Put the hat back on the surprise bread.

CIABATTA

Understand

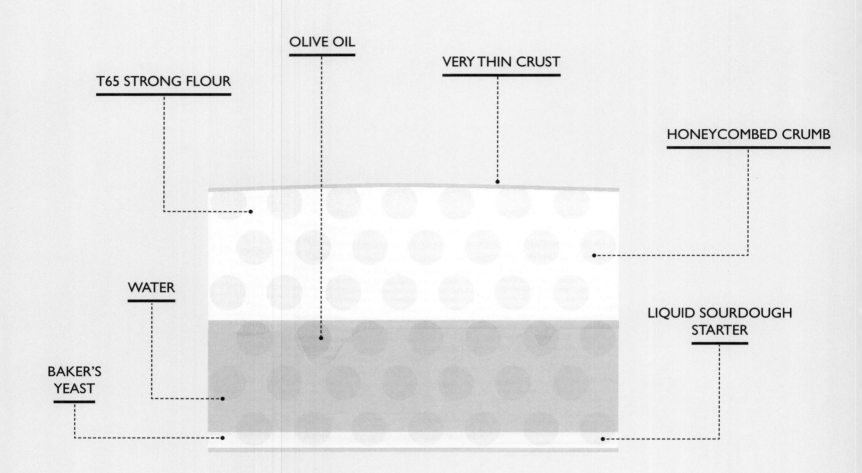

OLIVE OIL

VERY THIN CRUST

T65 STRONG FLOUR

HONEYCOMBED CRUMB

WATER

LIQUID SOURDOUGH STARTER

BAKER'S YEAST

WHAT IS IT?

Bread made with flour, liquid sourdough starter and olive oil, shaped into a rectangle.

CHARACTERISTICS

Weight: 200 g
Size: 15 cm
Crumb: honeycombed
Crust: very thin, soft
Taste: olive oil and very slightly acidic

TIME TO MAKE

Preparation: 30 minutes
Fermentation: 3 hours (1 hour of pointage, 2 hours proving)
Baking: 15 minutes

EQUIPMENT

Electric mixer with dough hook (optional)
Sieve

TECHNIQUES TO MASTER
Kneading (pages 30–33)
Rabat (folding; page 37)
Shaping (page 41)

THEY'RE READY . . .
When the bread starts to colour slightly.

STORAGE
About 2 days protected from the air.

Learn

MAKES 2

DOUGH

205 g T65 strong flour
145 g water
4 g salt
25 g liquid sourdough starter (page 20)
1 g fresh baker's yeast
20 g olive oil

OR DOUGH WITHOUT SOURDOUGH

220 g T55 plain flour
155 g water at room temperature
4 g salt
4 g fresh baker's yeast
18 g olive oil

TO FINISH

10 g T55 plain flour

1   Put the flour, water, salt, liquid starter and crumbled yeast in the bowl of an electric mixer.

2   Knead (see pages 32–33) for 4 minutes at the lowest speed, then 6 minutes at medium speed. (For kneading by hand, see pages 30–31.)

3   Continue to knead slowly while adding the olive oil in a thin stream until it is all completely incorporated.

4   Transfer the dough to a round-bottomed bowl. Cover with a clean tea towel and leave to undergo pointage for 30 minutes in a warm place (25–28°C).

5   Make a rabat (fold; see page 37). Leave to undergo further pointage for 30 minutes, covered with the tea towel, in a warm place (25–28°C).

6   Divide the dough into two 200 g pieces. Shape (see page 41) each piece into a rectangle.

7   Place the dough pieces on a sheet of baking paper, seam side down, cover with the tea towel, and leave to prove for 2 hours in a warm place (25–28°C).

8   Place a baking sheet and a heatproof bowl filled with water in the oven and preheat to 260°C (conventional oven). Lightly dust the top of the bread with flour. Remove the warmed baking sheet from the oven and slide the baking paper with the bread onto it. Spray the bottom of the oven with water and bake the bread for 15 minutes (keeping the bowl in the oven).

FOCACCIA

Understand

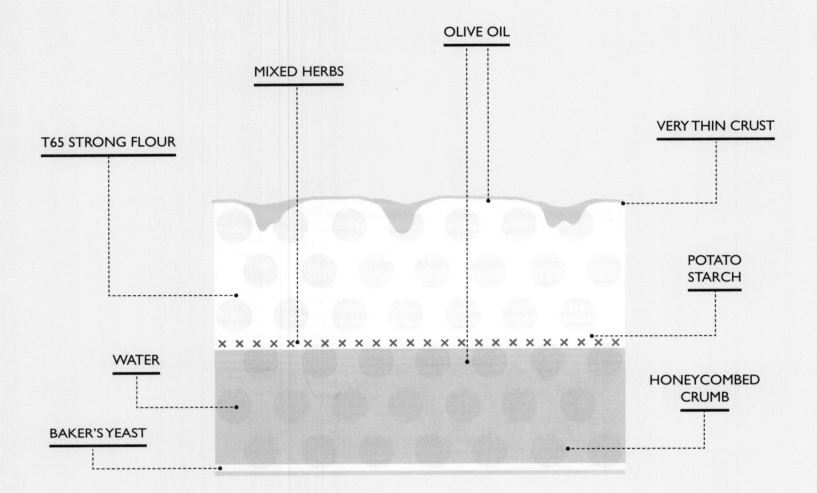

OLIVE OIL

MIXED HERBS

VERY THIN CRUST

T65 STRONG FLOUR

POTATO STARCH

WATER

HONEYCOMBED CRUMB

BAKER'S YEAST

WHAT IS IT?

Bread made with olive oil, shaped into a flat rectangle.

CHARACTERISTICS

Weight: 200 g
Size: about 20 cm × 15 cm
Crumb: honeycombed
Crust: very thin, soft

TIME TO MAKE

Preparation: 20 minutes
Fermentation: 2 hours 30 minutes (1 hour of pointage, 30 minutes resting, 1 hour proving)
Baking: 10 minutes

EQUIPMENT

Electric mixer with dough hook (optional)
Dough cutter
Pastry brush
Pastry rolling pin

DERIVATION

Focaccia topped like a pizza.

TRICKY ASPECT

Not tearing the dough.

TECHNIQUES TO MASTER

Kneading (pages 30–33)
Rabat (folding; page 37)
Pre-shaping into a ball (page 41)

THEY'RE READY . . .

When the focaccias are lightly browned and still very moist.

STORAGE

The dough will keep, wrapped in plastic wrap, for 24 hours in the refrigerator.

WHAT IS THE DIFFERENCE BETWEEN FOCACCIA AND CIABATTA?

Focaccia contains no sourdough, so its aromatic notes are less acidic. The fermentation time for focaccia is shorter, which gives it a less airy texture.

1

2

3

MAKES 2

1 DOUGH

190 g T65 strong flour
140 g water
4 g salt
6 g fresh baker's yeast
35 g potato starch

2 FLAVOURING

2 g mixed herbs (herbes de Provence)
25 g olive oil

3 TO FINISH

5 g olive oil

Making focaccia

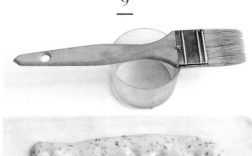

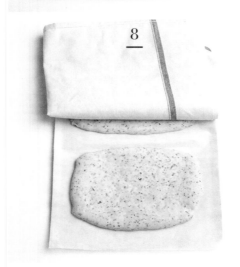

1 Knead the flour, water, salt, crumbled yeast, potato starch and mixed herbs using an electric mixer (see pages 32–33) for 4 minutes at the lowest speed, then 6 minutes at medium speed. The dough should pull away from the side of the bowl. (For kneading by hand, see pages 30–31.)

2 Continue to knead at the lowest speed while adding the olive oil in a thin stream until it is all completely incorporated.

3 Transfer the dough to a round-bottomed bowl. Cover with a clean tea towel and leave to undergo pointage for 30 minutes in a warm place (25–28°C).

4 Make a rabat (fold; see page 37). Return to the bowl, cover with the tea towel and leave to undergo pointage for a further 30 minutes in a warm place (25–28°C).

5 Divide the dough into two 200 g pieces using a dough cutter. Pre-shape each piece into a ball (see page 41), pulling tight.

6 Place the dough pieces on a sheet of baking paper, cover with the tea towel and leave to rest for 30 minutes in a warm place (25–28°C).

7 Using a rolling pin, roll each dough piece (see page 283) into a 20 cm × 15 cm rectangle about 2 cm thick.

8 Cover with the tea towel. Leave to prove for about 1 hour in a warm place (25–28°C).

9 Place a baking sheet and a heatproof bowl filled with water in the oven and preheat to 260°C (conventional oven). Remove the warmed baking sheet from the oven and slide the baking paper with the bread onto it. Make about 30 holes in the dough with your fingers without tearing the bottom, and fill them with olive oil using a pastry brush.

10 Spray the bottom of the oven with water and bake the bread for 10 minutes (keeping the bowl in the oven).

FOUGASSE

Understand

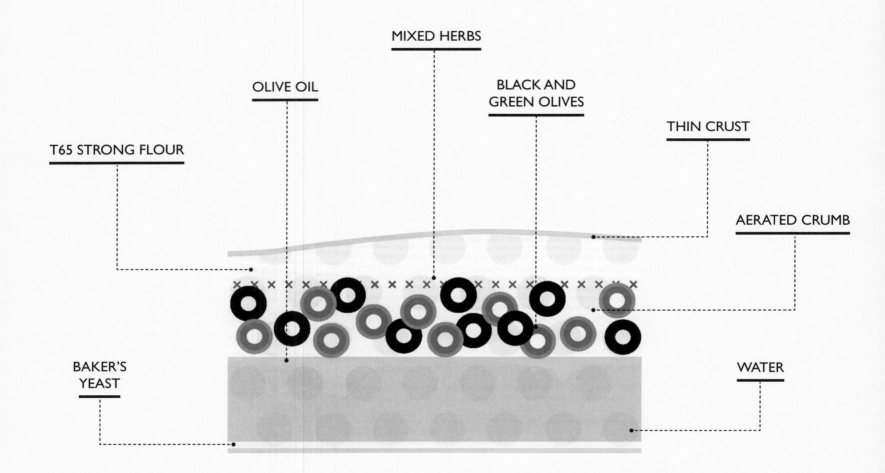

MIXED HERBS

OLIVE OIL

BLACK AND
GREEN OLIVES

THIN CRUST

T65 STRONG FLOUR

AERATED CRUMB

BAKER'S
YEAST

WATER

WHAT IS IT?

Bread made with T65 strong flour, baker's
yeast and olive oil, flavoured with mixed
herbs and enriched with olives. It is shaped
into a flat rectangle then slashed all the way
through.

CHARACTERISTICS

Weight: 300 g
Size: 15 cm × 30 cm
Crumb: honeycombed
Crust: thin

TIME TO MAKE

Preparation: 45 minutes
Fermentation: 45 minutes (pointage)
Baking: 12 minutes

EQUIPMENT

Electric mixer with dough hook (optional)
Pastry rolling pin
Dough cutter

TRICKY ASPECT

Making the holes.

TECHNIQUES TO MASTER

Kneading (pages 30–33)
Slashing (page 51)

WHAT DO THE HOLES DO?

*They increase the surface area of crust
and therefore the crunchiness. The
ratio of crumb to crust is more even.*

MAKES 1

1 DOUGH

140 g T65 strong flour
95 g water
3 g salt
3 g fresh baker's yeast
5 g mixed herbs (herbes de Provence)
10 g olive oil

2 FLAVOURING

60 g sliced olives

2

3a

3b

4

5

6

1 Knead the flour, water, salt, crumbled yeast and mixed herbs using an electric mixer (see pages 32–33) for 4 minutes at the lowest speed, then 6 minutes at medium speed. The dough should pull away from the side of the bowl. (For kneading by hand, see pages 30–31.)

2 Continue to knead at the lowest speed while adding the olive oil in a thin stream until it is all completely incorporated. Add the olives and knead again to incorporate into the dough.

3 Transfer the dough to a round-bottomed bowl, cover with plastic wrap and leave to undergo pointage for 45 minutes in a warm place (25–28°C).

4 Shape into a large rectangle (see page 41). Place on a sheet of floured baking paper.

5 Turn the paper so that the dough is on a diagonal in front of you and roll it out with a rolling pin (see page 283) to about 2 cm thick. Make four holes with a dough cutter and stretch them well with your hands.

6 Preheat the oven to 260°C (conventional oven) with a baking sheet inside. Remove the warmed baking sheet from the oven and slide the baking paper with the fougasse onto it. Bake for 12 minutes.

GRISSINI

Understand

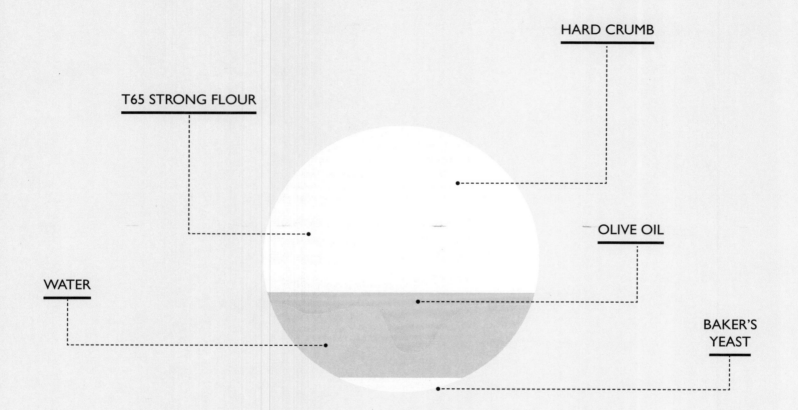

HARD CRUMB

T65 STRONG FLOUR

OLIVE OIL

WATER

BAKER'S YEAST

WHAT ARE THEY?

Bread shaped into thins and long sticks, brushed with olive oil. Originally from Turin, they can be plain, flavoured with herbs or spices, or covered with seeds.

CHARACTERISTICS

Weight: 20 g
Size: about 50 cm
Crumb: like a biscuit
Crust: no crust

TIME TO MAKE

Preparation: 30 minutes
Fermentation: 30 minutes (pointage)
Baking: 10 minutes

EQUIPMENT

Electric mixer with dough hook (optional)
Pastry rolling pin
Pastry brush

TECHNIQUE TO MASTER

Kneading (pages 30–33)

TIP
Pinch the ends of the grissini with wet hands so they don't move during cooking.

THEY'RE READY . . .
When the grissini are golden and dry.

STORAGE
4–5 days

1

4

5

6

MAKES 15–20

DOUGH

225 g T65 strong flour
7 g fresh baker's yeast
5 g salt
135 g water at 20–25°C

TO FINISH

40 g fleur de sel, chilli powder, garlic, sesame
 seeds, pepper, tomato paste or tandoori spices
20 g olive oil

1 Put the flour, crumbled yeast, salt and
water in the bowl of an electric mixer.

2 Knead (see pages 32–33) at the lowest speed
for 4 minutes or until the dough becomes smooth,
then at medium speed for 6 minutes or until
the dough pulls away from the side of the bowl.
(For kneading by hand, see pages 30–31.)

3 Transfer the dough to a round-bottomed bowl.
Cover with plastic wrap (see page 285) and leave to
undergo pointage for 30 minutes at room temperature.

4 Preheat the oven to 270°C. Using a rolling pin,
roll the dough (see page 283) to 1 cm thick. Cut
into strips as long as the dough and 1 cm wide.

5 Top with your chosen ingredients. Take the
ends of each grissini in your hands and twist them
to stretch them to 50–60 cm long. Place them
on a baking sheet lined with baking paper.

6 Brush the grissini with olive oil using
a pastry brush.

7 Pour any remaining olive oil over the grissini in a
thin stream. Bake for 10 minutes.

SOFT WHITE

Understand

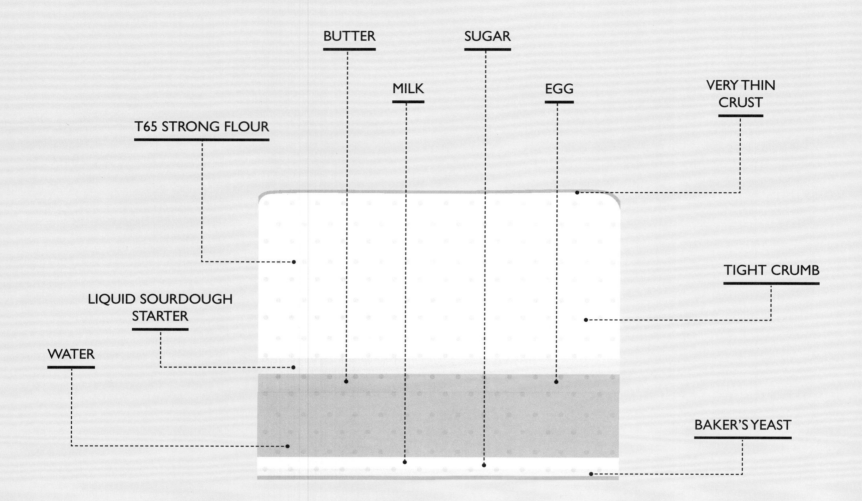

BUTTER   SUGAR

MILK   EGG   VERY THIN CRUST

T65 STRONG FLOUR

TIGHT CRUMB

LIQUID SOURDOUGH STARTER

WATER

BAKER'S YEAST

WHAT IS IT?

Slightly sweet white bread cooked in a rectangular tin.

CHARACTERISTICS

Weight: 450 g
Size: 18 cm long
Crumb: tight, moist
Crust: very thin, soft

TIME TO MAKE

Preparation: 25 minutes

Fermentation: 2 hours 30 minutes to
3 hours (1 hour 30 minutes of pointage,
1 hour to 1 hour 30 minutes proving)
Baking: 25 minutes

EQUIPMENT

Electric mixer with dough hook (optional)
Loaf tin with a lid, 18 cm long
and 8 cm high (see tip)
Pastry brush

TRICKY ASPECTS

Knowing when to put it in the oven: the
bread must not have risen too much.
Baking: it must stay soft and moist.

TECHNIQUES TO MASTER

Kneading (pages 30–33)
Rabat (folding; page 37)
Pre-shaping into a ball (page 41)
Shaping (page 41)

TIP

If you have no tin with a lid, rest a baking
sheet on top of the tin, then a weight on top.

IT'S READY . . .

When the bread has a well-developed,
well-coloured crust.

STORAGE

3 days in the refrigerator (to prevent
mould developing).

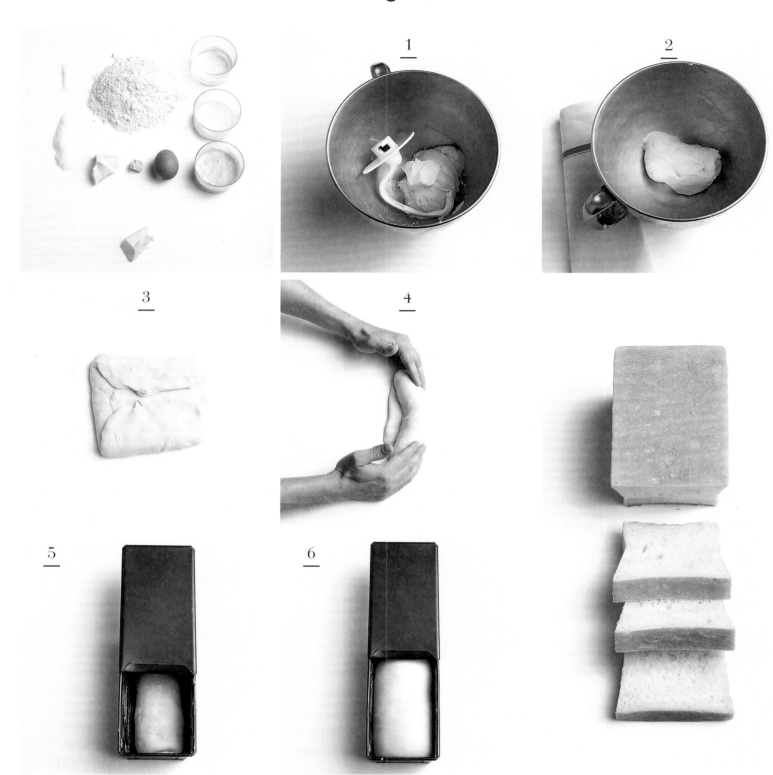

MAKES 1 LOAF

170 g T65 strong flour

80 g cold water

20 g liquid sourdough starter (page 20)

3 g fresh baker's yeast

15 g caster sugar

10 g milk

3 g salt

10 g egg

25 g unsalted butter, plus 15 g,
   softened, for greasing

1　Knead all the ingredients except the butter using an electric mixer (see pages 32–33) at the lowest speed for 6 minutes, then 5 minutes one click higher. The dough should pull away from the side of the bowl. (For kneading by hand, see pages 30–31.) Add the butter and knead at the lowest speed until well incorporated.

2　Cover with a clean tea towel and leave to undergo pointage for 1 hour 30 minutes in a warm place (25–28°C).

3　After 45 minutes, make a rabat (fold; see page 37).

4　Pre-shape into a ball (see page 41) then elongate (see page 41) into a sausage the length of the tin.

5　Grease the tin with the extra softened butter using a pastry brush. Lay the dough inside the tin, seam side down.

6　Close with the lid and leave to prove for 1 hour to 1 hour 30 minutes in a warm place (25–28°C). After proving, the dough should be 5 mm from the rim of the tin.

7　Preheat the oven to 200°C. Bake for 25 minutes with the lid closed.

BAGELS

Understand

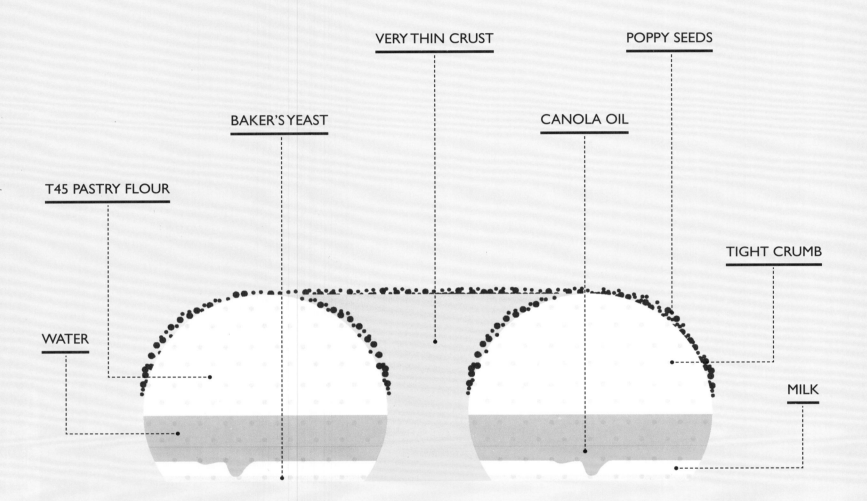

VERY THIN CRUST

POPPY SEEDS

BAKER'S YEAST

CANOLA OIL

T45 PASTRY FLOUR

TIGHT CRUMB

WATER

MILK

WHAT ARE THEY?

Bread dough made with T45 pastry flour and milk, lightly sweetened, shaped into small crowns, poached then baked.

CHARACTERISTICS

Weight: 150 g
Size: 15 cm diameter
Crumb: tight, moist
Crust: very thin, soft

TIME TO MAKE

Preparation: 1 hour
Fermentation: 1 hour 45 minutes to 2 hours 15 minutes (45 minutes resting, 1 hour to 1 hour 30 minutes proving)
Baking: 12–13 minutes

EQUIPMENT

Electric mixer with dough hook (optional)
Dough cutter

TRICKY ASPECTS

Shaping
Poaching

TECHNIQUES TO MASTER

Kneading (pages 30–33)
Pre-shaping into a ball (page 41)
Shaping into a crown (page 46)

THEY'RE READY . . .
When the bagels are lightly browned.

STORAGE
2 days

WHY POACH THE BAGELS
BEFORE BAKING?

So that the crust is very soft after baking: the boiling water makes the starch gelatinise at the surface. And to obtain a much moister texture: during poaching, steam forms within the dough and makes it swell.

Learn

1

2–3

MAKES 8

1 DOUGH

700 g T45 pastry flour
300 g water
25 g fresh baker's yeast
50 g milk
15 g caster sugar
15 g salt
50 g canola oil

2 COOKING

1 tablespoon white vinegar

3 TO FINISH

30 g poppy seeds

Making bagels

4

5

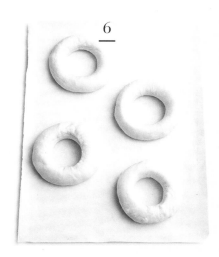

6

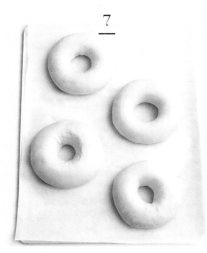

7

8

9

1 Knead the flour, water, crumbled yeast, milk, sugar and salt using an electric mixer (see pages 32–33) at the lowest speed until the mixture is smooth, then for 6 minutes at a higher speed. (For kneading by hand, see pages 30–31.)

2 Add the canola oil and knead for a few moments at the lowest speed to incorporate it well.

3 Leave to rest for 15 minutes under a clean tea towel at room temperature.

4 Cut the dough into eight 150 g pieces using a dough cutter. Pre-shape each piece into a ball (see page 41). Leave to rest for 30 minutes under a clean tea towel.

5 Make a hole in the centre of each dough piece with your thumb, then lightly coat your fingers in flour.

6 Shape each dough piece into a crown (see page 46) with an outside diameter of 15 cm.

7 Place them on two sheets of baking paper with four on each, cover with the tea towel and leave to prove in a warm place (25–28°C) until almost doubled in volume (1 hour to 1 hour 30 minutes).

8 Preheat the oven to 240°C (conventional oven). Bring a large saucepan of water with the white vinegar added to the boil. Poach the dough pieces two at a time for 30 seconds on each side. Remove them using a skimmer or slotted spoon and drain on a wire rack.

9 Dip the top of the bagels in the poppy seeds, then place on a baking sheet lined with baking paper.

10 Bake for 12–13 minutes.

BUNS

Understand

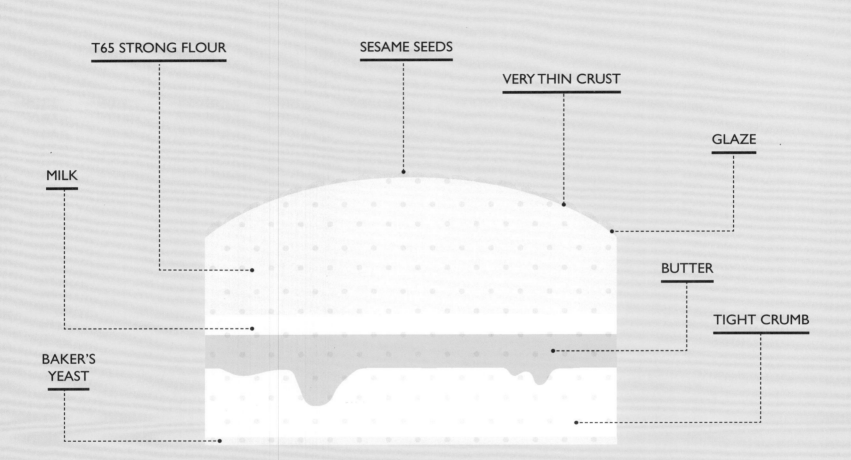

T65 STRONG FLOUR

SESAME SEEDS

VERY THIN CRUST

GLAZE

MILK

BUTTER

TIGHT CRUMB

BAKER'S YEAST

WHAT ARE THEY?

Vienna dough shaped into balls and coated in sesame seeds.

CHARACTERISTICS

Weight: 80 g
Size: 10 cm diameter
Crumb: tight
Crust: very thin, soft

TIME TO MAKE

Preparation: 3 hours
Fermentation: 6 hours (4 hours 30 minutes resting, 1 hour 30 minutes proving)
Baking: 10–15 minutes

EQUIPMENT

Electric mixer with dough hook (optional)
Dough cutter
Pastry brush

TRICKY ASPECT

Shaping into their final form: if the buns are flattened too much the dough will lose its gas and will be flat after baking.

TECHNIQUES TO MASTER

Kneading (pages 30–33)
Shaping into a ball (page 42)
Glazing (page 49)

THEY'RE READY . . .

When the buns are golden.

STORAGE

Up to 2 days at room temperature.
A few weeks in the freezer.

HOW ARE THE BUNS SO MOIST?

They are made with Vienna dough (which contains milk and butter). The dough contains less butter, however, than a milk bread or brioche, and above all no egg, two ingredients that promote the incorporation of air into a dough and silkier textures.

Learn

$\underline{1}$

$\underline{2}$

$\underline{3}$

MAKES 4

1 VIENNA DOUGH

240 g T65 strong flour
145 g milk
4 g salt
4 g fresh baker's yeast
20 g caster sugar
35 g unsalted butter at room temperature

2 GLAZE

1 egg
3 g (½ teaspoon) milk
pinch of salt

3 TO FINISH

20 g white sesame seeds (or black
    sesame or poppy seeds)

Making buns

1 Knead the flour, milk, salt, crumbled yeast and sugar using an electric mixer (see pages 32–33) for 4 minutes at the lowest speed, then 6 minutes at medium speed. The dough should pull away from the side of the bowl. (For kneading by hand, see pages 30–31.)

2 Add the soft butter and knead until completely incorporated.

3 Transfer the dough to a round-bottomed bowl. Cover with plastic wrap and leave to rest for 4 hours in the refrigerator.

4 Divide the dough into four 100 g pieces using a dough cutter. Pre-shape each piece into a ball (see page 41). Place the dough pieces on a sheet of baking paper, seam side down, and leave to rest for another 30 minutes in the refrigerator.

5 Flatten the dough pieces lightly by pressing on them with the flat of your hand.

6 Make the glaze (see page 49). Glaze the buns using a pastry brush. Sprinkle with the sesame seeds. Leave to prove, protected from the air, for 1 hour 30 minutes in a warm place (25–28°C).

7 Place a baking sheet and a heatproof bowl filled with water in the oven and preheat to 260°C (conventional oven). Remove the warmed baking sheet from the oven and slide the baking paper with the bread onto it. Bake for 10–15 minutes (keeping the bowl in the oven).

CROISSANTS

Understand

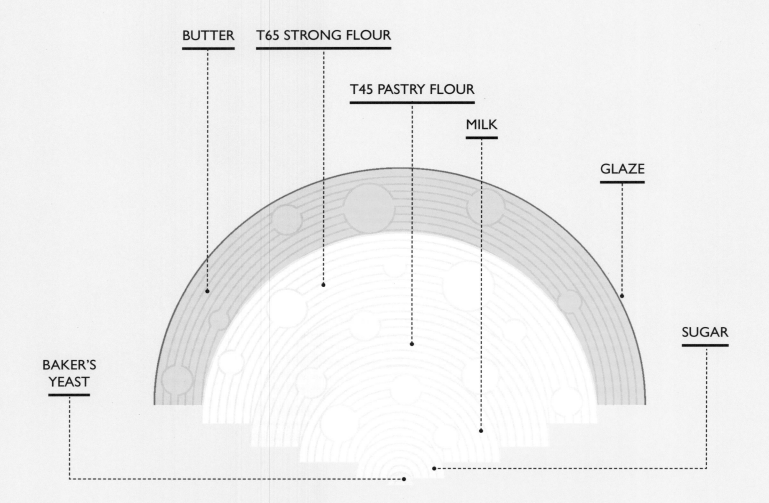

BUTTER

T65 STRONG FLOUR

T45 PASTRY FLOUR

MILK

GLAZE

SUGAR

BAKER'S YEAST

WHAT ARE THEY?

Layered yeast dough cut into triangles then rolled.

CHARACTERISTICS

Weight: 80–90 g
Size: 12 cm
Layering: very honeycombed

TIME TO MAKE

Preparation: 1 hour 30 minutes
Resting: 6 hours (3 hours in the refrigerator, 3 hours resting)
Baking: 15 minutes

EQUIPMENT

Electric mixer with dough hook (optional)
Pastry rolling pin
Pastry brush

TRICKY ASPECT

Rolling out the dough: don't overdo it. The layers of détrempe (base dough) and butter must not mix or the layering will not develop.

TECHNIQUES TO MASTER

Kneading (pages 30–33)
Shaping into a ball (page 42)
Rolling out dough (page 283)
Glazing (page 49)

THEY'RE READY . . .

When the croissants are golden and puffy.

WHAT MAKES THE LAYERS SO AIRY?

Due to the balance between the layers of détrempe and butter, during baking, the external layers of the pastry separate and dry out (due to the butter, which makes them impermeable) to form layers, while the internal layers stay moist and form leaf-like bread layers.

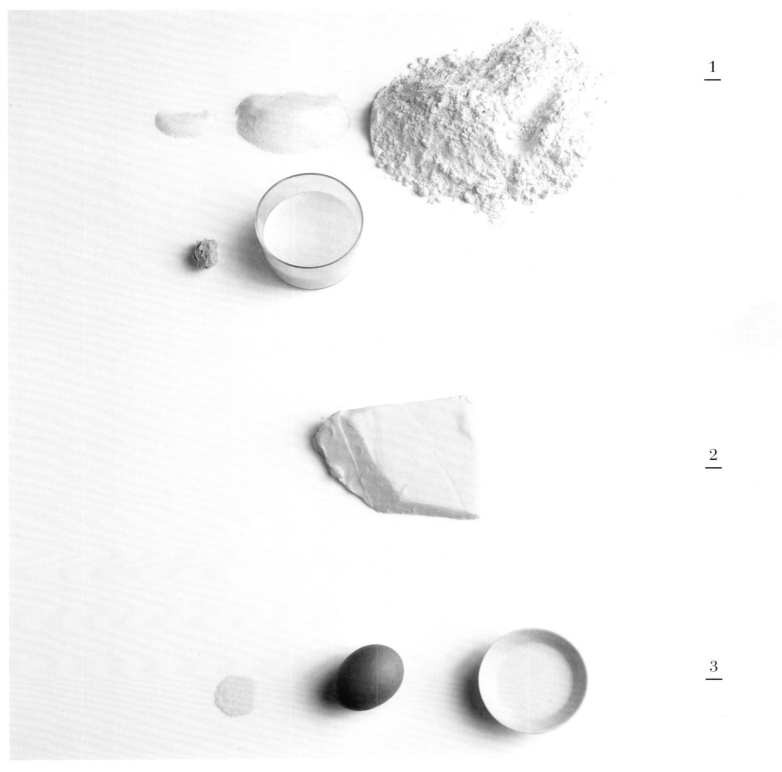

MAKES 6

1 DÉTREMPE

110 g T65 strong flour
110 g T45 pastry flour
30 g caster sugar
4 g salt
105 g cold milk
7 g fresh baker's yeast

2 LAYERING

120 g unsalted butter

3 GLAZE

1 egg
3 g (½ teaspoon) milk
pinch of salt

Making croissants

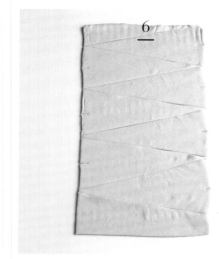

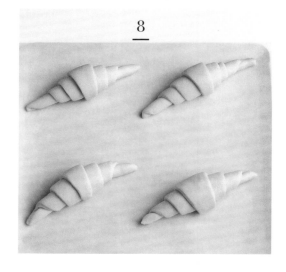

1 Make the détrempe: knead the flours, sugar, salt, milk and crumbled yeast using an electric mixer (see pages 32–33) for 5 minutes at the lowest speed, then 5 minutes at medium speed. (For kneading by hand, see pages 30–31.) Shape into a ball (see page 42), pulling the dough very tight, wrap in plastic wrap and leave to rest for 1 hour in the refrigerator.

2 Tap the butter with a pastry rolling pin to soften it. Roll it out to obtain a neat even square 1 cm thick and 8 cm on each side.

3 Roll out the détrempe to the same width and twice as long as the butter (16 cm).

4 Lay the butter in the middle of the dough and fold the two sides of the dough over the butter, joining them in the middle. Make a quarter turn with the dough so that the join is vertical.

5 Make a simple turn (see page 283): using a rolling pin, roll the dough out in front of you (with the join still vertical) to 24 cm long. Fold in three to make a square of dough. Cover with plastic wrap and freeze for 10 minutes, then refrigerate for 30 minutes. Repeat this step twice.

6 Roll the dough out (see page 283) to 2.5 mm thick and 24 cm wide. Cut into triangles, each with a base measuring 9 cm and sides 24 cm long.

7 Cut a little 5 mm notch in the middle of the base of each triangle. Spread apart the two corners of the base of each triangle and roll up the dough without rolling too tight. The point should end up underneath.

8 Place the croissants on a baking sheet lined with baking paper, spacing them 3–4 cm apart. Make the glaze (see page 49). Glaze the croissants using a pastry brush.

9 Leave to rest, uncovered, for 3 hours in a warm place (25–28°C).

10 Preheat the oven to 180°C (fan-forced). Glaze the croissants once more. Bake for about 15 minutes.

PAINS AU CHOCOLAT

Understand

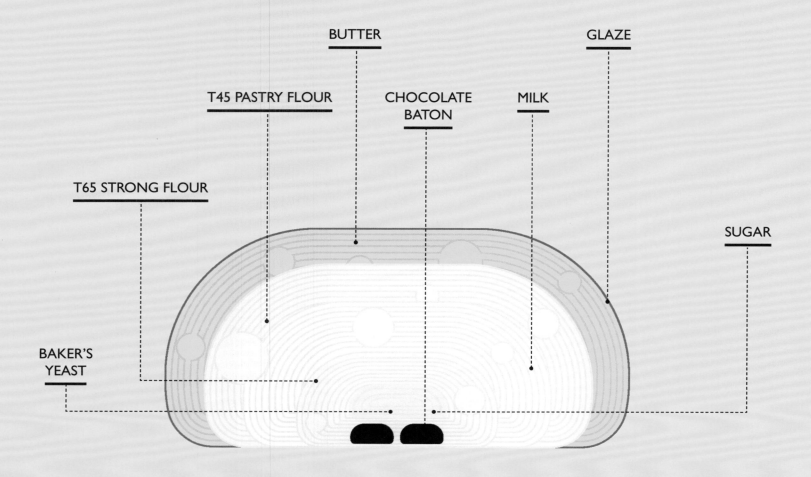

BUTTER

GLAZE

T45 PASTRY FLOUR

CHOCOLATE
BATON

MILK

T65 STRONG FLOUR

SUGAR

BAKER'S
YEAST

WHAT ARE THEY?

Layered yeast dough, cut into rectangles,
filled with two chocolate batons, then rolled.

CHARACTERISTICS

Weight: 80–90 g
Size: 10 cm
Layering: very honeycombed

TIME TO MAKE

Preparation: 1 hour
Fermentation: 5 hours 30 minutes (3 hours in
the refrigerator, 2 hours 30 minutes proving)
Baking: 15 minutes

EQUIPMENT

Electric mixer with dough hook (optional)
Pastry rolling pin
Pastry brush

TRICKY ASPECT

Rolling out the dough: don't overdo it. The
layers of détrempe (base dough) and butter
must not mix or the layering won't develop.

TECHNIQUES TO MASTER

Kneading (pages 30–33)
Shaping into a ball (page 42)
Rolling out dough (page 283)
Glazing (page 49)

TIP

If you cannot obtain chocolate batons
made for Viennese pastry, use a row
of cooking chocolate squares.

THEY'RE READY . . .

When the pains au chocolat are well
browned and have puffed up nicely.

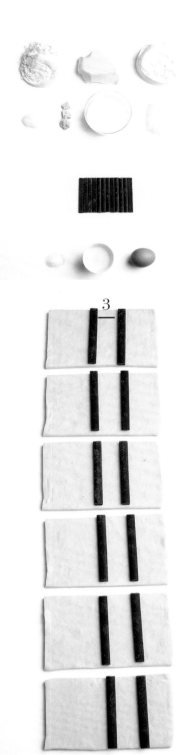

MAKES ABOUT 6

LAYERED YEAST DOUGH

110 g T65 strong flour
110 g T45 pastry flour
105 g milk
30 g caster sugar
4 g salt
7 g fresh baker's yeast
120 g unsalted butter (for layering)

FILLING

12 chocolate batons for Viennese pastries
(available from specialist pastry suppliers)

GLAZE

1 egg
3 g (½ teaspoon) milk
pinch of salt

1   Make the layered yeast dough (see page 64).

2   Roll the dough out (see page 283) to 2.5 mm thick
and 13 cm wide.

3   Cut into rectangles 13 cm long and
10 cm wide. Place two chocolate batons on
each rectangle, one 2 cm from the top edge
and the other 3 cm from the bottom.

4   Roll the rectangles of dough, starting from the
top and folding the dough over the first chocolate
baton. Continue rolling until you reach the bottom.
The seam should be underneath the pain au chocolat.

5   Make the glaze (see page 49). Glaze the pains
au chocolat using a pastry brush. Leave to rest,
uncovered, for 2 hours 30 minutes in a warm place
(25–28°C).

6   Preheat the oven to 180°C (conventional
oven). Place the pains au chocolat on a baking
tray lined with baking paper, glaze them a
second time, then bake for 15 minutes.

PAINS AUX SULTANAS

Understand

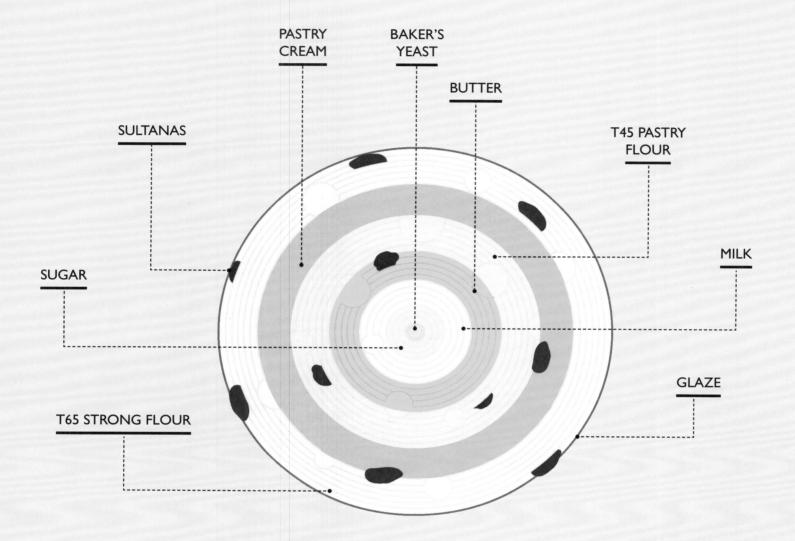

PASTRY CREAM

BAKER'S YEAST

BUTTER

SULTANAS

T45 PASTRY FLOUR

MILK

SUGAR

GLAZE

T65 STRONG FLOUR

WHAT ARE THEY?

Layered yeast dough filled with pastry cream and sultanas then rolled up like a snail.

CHARACTERISTICS

Weight: 120 g
Size: 20 cm diameter
Layering: very honeycombed

TIME TO MAKE

Soaking: overnight
Preparation: 1 hour 30 minutes
Fermentation: 6 hours 30 minutes (4 hours in refrigerator, 2 hours 30 minutes proving)
Baking: 15 minutes

EQUIPMENT

Electric mixer with dough hook (optional)
Pastry rolling pin
Pastry brush

TRICKY ASPECTS

Rolling out the dough: don't overdo it. The layers of détrempe (base dough) and butter must not mix or the layering will not develop. Rolling up in a spiral.

TECHNIQUES TO MASTER

Blanching egg yolks (page 284)
Kneading (pages 30–33)
Shaping into a ball (page 42)
Rolling out dough (page 283)
Glazing (page 49)

THEY'RE READY . . .

When the pains aux sultanas are well browned and have puffed up nicely.

STORAGE

No more than 1–2 days.

 1

 2

 3–5

MAKES ABOUT 6

1 LAYERED YEAST DOUGH

120 g T65 strong flour
120 g T45 pastry flour
115 g milk
30 g caster sugar
5 g salt
7 g fresh baker's yeast
120 g unsalted butter (for layering)

2 PASTRY CREAM

250 g milk
100 g caster sugar
25 g cornflour
2 eggs

3 FILLING

200 g sultanas

4 GLAZE

1 egg
3 g (½ teaspoon) milk
pinch of salt

5 SYRUP

25 g water
25 g caster sugar

Making pains aux sultanas

2

6

7

3

5

9

10

THE DAY BEFORE

1 Soak the sultanas in slightly warm water overnight.

ON THE DAY

2 Make the pastry cream (see page 76). Pour it into a baking tray, cover with plastic wrap, with plastic touching the surface of the cream (see page 285) and refrigerate for 1 hour to set.

3 Make the layered yeast dough (see page 64). Roll it out (see page 283) to 2.5 mm thick and 30 cm wide. Spread the pastry cream over the dough.

4 Drain the sultanas and scatter them over the pastry cream, putting more of them at the bottom (the outside of the snail once it is rolled up).

5 Roll up tightly, starting at the top.

6 Cut the roll into 4 cm slices to make the pains aux sultanas.

7 Tuck the outside edge of the dough of each pain aux sultanas underneath and place them on a baking sheet lined with baking paper. Make the glaze (see page 49). Glaze the pains aux raisins using a pastry brush.

8 Leave to prove for 2 hours 30 minutes in a warm place (25–28°C).

9 Preheat the oven to 180°C. Glaze once more. Bake for 15 minutes.

10 Make the syrup: bring the water and sugar to the boil in a small saucepan then remove from the heat. Use a pastry brush to spread the syrup over the pains aux sultanas when they come out of the oven.

SWISS BRIOCHES

Understand

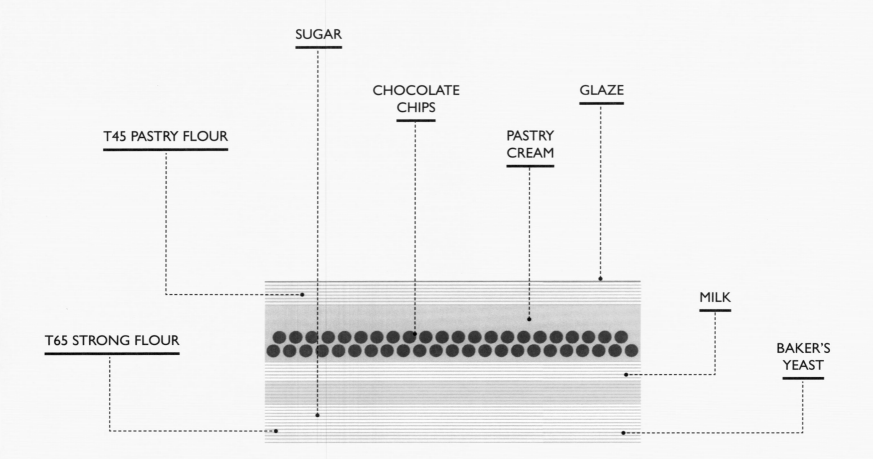

SUGAR

CHOCOLATE
CHIPS

GLAZE

T45 PASTRY FLOUR

PASTRY
CREAM

T65 STRONG FLOUR

MILK

BAKER'S
YEAST

WHAT ARE THEY?

Two stacked layers of layered yeast dough
filled with pastry cream and chocolate chips.

CHARACTERISTICS

Weight: 120 g
Size: 10 cm
Layering: honeycombed

TIME TO MAKE

Preparation: 2 hours
Fermentation: 4 hours (3 hours
refrigeration, 1 hour proving)
Baking: 30 minutes

EQUIPMENT

Electric mixer with dough hook (optional)
Dough cutter
Pastry brush

TECHNIQUES TO MASTER
Kneading (pages 30–33)
Rolling out dough (page 283)
Glazing (page 49)

THEY'RE READY . . .
When the Swiss brioches are golden
and the pastry has lifted slightly.

STORAGE
1–2 days at room temperature.

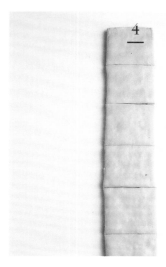

MAKES 6

LAYERED YEAST DOUGH

120 g T65 strong flour
120 g T45 pastry flour
115 g milk
30 g caster sugar
5 g salt
7 g fresh baker's yeast
120 g unsalted butter

PASTRY CREAM

250 g milk
50 g caster sugar
25 g cornflour
2 eggs

FILLING

60 g chocolate chips

GLAZE

1 egg
3 g (½ teaspoon) milk or cream
pinch of salt

1 Make the pastry cream (see page 76). Make the layered yeast dough (see page 64). Cut the dough into two pieces using a dough cutter, then roll each one out (see page 283) to 2.5 mm thick and 10 cm wide.

2 Spread the pastry cream on one of the two strips of dough, leaving 5 mm bare at the edges. Scatter over the chocolate chips.

3 Cover with the other strip of dough.

4 Using a knife, cut the strip every 10 cm to make 10 cm × 10 cm squares.

5 Place the Swiss brioches on a sheet of baking paper. Make the glaze (see page 49). Glaze the Swiss brioches using a pastry brush. Cover with a clean tea towel and leave to prove for 1 hour in a warm place (25–28°C).

6 Preheat the oven to 180°C (conventional oven) with a baking sheet inside. Remove the warmed baking sheet from the oven and slide the baking paper with the pastries onto it. Glaze once more and bake for 30 minutes.

ALMOND
CROISSANTS

Understand

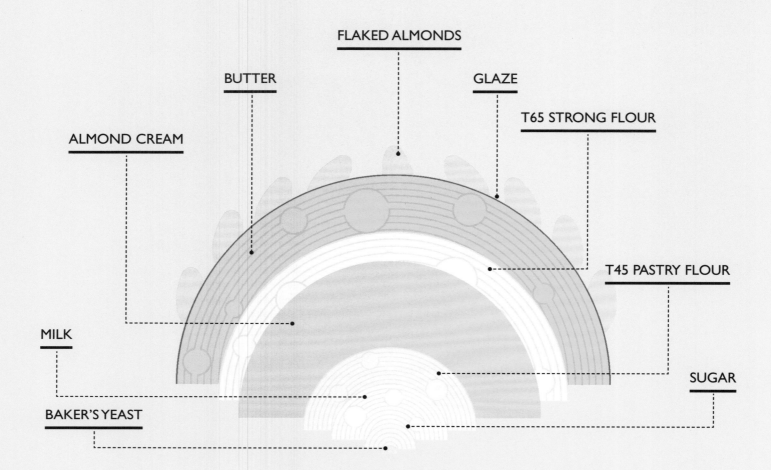

FLAKED ALMONDS

BUTTER

GLAZE

ALMOND CREAM

T65 STRONG FLOUR

T45 PASTRY FLOUR

MILK

SUGAR

BAKER'S YEAST

WHAT ARE THEY?

Cooked croissants filled with almond cream and topped with flaked almonds, then baked once more.

TIME TO MAKE

Preparation: 30 minutes
Baking: 30 minutes

CHARACTERISTICS

Weight: about 100 g
Size: 12 cm
Layering: honeycombed

EQUIPMENT

Bread knife
Pastry brush
Piping bag and basket-weave
    nozzle (or a knife)
Sieve

TECHNIQUES TO MASTER
Creaming butter and sugar (page 284)
Softening butter (page 284)

THEY'RE READY . . .
When the exposed almond cream and the flaked almonds are golden.

STORAGE
No more than 1–2 days exposed to the air.

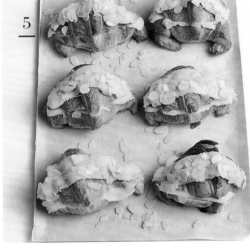

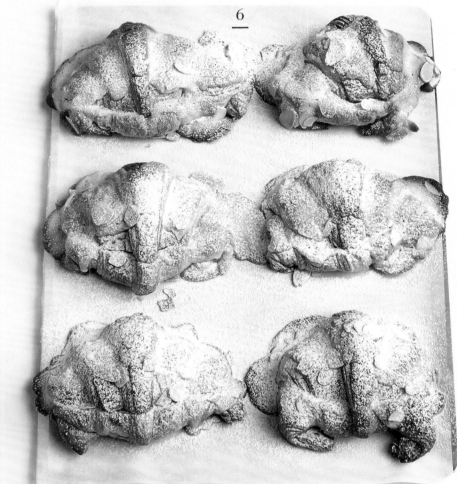

MAKES 6

VIENNESE PASTRIES

6 croissants or pains au chocolat

ALMOND CREAM

50 g softened unsalted butter (page 284)
50 g caster sugar
50 g ground almonds
5 g cornflour
1 egg

SYRUP

100 g water
100 g caster sugar

TO FINISH

60 g flaked almonds
icing sugar

1   Make the syrup by heating the water and sugar in a small saucepan. Remove from the heat as soon as the mixture starts boiling.

2   Preheat the oven to 180°C. Make the almond cream (see page 78).

3   Cut the Viennese pastries in half horizontally using a bread knife, without cutting all the way through. Brush the interior and exterior generously with the syrup using a pastry brush. Place the pastries on a baking sheet lined with baking paper.

4   Use the almond cream to fill a piping bag fitted with a basket-weave nozzle. Pipe the cream in the centre of the pastries, then close them.

5   Add a little almond cream on top of the pastries and scatter over the flaked almonds. Press with your fingers to make sure the almonds stick to the cream.

6   Bake for 30 minutes. Allow to cool, then sift the icing sugar over the top.

APPLE
TURNOVERS

Understand

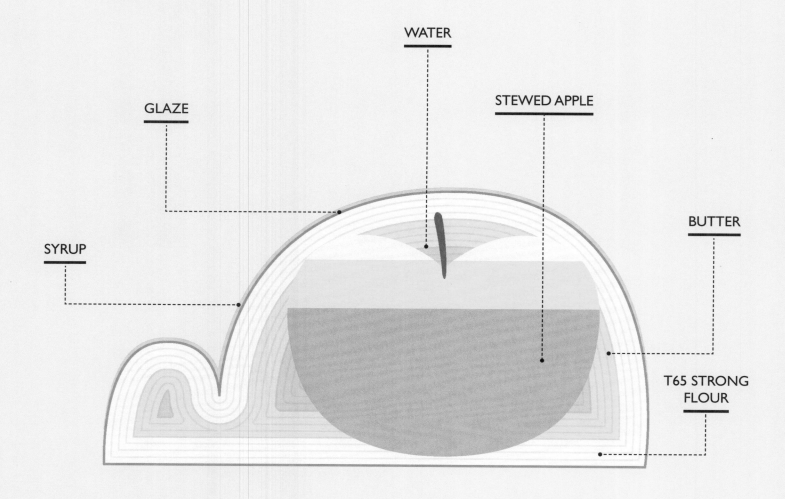

GLAZE

WATER

STEWED APPLE

BUTTER

SYRUP

T65 STRONG FLOUR

WHAT ARE THEY?

Inverse puff pastry filled with stewed apple and folded to form a turnover.

CHARACTERISTICS

Weight: 100 g
Size: 7.5 cm
Layering: airy, crisp

TIME TO MAKE

Preparation: 1 hour 30 minutes
Resting in the refrigerator: 12 hours
Cooking: 1 hour stewing apple,
30 minutes baking

EQUIPMENT

13 cm fluted biscuit cutter
Electric mixer with dough hook and beater
Pastry rolling pin
Pastry brush

TECHNIQUES TO MASTER

Kneading (pages 30–33)
Rolling out dough (page 283)
Glazing (page 49)
Slashing in sausage style (page 51)

TIP

Turn over the turnovers before cooking to retain a neat shape.

THEY'RE READY . . .

When the turnovers are golden.

STORAGE

No more than 1–2 days.

WHAT MAKES THE TURNOVERS SHINY?

The syrup applied after cooking. When a sugar solution boils, the water molecules evaporate. During cooling, the sugar molecules bond with each other and form a shiny coating.

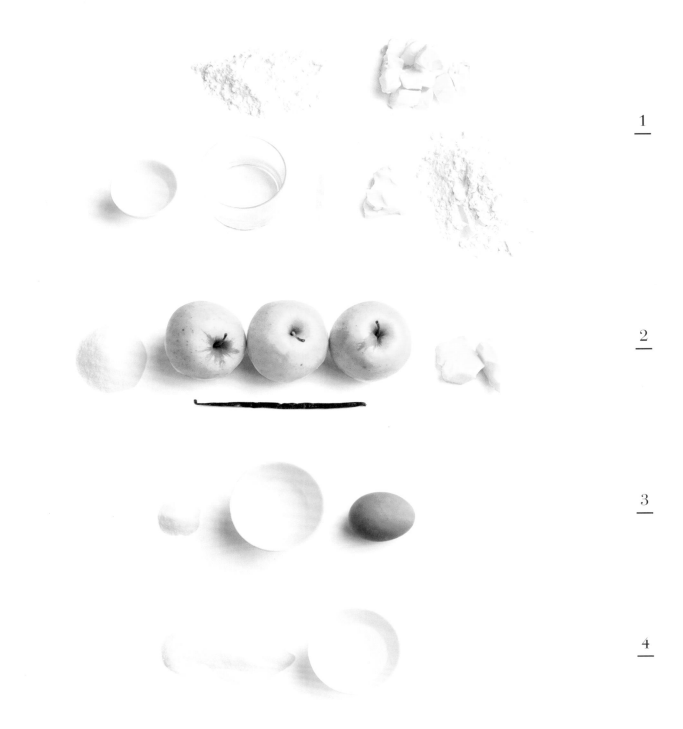

MAKES 8

1 INVERSE PUFF PASTRY (300 G)

Beurre manié (kneaded butter)
100 g softened unsalted butter
   (page 284), cut into cubes
40 g T65 strong flour

Détrempe
90 g T65 strong flour
40 g cold water
5 g salt
30 g softened unsalted butter (page 284)
1 g white vinegar

2 STEWED APPLE (600 G)

530 g apples
30 g caster sugar
40 g unsalted butter
1 vanilla bean

3 GLAZE

1 egg
3 g (½ teaspoon) milk
pinch of salt

4 SYRUP

25 g water
25 g caster sugar

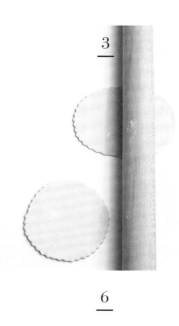

1 Make the stewed apple (see page 80).

2 Make the inverse puff pastry (see page 68). Preheat the oven to 180°C (conventional oven). Roll out the dough (see page 283) to 2.5 mm thick using a rolling pin. Cut out eight round discs of dough using the biscuit cutter.

3 Slightly stretch each disc to form an oval. Place the apple tunovers on a sheet of baking paper.

4 Make the glaze (see page 49). Glaze the perimeter of each pastry disc.

5 Put some stewed apple on one half of each oval, leaving a 1 cm border. Fold the other half over the apple and gently pinch the edges of the pastry to join them together.

6 Turn over the turnovers. Using a pastry brush, coat them with the remaining glaze. Slash the top of the pastry in sausage style (see page 51) using a knife.

7 Bake for 30 minutes.

8 Make a syrup: bring the water and sugar to the boil in a small saucepan then remove from the heat. Using a pastry brush, spread the syrup over the turnovers when they come out of the oven.

APPLE LATTICE TART

Understand

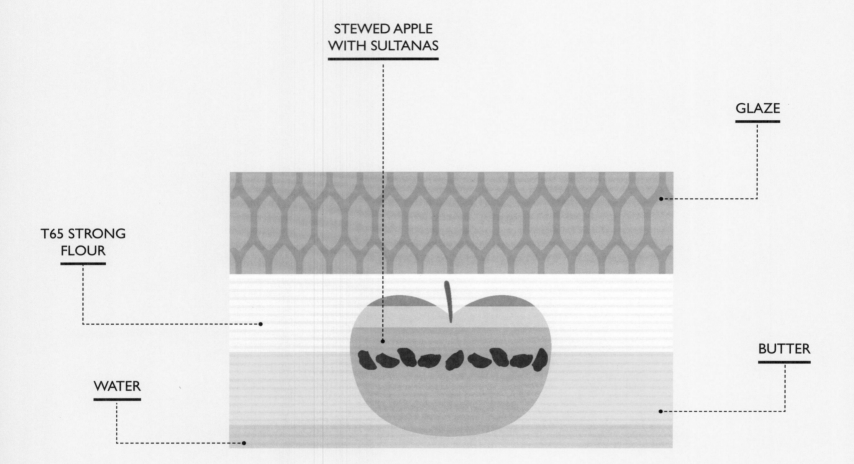

STEWED APPLE
WITH SULTANAS

GLAZE

T65 STRONG
FLOUR

BUTTER

WATER

WHAT IS IT?

Inverse puff pastry topped with stewed
apple and covered with inverse puff
pastry cut with a lattice roller.

TIME TO MAKE

Preparation: 30 minutes
Resting in the refrigerator: 12 hours
Cooking: 45 minutes stewing
apple, 45 minutes baking

EQUIPMENT

Electric mixer with beater
40 cm × 60 cm baking sheet
Pastry rolling pin
Lattice roller
Pastry brush

TRICKY ASPECT
Manipulating the pastry lattice.

TECHNIQUES TO MASTER
Kneading (pages 30–33)
Lining with dough (page 283)
Rolling out dough (page 283)
Glazing (page 49)

TIPS
Leave the pastry in the refrigerator for
a day (12 hours) before working with
it, to obtain a more even lattice.
If you don't have a lattice roller, cut
thin strips of puff pastry (about 1.5 cm
wide), criss-cross them to make a
lattice, then cut off any overhang.

IT'S READY . . .
When the pastry is a light golden colour.

STORAGE
2–3 days

1

2

SERVES 8

1 INVERSE PUFF PASTRY (300 G)

Beurre manié (kneaded butter)
100 g soft unsalted butter
   (page 284), cut into cubes
40 g T65 flour

Détrempe
90 g T65 strong flour
40 g cold water
5 g salt
30 g softened unsalted butter (page 284)
1 g white vinegar

2 STEWED APPLE

1 kg golden delicious apples
50 g raw sugar
150 g water
50 g sultanas
1 vanilla bean, split lengthways and seeds scraped
2 g ground cinnamon

3 GLAZE

1 egg
3 g (½ teaspoon) milk or cream
pinch of salt

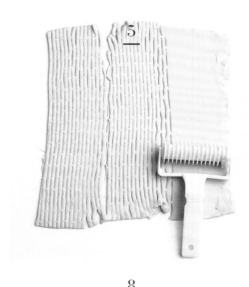

1 Make the inverse puff pastry (see page 60). Peel and core the apples, then cut into large pieces.

2 Put the apples in a saucepan with the sugar, water, sultanas, and the vanilla bean and scraped seeds. Bring to the boil, then reduce the heat and simmer for about 30 minutes, stirring from time to time. Stir in the cinnamon, then continue cooking for a further 15 minutes over a very low heat. Transfer to a bowl and set aside to cool.

3 Cut the pastry into two pieces. Roll out (see page 283) one half to 2.5 mm thick.

4 Line a baking sheet with baking paper. Spread the stewed apple over the rolled pastry, leaving a 1 cm border and making a slight bulge in the middle.

5 Roll out the second half of the dough to 2 mm thick. Run the lattice roller over it and pull on the sides to make a lattice.

6 Roll the lattice onto the rolling pin then unroll it over the stewed apple.

7 Make the glaze (see page 49). Glaze the lattice using a pastry brush.

8 Preheat the oven to 160°C (conventional oven). Bake for 45 minutes.

APPLE
TARTLETS

Understand

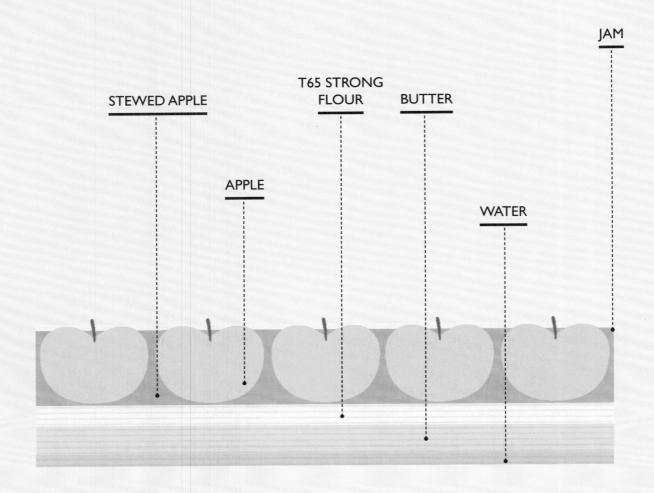

JAM

STEWED APPLE

T65 STRONG
FLOUR

BUTTER

APPLE

WATER

WHAT ARE THEY?

Inverse puff pastry bases topped with
stewed apple and thin slices of apple.

TIME TO MAKE

Preparation: 1 hour 15 minutes
Resting in the refrigerator: 12 hours
Cooking: 1 hour stewing apple,
25 minutes baking

EQUIPMENT

Electric mixer with beater
Pastry rolling pin
10 cm biscuit cutter or tart ring
Pastry brush

VARIATIONS

Apricots
Mirabelle plums
Fresh pears/figs

TRICKY ASPECT

Arranging the apples.

TECHNIQUE TO MASTER
Kneading (pages 30–33)

TIP

Put pieces of fresh apple in the stewed apple
to give the tart a good volume after cooking.

THEY'RE READY . . .

When the apple slices are golden
and the dough is lightly golden on
top and coloured underneath.

STORAGE

Up to 3 days in the refrigerator.

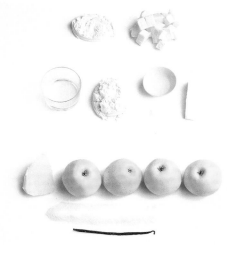

MAKES 4

INVERSE PUFF PASTRY (300 G)

Beurre manié (kneaded butter)
100 g softened unsalted butter
   (page 284), cut into cubes
40 g T65 strong flour

Détrempe
90 g T65 strong flour
40 g cold water
5 g salt
30 g softened unsalted butter (page 284)
1 g white vinegar

STEWED APPLE

180 g apples
10 g caster sugar
15 g unsalted butter
½ vanilla bean

TOPPING

2–3 apples
10 g apple or apricot jam, melted

1 Make the stewed apple (see page 80).

2 Make the inverse puff pastry (see page 68). Roll out the dough (see page 283) to 2 mm thick using a rolling pin. Preheat the oven to 150°C (fan-forced).

3 Cut out four pastry discs using the biscuit cutter or dessert ring. Lay them on a baking sheet lined with baking paper.

4 Spread a generous layer of stewed apple over each tart base, forming a dome in the centre.

5 Peel and core the apples. Cut them in half then in very thin slices.

6 Arrange the apple slices in a rose on top of the stewed apple, working from the outside in.

7 Bake for 25 minutes. Brush the tarts with the apple or apricot jam using a pastry brush.

EPIPHANY CAKE

Understand

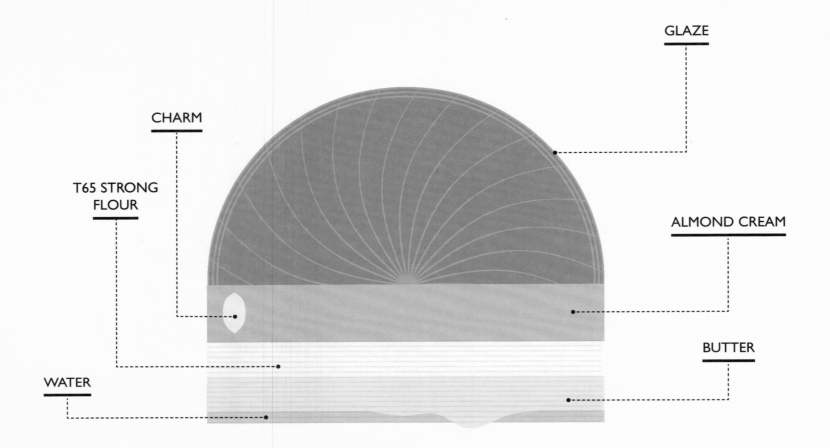

GLAZE

CHARM

T65 STRONG
FLOUR

ALMOND CREAM

BUTTER

WATER

WHAT IS IT?

Also called a Twelfth Night cake. Two
discs of puff pastry filled with almond
cream. Traditionally a dried bean is placed
in the cake but it's now more commonly
a 'charm', such as a little porcelain
figurine. Whoever receives the charm
is crowned king or queen for the day.

TIME TO MAKE

Preparation: 30 minutes
Resting in the refrigerator: 13 hours
Baking: 40–45 minutes

EQUIPMENT

Electric mixer with dough hook and beater
Pastry rolling pin
32 cm cutting ring
Pastry brush
Piping bag and plain no. 8 nozzle

DERIVATION

Frangipane Epiphany cake: two-thirds
almond cream, one-third pastry cream.

TRICKY ASPECT

Turning the cake over.

TECHNIQUES TO MASTER

Kneading (pages 30–33)
Glazing (page 49)
Creaming butter and sugar (page 284)
Pinching the edges (page 283)

TIPS

Make the almond cream the day before
to make piping easier. Refrigerate the
pastry discs for 1 hour before assembling
the cake, to make it easier to manage.

IT'S READY . . .

When the cake is lightly golden and shiny.

STORAGE

No more than 1–2 days (before
the cream dries out).

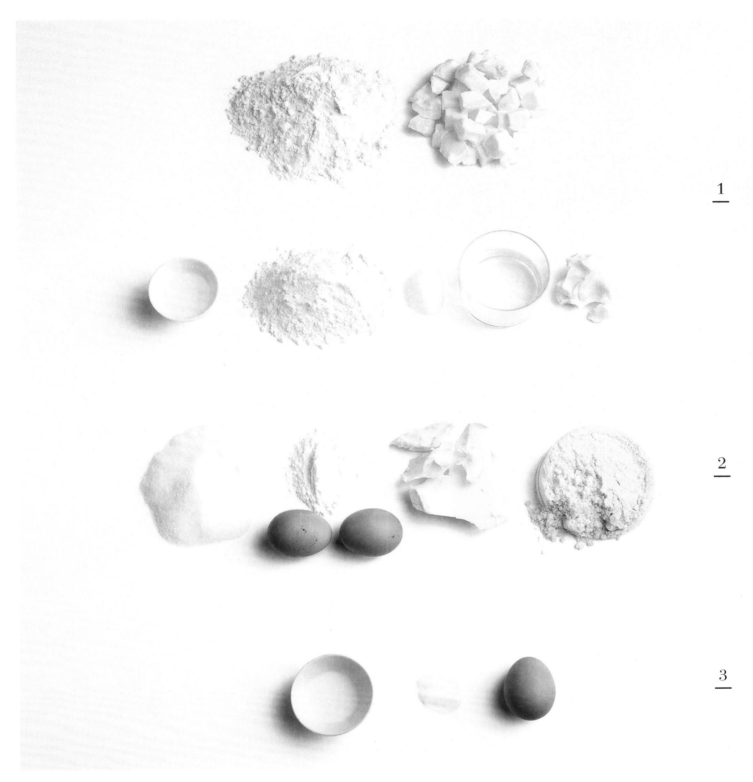

SERVES 8

1 INVERSE PUFF PASTRY (600 G)

Beurre manié (kneaded butter)
200 g soft unsalted butter
  (page 284), cut into cubes
80 g T65 strong flour

Détrempe
180 g T65 strong flour
80 g cold water
10 g salt
60 g softened unsalted butter (page 284)
2 g white vinegar

2 ALMOND CREAM (400 G)

100 g unsalted butter
100 g caster sugar
100 g ground almonds
10 g cornflour
2 eggs

3 GLAZE

1 egg
3 g (½ teaspoon) milk
pinch of salt

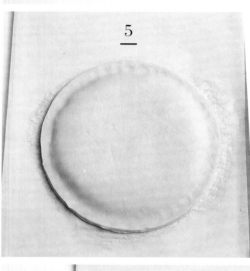

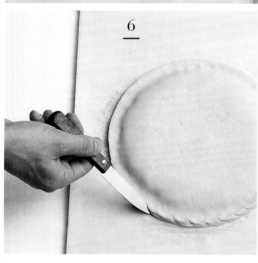

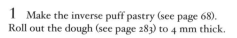

1 Make the inverse puff pastry (see page 68). Roll out the dough (see page 283) to 4 mm thick.

2 Cut out two pastry discs using the cutting ring.

3 Lay one of the discs on a baking sheet lined with baking paper. Make the glaze (see page 49). Glaze a 2 cm wide strip around the edge of the dough.

4 Make the almond cream (see page 78). Use it to fill a piping bag fitted with a plain no. 8 nozzle. Pipe the almond cream on the pastry in a spiral, starting from the middle of the disc. Place a charm in the cream.

5 Dust the rolling pin and the second pastry disc with flour, then roll the disc up on the rolling pin. Unroll the pastry over the almond cream on the other disc. Join the two discs together by pressing the edges lightly with your fingers.

6 Pinch or notch the edges (see page 283) by making a light incision with the back of a knife.

7 Using a pastry brush, glaze the whole top surface of the cake with the remaining glaze.

8 Preheat the oven to 180°C. Score the top of the cake with the back of a knife, making grooves starting at the centre and moving towards the edge.

9 Bake for 40–45 minutes.

SWEET ROLLS

Understand

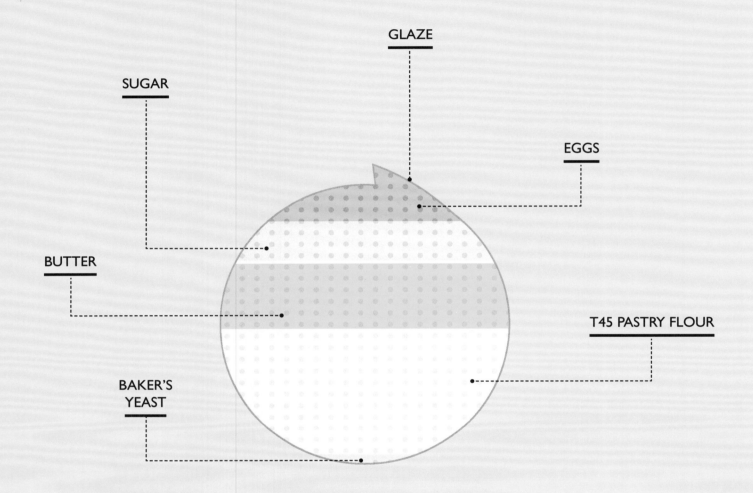

GLAZE

SUGAR

EGGS

BUTTER

T45 PASTRY FLOUR

BAKER'S
YEAST

WHAT ARE THEY?

Sweet yeast dough shaped into rolls.

CHARACTERISTICS

Weight: 50 g
Size: 18 cm
Crumb: tight, moist

EQUIPMENT

Electric mixer with dough hook
Pastry brush
Scissors

TIME TO MAKE

Preparation: 45 minutes
Fermentation: 30 minutes of pointage,
overnight and 1 hour 45 minutes on
the day (15 minutes in the refrigerator,
1 hour 30 minutes proving)
Baking: 10 minutes

TRICKY ASPECT

Incorporating the butter after
kneading without it melting, and so
the dough retains its consistency.

TECHNIQUES TO MASTER

Kneading (pages 33–30)
Rabat (folding; page 37)
Pre-shaping into a ball (page 41)
Shaping into a torpedo loaf (page 45)
Elongating dough (page 41)
Glazing (page 49)

THEY'RE READY . . .

When the bread is golden.

STORAGE

2–3 days

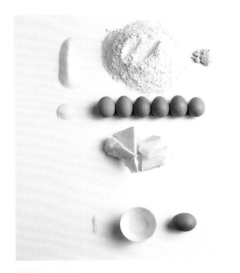

MAKES 16

YEAST DOUGH

450 g T45 pastry flour
6 eggs
8 g salt
14 g fresh baker's yeast
60 g caster sugar
200 g soft unsalted butter
   (page 284), cut into cubes

GLAZE

1 egg
3 g (½ teaspoon) milk
pinch of salt

1 Knead the flour, eggs, salt, crumbled yeast and sugar using an electric mixer (see pages 32–33) for 4 minutes at the lowest speed, then 6 minutes at medium speed. The dough should pull away from the side of the bowl. Return to the lowest speed and add the butter. Mix gently until the cubes are incorporated.

2 Transfer the dough to a round-bottomed bowl, cover with plastic wrap and leave to undergo pointage for 30 minutes at room temperature. Make a rabat (fold; see page 37), return to the bowl, cover with plastic wrap and refrigerate overnight.

3 Divide the dough into 16 pieces about 60 g each and pre-shape each one into a ball (see page 41). Shape into torpedo loaves (see page 45), cover with plastic wrap and refrigerate for 15 minutes.

4 Elongate the rolls (see page 41) to 18 cm long: rest both hands in the centre of the dough and roll it while moving your hands towards the ends.

5 Lay the rolls on a sheet of baking paper. Make the glaze (see page 49). Glaze the rolls using a pastry brush. Leave to prove, uncovered, for 1 hour 30 minutes in a warm place (25–28°C).

6 Dip the scissors in the glaze (so they don't stick), hold them at a 45-degree angle and snip chevrons in the top about 1 cm deep without lifting the scissors.

7 Preheat the oven to 180°C (conventional oven) with a baking sheet in it. Remove the baking sheet from the oven and slide the baking paper with the rolls onto it. Glaze again and bake for 10 minutes.

VIENNESE BAGUETTES

Understand

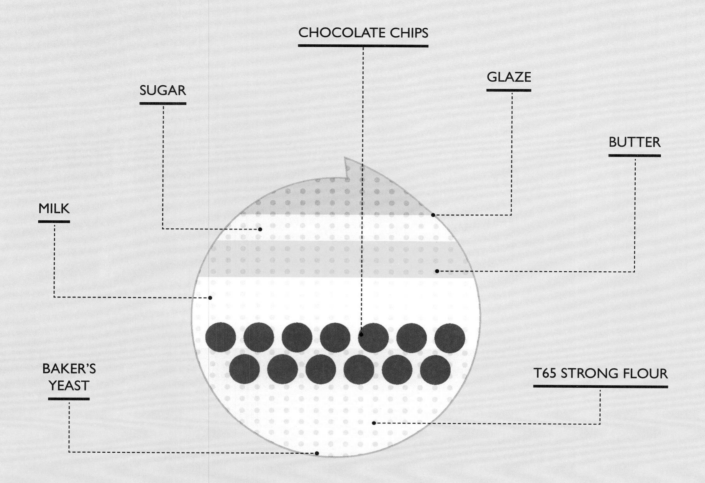

CHOCOLATE CHIPS

GLAZE

BUTTER

SUGAR

MILK

BAKER'S YEAST

T65 STRONG FLOUR

WHAT ARE THEY?

Vienna dough shaped into little baguettes, enriched or not with chocolate chips.

CHARACTERISTICS

Weight: 120 g
Size: 25 cm
Crumb: tight, moist
Crust: very thin, soft

TIME TO MAKE

Preparation: 40 minutes
Fermentation: 6 hours 30 minutes
(5 hours 15 minutes resting in the refrigerator, 1 hour 15 minutes proving)
Baking: 15–20 minutes

EQUIPMENT

Electric mixer with dough hook (optional)
Bread lame (razor)
Dough cutter
Pastry brush

TECHNIQUES TO MASTER

Kneading (pages 30–33)
Shaping into a baguette (page 43)
Glazing (page 49)
Slashing in sausage style (page 51)

THEY'RE READY . . .

As soon as the baguettes are golden.

STORAGE

2 days

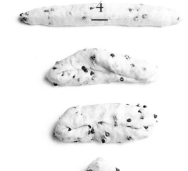

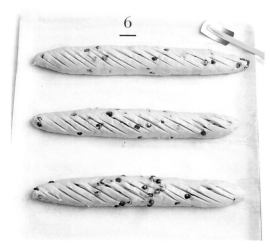

MAKES 4

VIENNA DOUGH

340 g T65 strong flour
210 g milk
7 g salt
7 g fresh baker's yeast
30 g caster sugar
55 g unsalted butter, cut into small cubes

FLAVOURING (OPTIONAL)

90 g chocolate chips

GLAZE

1 egg
3 g (½ teaspoon) milk
pinch of salt

1   Make the Vienna dough (see page 60).

2   For the chocolate baguettes, add the chocolate chips after having incorporated the butter. Knead a little to spread them through the dough.

3   Transfer the dough to a round-bottomed bowl, cover with plastic wrap and refrigerate for 5 hours.

4   Divide the dough into four pieces using a dough cutter. Shape each piece into a baguette (see page 43). Cover with plastic wrap and refrigerate for 15 minutes.

5   Make the glaze (see page 49). Glaze the baguettes using a pastry brush.

6   Slash the baguettes in sausage style (see page 51) using a bread lame (razor). Leave to prove, uncovered, for 1 hour 15 minutes in a warm place (25–28°C).

7   Preheat the oven to 180°C (conventional oven) with a baking sheet inside. Glaze the baguettes again using the pastry brush.

8   Remove the baking sheet from the oven and line it with baking paper. Place the baguettes on the sheet and bake for 15–20 minutes.

JAM DOUGHNUTS

Understand

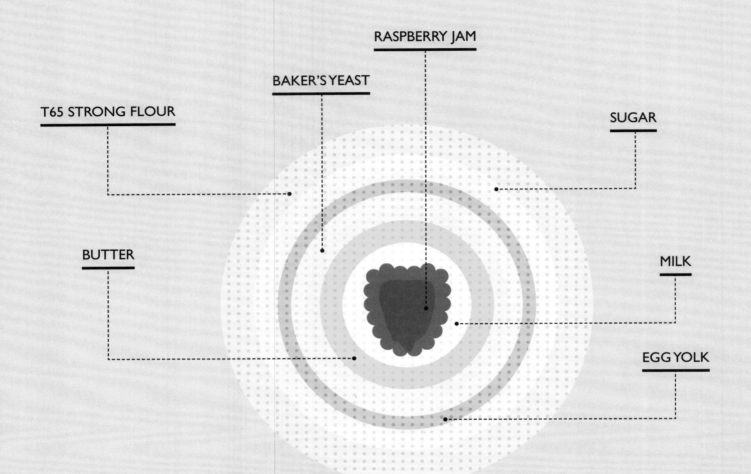

RASPBERRY JAM

BAKER'S YEAST

T65 STRONG FLOUR

SUGAR

BUTTER

MILK

EGG YOLK

WHAT ARE THEY?

Sweetened yeast dough shaped into smallish balls. The balls are fried, rolled in a mixture of sugar and cinnamon then filled with raspberry jam.

CHARACTERISTICS

Weight: 100 g
Size: 10 cm diameter
Crumb: tight, moist

TIME TO MAKE

Preparation: 1 hour
Fermentation: 6 hours to 6 hours 30 minutes
(1 hour 30 minutes resting at 24°C, 3 hours in th refrigerator, 1 hour 30 minuts to 2 hours proving)
Frying: 12 minutes

EQUIPMENT

Electric mixer with dough hook
Dough cutter
Piping bag and plain no. 6 nozzle

FILLING VARIATIONS

Stewed apple
Pastry cream
Chocolate paste

TRICKY ASPECTS

Frying: controlling the temperature of the oil.
Filling.

TECHNIQUES TO MASTER

Kneading (pages 30–33)
Shaping into a ball (page 42)

TIP

The dough is risen when a light push with a finger leaves no trace.

THEY'RE READY . . .

When the doughnuts are well browned.

STORAGE

2 days at room temperature.

1

2

3

4–5

WHY IS THERE A PALE LINE AROUND THE MIDDLE OF THE DOUGHNUT?

The doughnuts float on the surface, and they must be turned to cook both sides. The white line is the flotation line.

MAKES 12

1 YEAST DOUGH

125 g T65 strong flour
50 g egg yolk
35 g caster sugar
30 g fresh baker's yeast
20 g milk
6 g salt
35 g unsalted butter, cut into cubes

2 LEAVEN

140 g flour
3 g fresh baker's yeast
90 g water

3 FRYING

1 litre canola oil

4 RASPBERRY JAM (300 G)

120 g caster sugar
3 g pectin
250 g raspberries

5 TO FINISH

100 g caster sugar
10 g ground cinnamon

Making jam doughnuts

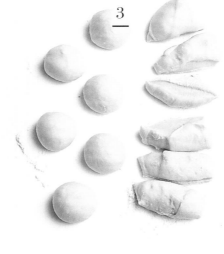

1   Make the leaven: mix the flour, crumbled yeast and water. Leave to rest for 1 hour 30 minutes at 24°C. Knead all the dough ingredients (except the butter) and the leaven using an electric mixer (see pages 32–33) for 6–8 minutes at the lowest speed, then 6–8 minutes one click higher. Add the butter and knead quickly to incorporate.

2   When the dough pulls away from the side of the bowl, cover it with plastic wrap and refrigerate until completely cool (3 hours).

3   Using a dough cutter, divide the dough into 12 pieces about 40 g each. Shape each into a ball (see page 42). Place on a clean well-floured tea towel.

4   Cover with another clean tea towel and leave to prove for 1 hour 30 minutes to 2 hours in a warm place (25–28°C): the dough should double in volume.

5   Heat the canola oil to 140–150°C. Immerse the doughnuts in the hot oil and cook for 30 seconds on each side. Remove using a skimmer and drain on paper towel.

6   Once cooled, roll them in the mixed sugar and cinnamon.

7   Prepare the raspberry jam (see page 268). Allow to cool, then use to fill a piping bag fitted with a plain no. 6 nozzle. Make a hole in the side of each doughnut and fill them with the raspberry jam.

PARISIAN BRIOCHES

Understand

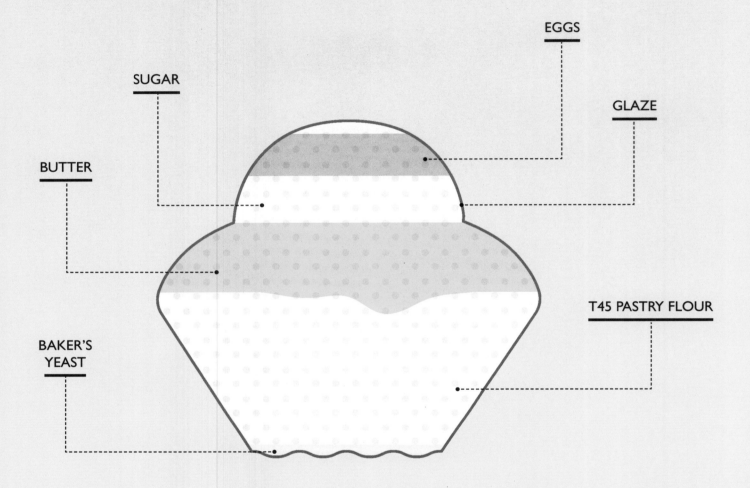

SUGAR

EGGS

GLAZE

BUTTER

BAKER'S
YEAST

T45 PASTRY FLOUR

WHAT ARE THEY?

Brioche dough shaped into two elements:
round head and fluted body.

CHARACTERISTICS

Size (small): 6 cm
Size (large): 12 cm
Weight (small): 50 g each
Weight (large): 350 g
Crumb: tight, silky

TIME TO MAKE

Preparation: 1 hour 20 minutes
Fermentation: overnight pointage,
2 hours 45 minutes (15 minutes resting in
refrigerator, 2 hours 30 minutes proving)
Baking: 10–15 minutes

EQUIPMENT

4 × 8 cm fluted brioche tins
1 × 18 cm fluted brioche tin
Electric mixer with dough hook
Dough cutter
Pastry brush

TRICKY ASPECT
Making the heads of the brioches.

TECHNIQUES TO MASTER
Kneading (pages 30–33)
Shaping into a ball (page 42)
Glazing (page 49)
Rabat (folding; page 37)

TIP
Push the edges of the head well
into the body using your fingers,
to help it rise, otherwise it will be
flattened at the end of cooking.

THEY'RE READY . . .
When the heads of the brioches are nicely
swollen and the brioches are golden.

STORAGE
2–3 days

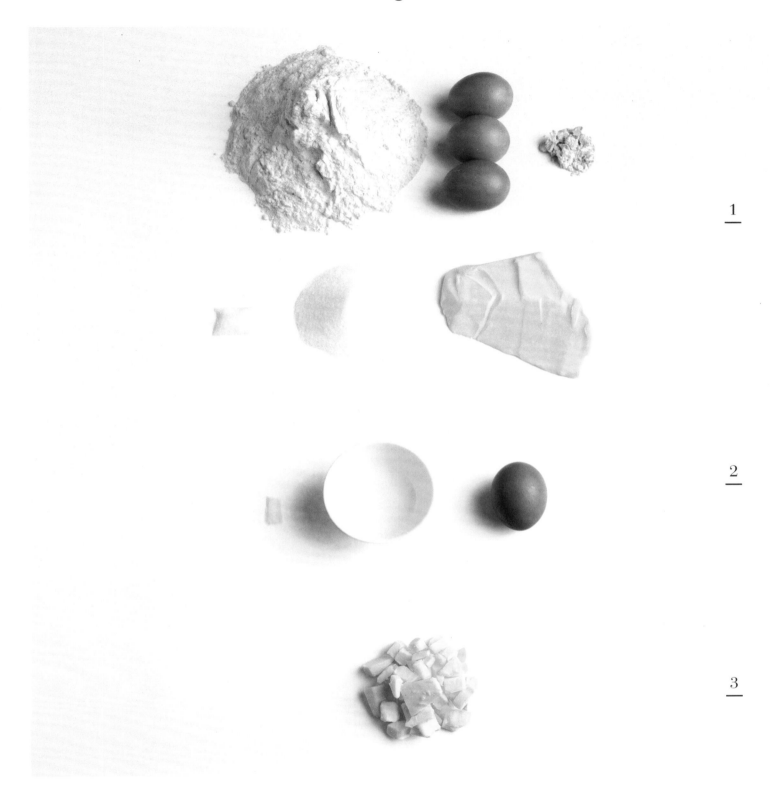

1

2

3

MAKES 4 × 50 G AND 1 × 350 G

1 BRIOCHE DOUGH

240 g T45 pastry flour
3 eggs
5 g salt
8 g fresh baker's yeast
40 g caster sugar
130 g unsalted butter, cut into cubes

2 GLAZE

1 egg
3 g (½ teaspoon) milk
pinch of salt

3 GREASING

softened butter

217

Making Parisian brioches

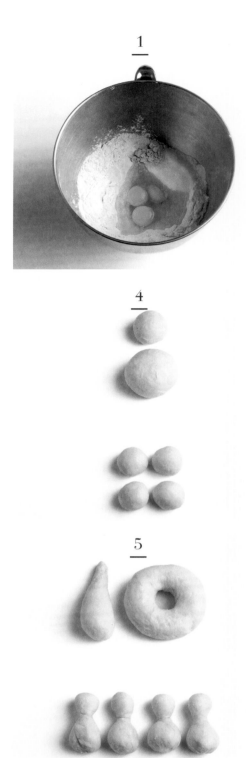

THE DAY BEFORE

1 Cool all the ingredients in the refrigerator before using. Knead the flour, eggs, salt, crumbled yeast and sugar using an electric mixer (see pages 32–33) for 4 minutes at the lowest speed, then 6 minutes at medium speed. The dough should pull away from the side of the bowl.

2 Add the butter, then continue to knead until completely incorporated.

3 Transfer the dough to a round-bottomed bowl. Cover with plastic wrap (plastic touching the dough; see page 285) and leave to undergo pointage for 30 minutes. Make a rabat (fold; see page 37). Return to the bowl, cover with plastic wrap (plastic touching the dough) and refrigerate overnight.

ON THE DAY

4 Using a dough cutter, cut the dough into four 50 g pieces, one 250 g piece and a last piece of 100 g. Shape each piece into a ball (see page 42), cover with plastic wrap and refrigerate for 15 minutes.

5 Using a pastry brush, grease the tins with the softened butter. Squeeze the four small pieces of dough two-thirds of the way up, without breaking, to form the heads of the small brioches. For the large brioche: make a crown (see page 46) with the largest piece and roll the remaining (100 g) piece into a pear shape.

6 Place the four small dough pieces in the small tins with the heads up. For the large brioche, push the thin end of the pear-shaped dough piece into the hole in the crown, join the end under the crown and place in the large tin. Using your fingers, push the edges of the five brioche heads into the bodies to join.

7 Make the glaze (see page 49). Glaze the brioches using a pastry brush. Leave to prove for 2 hours 30 minutes in a warm place (25–28°C).

8 Preheat the oven to 260°C (conventional oven) with a baking sheet inside. Remove the baking sheet from the oven and place the brioche tins on it. Glaze once more, then bake for 10–15 minutes. Leave the brioches to rest for 5 minutes before turning them out of their tins.

PRALINE
BRIOCHES

Understand

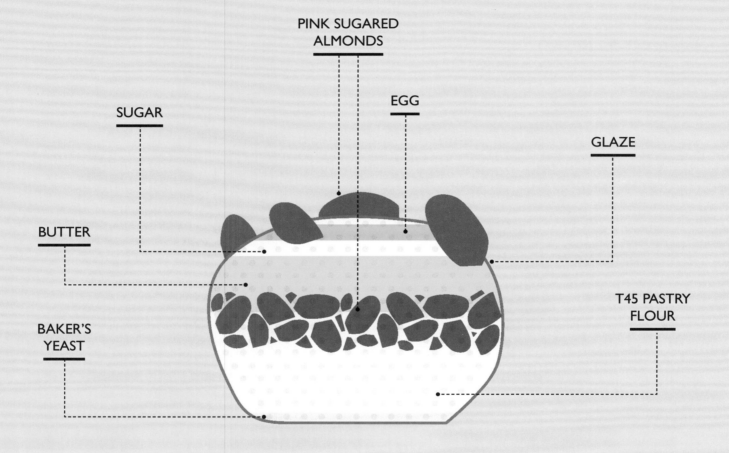

PINK SUGARED
ALMONDS

SUGAR

EGG

GLAZE

BUTTER

BAKER'S
YEAST

T45 PASTRY
FLOUR

WHAT ARE THEY?

Brioche dough enriched with pink
sugared almonds and shaped into balls.

CHARACTERISTICS

Weight: 40 g each
Size: small
Crumb: dense, silky

TIME TO MAKE

Preparation: 1 hour 10 minutes
Fermentation: overnight pointage,
2 hours 30 minutes proving (plus
15 minutes chilling, if necessary)
Baking: 10 minutes

EQUIPMENT

Electric mixer with dough hook
Pastry brush
Dough cutter

TRICKY ASPECT

Shaping: so that the sugared almonds
stay in the brioches during baking.

TECHNIQUES TO MASTER

Kneading (pages 30–33)
Rabat (folding; page 37)
Shaping into a ball (page 42)
Glazing (page 49)

DERIVATIONS

Chocolate chip brioches: incorporate
the choc chips with the electric
mixer, after the butter.

THEY'RE READY . . .

When the brioches are well browned.

STORAGE

2–3 days

MAKES 4

1 BRIOCHE DOUGH

80 g T45 pastry flour
1 egg
2 g salt
3 g fresh baker's yeast
15 g caster sugar
40 g unsalted butter at room
    temperature, cut into cubes

2 GLAZE

1 egg
3 g (½ teaspoon) milk or cream
pinch of salt

3 FILLING

60 g pink sugared almonds, roughly chopped

Making praline brioches

1

3

5

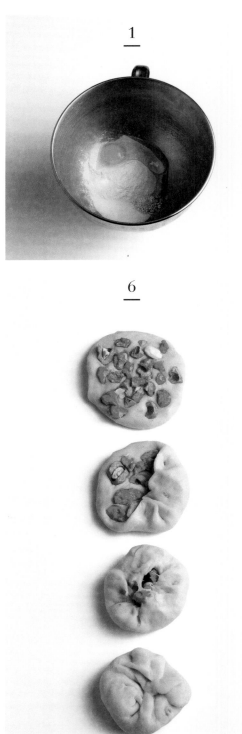

6

7

8

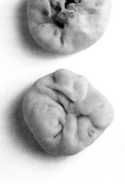

THE DAY BEFORE

1 Cool all the brioche dough ingredients except the butter in the refrigerator before using. Knead the flour, egg, salt, crumbled yeast and sugar using an electric mixer (see pages 30–33) for 4 minutes at the lowest speed, then 6 minutes at medium speed.

2 Return to the lowest speed and add the butter. Mix slowly until the cubes are incorporated.

3 Leave in the mixer bowl and cover with plastic wrap (plastic touching the dough; see page 285) to undergo pointage for 30 minutes at room temperature, then make a rabat (fold; see page 37). Cover with plastic wrap (plastic touching the dough; see page 285) and refrigerate overnight.

ON THE DAY

4 Using a dough cutter, divide the dough into four 60 g pieces. Shape each into a ball (see page 42). Return the pieces to the refrigerator for 15 minutes if they are too warm.

5 Flatten each dough piece into a 10 cm disc. Set aside some of the sugared almonds to top the brioches, then scatter the remainder over one side of each disc and press them in with your palm.

6 Close up the dough over the almonds and reshape into a ball. The almonds should all be inside the dough.

7 Place the brioches on a sheet of baking paper, seam side down. Make the glaze (see page 49). Glaze the brioches using a pastry brush. Leave to prove for 2 hours 30 minutes in a warm place (25–28°C).

8 Preheat the oven to 180°C (conventional oven) with a baking sheet inside. Remove the baking sheet from the oven and slide the baking paper with the brioches onto it. Glaze the brioches again, and lightly press the reserved sugared almonds onto the tops. Bake for 10 minutes.

PLAITED
BRIOCHE

Understand

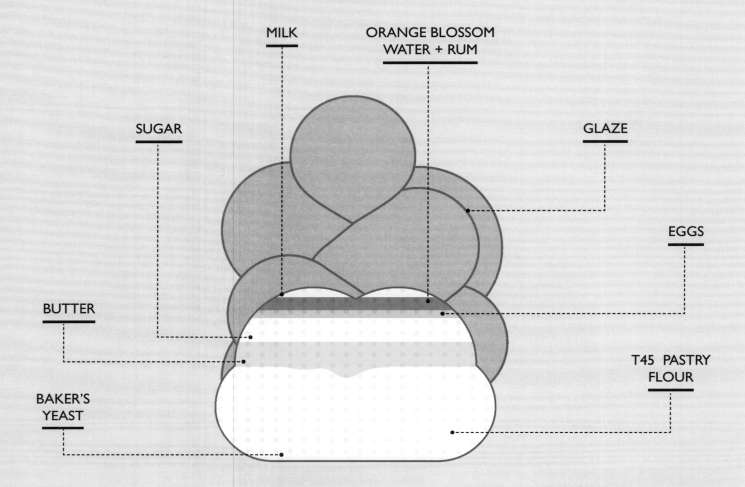

MILK

ORANGE BLOSSOM
WATER + RUM

SUGAR

GLAZE

EGGS

BUTTER

T45 PASTRY
FLOUR

BAKER'S
YEAST

WHAT IS IT?

Brioche dough flavoured with orange
blossom water and rum, shaped into a plait.

CHARACTERISTICS

Weight: 350 g
Size: 40 cm
Crumb: fibrous

TIME TO MAKE

Preparation: 1 hour plus 1 hour
Fermentation: overnight
pointage, 4 hours proving
Baking: 25–30 minutes

EQUIPMENT

Electric mixer with dough hook
Dough scraper
Dough cutter
Pastry brush

TRICKY ASPECT

Plaiting loosely enough to allow the
brioche to rise during cooking.

TECHNIQUES TO MASTER

Kneading (pages 30–33)
Scraping out (page 282)
Rabat (folding; page 37)
Shaping into a plait (page 49)
Glazing (page 49)

IT'S READY . . .

When the crust is golden and the
dough is a little white and moist.

STORAGE

2–3 days

WHAT MAKES THE CRUMB
TEXTURE FIBROUS?

*Plaiting modifies the 'shape' of the
gluten network: the holes in the
network are stretched in the direction
of each strand of the plait.*

Learn

1

2

MAKES 1

1 BRIOCHE DOUGH

170 g T45 pastry flour
2 eggs
40 g caster sugar
10 g milk
2 g orange blossom water
10 g white rum
10 g fresh baker's yeast
3 g salt
50 g unsalted butter at room
    temperature, cut into small cubes

2 GLAZE

1 egg
3 g (½ teaspoon) milk
pinch of salt

Making a plaited brioche

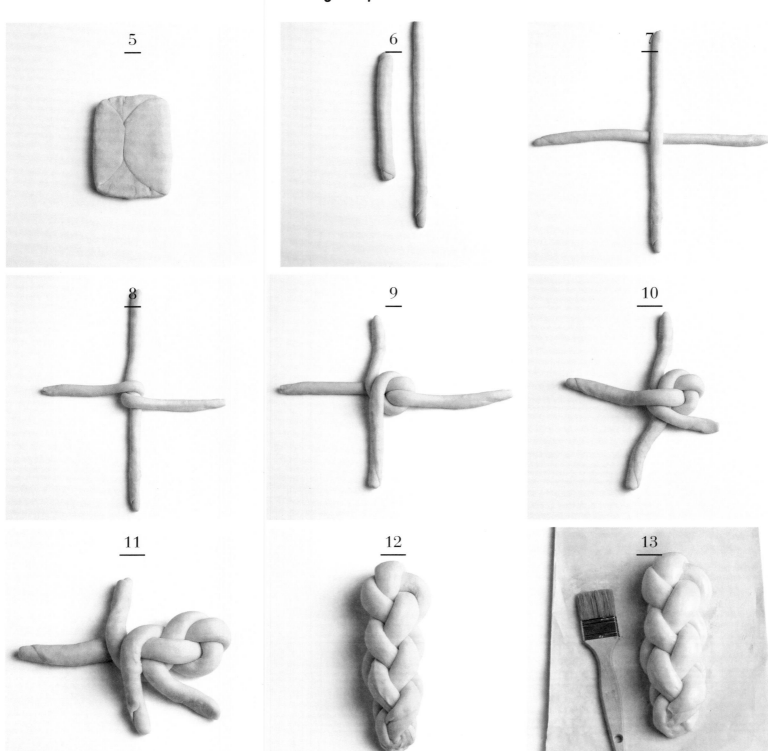

THE DAY BEFORE

1 Put the flour, eggs, sugar, milk, orange blossom water, rum, crumbled yeast and salt in the bowl of an electric mixer.

2 Knead (see pages 32–33) for 4 minutes at the lowest speed, then 8 minutes at medium speed, until the dough pulls away from the side of the bowl. During kneading, scrape down the side of the bowl regularly.

3 Return to the lowest speed and add the soft butter. Knead slowly until well incorporated.

4 Transfer the dough to a floured round-bottomed bowl, cover with plastic wrap (plastic touching the dough; see page 285) and leave to undergo pointage for 1 hour at room temperature.

5 Make a rabat (fold; see page 37). Return the dough to the bowl, cover with plastic wrap (plastic touching the dough; see page 285) and refrigerate overnight.

ON THE DAY

6 Divide the dough into two equal pieces using a dough cutter, and roll each under the palm of your hand to obtain two even sausages 60 cm long.

7 Shape into a plait with four strands. Make a cross with the two sausages, the vertical sausage on top of the horizontal sausage.

8 Cross over the horizontal strands, passing the strand from the right over the strand from the left.

9 Cross over the vertical strands, passing the top strand over the bottom strand.

10 Repeat: the strand from the right passes over the strand from the left.

11 The upper strand passes over the bottom strand.

12 Continue until you run out of strands. Join the ends.

13 Make the glaze (see page 49). Glaze the brioche using a pastry brush. Leave on a sheet of baking paper to prove for 4 hours in a warm place (25–28°C).

14 Preheat the oven to 180°C (fan-forced) with a baking sheet inside. Glaze the brioche again. Remove the sheet from the oven and slide the baking paper with the brioche onto it. Bake for 25–30 minutes.

LAYERED BRIOCHE

Understand

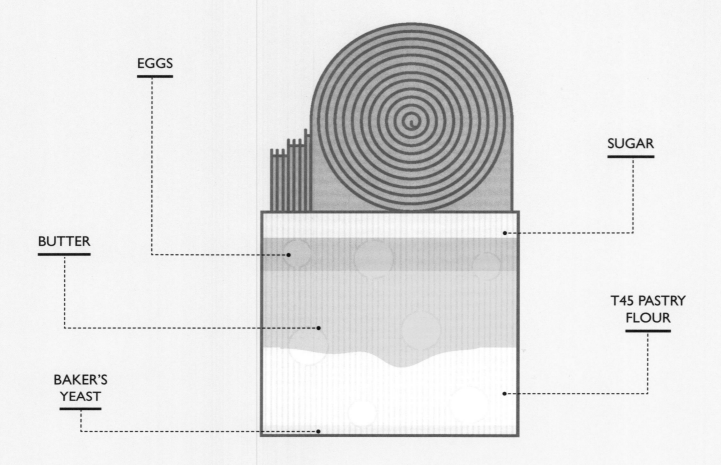

EGGS

SUGAR

BUTTER

T45 PASTRY FLOUR

BAKER'S YEAST

WHAT IS IT?

Brioche dough rolled with a band of butter to create layers.

CHARACTERISTICS

Weight: 400 g
Size: 10 cm
Crumb: honeycombed
Crust: layered

TIME TO MAKE

Preparation: 45 minutes
Fermentation: overnight resting plus
3 hours 30 minutes (1 hour resting in the
refrigerator, 2 hours 30 minutes proving)
Baking: 35 minutes

EQUIPMENT

Electric mixer with dough hook (optional)
Pastry rolling pin
15 cm paper baking mould
Sieve
Pastry brush

TRICKY ASPECT

Not rolling out the dough too much, so
that the butter and dough layers don't mix.

TECHNIQUES TO MASTER

Kneading (pages 30–33)
Rabat (folding; page 37)
Glazing (page 49)

IT'S READY . . .

When the brioche is nicely
swollen and browned.

1

2

4

MAKES I

1 BRIOCHE DOUGH

180 g T45 pastry flour
2 eggs
3 g salt
30 g caster sugar
6 g fresh baker's yeast
90 g unsalted butter at room
    temperature, cut into small cubes

2 LAYERING

100 g unsalted butter

3 GLAZE

1 egg
3 g (½ teaspoon) milk
pinch of salt

4 TO FINISH

icing sugar

Making a layered brioche

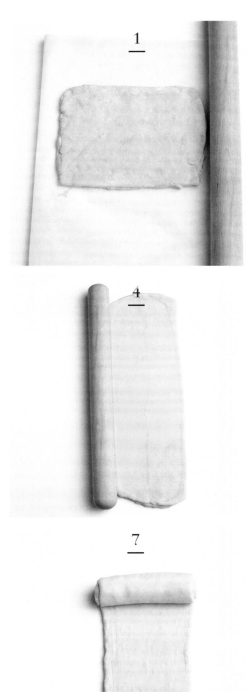

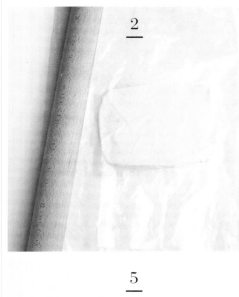

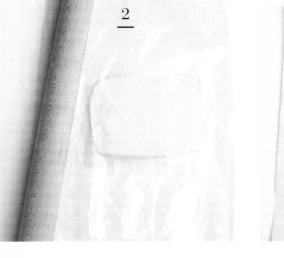

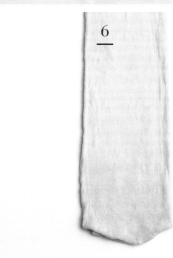

1 Make the brioche dough (see page 66). Roll the dough (see page 283) into a 30 cm × 20 cm rectangle using a rolling pin.

2 Place the butter on baking paper. Tap the butter with the rolling pin to loosen it.

3 Roll the butter into a rectangle 15 cm × 20 cm and place it in the centre of the dough. Fold the two sides of the dough over the butter, making a seam in the middle.

4 Make a simple turn (see page 283): roll out the dough away from you (in the direction of the seam), using a rolling pin. The aim is to obtain a strip of dough three times longer than wide.

5 Fold the dough into three. Cover with plastic wrap and refrigerate for 20 minutes. Make another simple turn: roll out the dough with the seam on the vertical, fold in three, cover with plastic wrap and refrigerate for another 20 minutes. Make a last simple turn, cover with plastic wrap and refrigerate for 20 minutes.

6 Using a rolling pin and with the seam on the vertical, roll out the dough to a width of 10 cm and a thickness of 0.5–1 cm.

7 Tightly roll the dough up on itself.

8 Put the dough in the mould with one end of the roll touching the bottom. Make the glaze (see page 49). Glaze the brioche using a pastry brush. Cover with a clean tea towel and leave to prove for 2 hours 30 minutes in a warm place (25–28°C).

9 Preheat the oven to 180°C (conventional oven). Glaze once more and bake for 35 minutes. Allow to cool, then sift over the icing sugar.

TARTES AU SUCRE

Understand

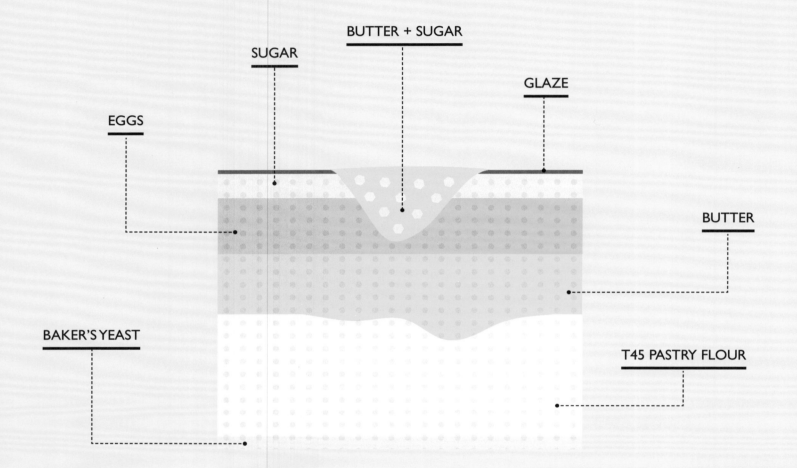

EGGS

SUGAR

BUTTER + SUGAR

GLAZE

BUTTER

BAKER'S YEAST

T45 PASTRY FLOUR

WHAT ARE THEY?

Brioche dough enriched with butter and sugar at the moment of shaping into tartlets.

TIME TO MAKE

Preparation: 50 minutes
Fermentation: overnight pointage,
3 hours (30 minutes relaxing,
2 hours 30 minutes proving)
Baking: 5–7 minutes

CHARACTERISTICS

Weight: 50 g
Size: 15 cm diameter
Crumb: tight, moist

EQUIPMENT

Electric mixer with dough hook (optional)
Dough cutter
Pastry rolling pin
Sieve
Pastry brush

TRICKY ASPECT

Rolling out the dough.

TECHNIQUES TO MASTER

Kneading (pages 30–33)
Rabat (folding; page 37)
Pre-shaping into a ball (page 41)
Glazing (page 49)

TIP

Carefully turn the dough regularly during rolling with a rolling pin, to retain the round shape.

THEY'RE READY . . .

When the tarts are lightly golden.

STORAGE

1–2 days at room temperature.

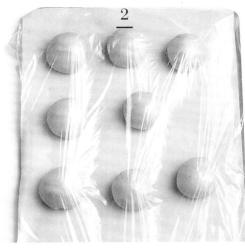

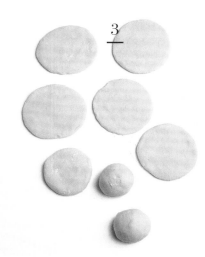

MAKES 8

BRIOCHE DOUGH

245 g T45 pastry flour
3 eggs
5 g salt
40 g caster sugar
8 g fresh baker's yeast
120 g unsalted butter at room
    temperature, cut into small cubes

GLAZE

1 egg
3 g (½ teaspoon) milk
pinch of salt

TOPPING

80 g unsalted butter
65 g caster sugar (or soft brown sugar)

1   Make the brioche dough (see page 66). Divide
the dough into eight 70 g pieces using a dough cutter.
Pre-shape each piece into a ball (see page 41).

2   Cover the dough pieces with plastic wrap
and refrigerate for at least 30 minutes to relax.

3   On a floured work surface using a rolling
pin, roll each piece (see page 283) into a
quite thin disc (about 5 mm thick). Keep
the bottom of the dough well floured.

4   Place the discs on a baking sheet lined with baking
paper, cover with a clean tea towel and leave to prove
for 2 hours 30 minutes in a warm place (25–28°C).

5   Preheat the oven to 180°C (conventional oven).
Make the glaze (see page 49). Glaze the tartlets using a
pastry brush.

6   Make five dents in each disc with your index
and middle fingers. Put small 2 g cubes of butter in
each hole and sprinkle over the sugar (about 8 g each)
using a sieve.

7   Bake for 5–7 minutes.

BRIOCHE BORDELAISE

Understand

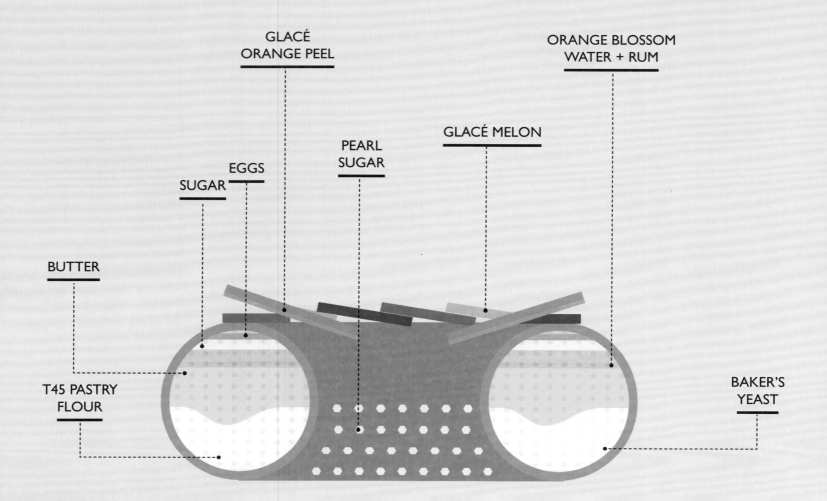

GLACÉ
ORANGE PEEL

ORANGE BLOSSOM
WATER + RUM

GLACÉ MELON

PEARL
SUGAR

EGGS

SUGAR

BUTTER

T45 PASTRY
FLOUR

BAKER'S
YEAST

WHAT IS IT?

Brioche dough flavoured with orange blossom water and enriched with glacé fruit, shaped into a crown and decorated with pearl sugar and glacé fruit.

CHARACTERISTICS

Weight: 500 g
Size: 25 cm diameter
Crumb: tight, moist

TIME TO MAKE

Preparation: 10 minutes
Fermentation: overnight plus
2 hours (30 minutes resting,
1 hour 30 minutes proving)
Baking: 30 minutes

EQUIPMENT

Electric mixer with dough hook
Pastry brush

TRICKY ASPECT

Incorporating the butter into the dough without it melting.

TECHNIQUES TO MASTER

Kneading (pages 30–33)
Rabat (folding; page 37)
Pre-shaping into a ball (page 41)
Shaping into a crown (page 46)
Glazing (page 49)

IT'S READY . . .

When the brioche is cooked and decorated.

STORAGE

2 days at room temperature.

MAKES 1

BRIOCHE DOUGH

200 g T45 pastry flour
20 g orange blossom water
10 g white rum
2 eggs
4 g salt
15 g caster sugar
6 g fresh baker's yeast
120 g unsalted butter
45 g orange peel, cut into small cubes
5 g lemon zest

GLAZE

1 egg, 3 g (½ teaspoon) milk, pinch of salt

TO FINISH

50 g pearl sugar
20 g strips of glacé orange peel and glacé melon

1   Put all the ingredients in the refrigerator two days before making. The next day make the brioche dough (see page 66), adding the orange blossom water and the rum with the flour. Add the orange peel and lemon zest after the butter and knead a little to incorporate them well. Leave to undergo pointage for 30 minutes, then make a rabat (fold; see page 37). Cover with plastic wrap and refrigerate overnight.

2   Pre-shape into a ball (see page 41) and refrigerate for 30 minutes to rest. Dip your index finger in flour then pierce the centre of the ball until you feel the work surface.

3   Shape into a crown (see page 46), finishing with an interior diameter of about 8 cm.

4   Place on a sheet of baking paper. Make the glaze (see page 49). Glaze using a pastry brush. Leave to prove for 1 hour 30 minutes in a warm place (25–28°C).

5   Preheat the oven to 260°C (conventional oven) with a baking sheet inside. Glaze again. Sprinkle the outside of the brioche with pearl sugar and top with the glacé fruit. Remove the sheet from the oven and slide the baking paper with the brioche onto it. Bake for 30 minutes.

TROPÉZIENNE TART

Understand

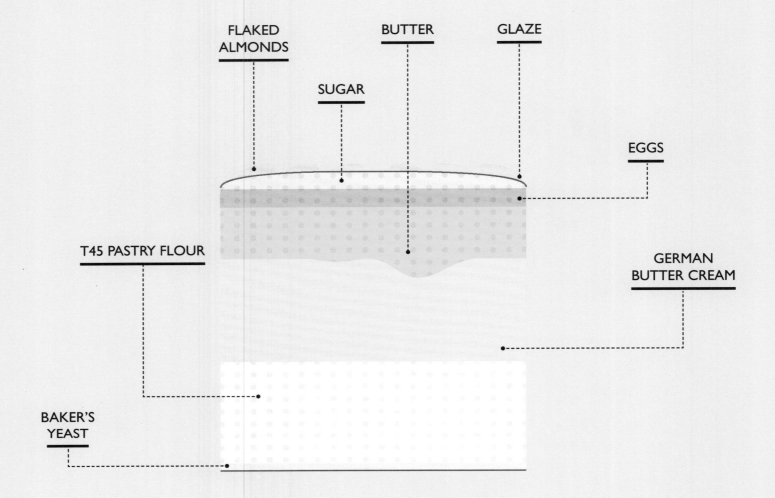

FLAKED ALMONDS

BUTTER

GLAZE

SUGAR

EGGS

T45 PASTRY FLOUR

GERMAN BUTTER CREAM

BAKER'S YEAST

WHAT IS IT?

Brioche filled with German butter cream flavoured with orange blossom water and vanilla, and topped with flaked almonds.

TIME TO MAKE

Preparation: 25 minutes
Fermentation: overnight pointage,
1 hour 30 minutes proving
Baking: 35 minutes

CHARACTERISTICS

Weight: 800 g
Size: 24 cm diameter
Crumb: tight, moist

EQUIPMENT

Electric mixer with dough hook (optional)
Pastry rolling pin
24 cm tart ring
Pastry brush
Palette knife

TECHNIQUES TO MASTER

Kneading (pages 30–33)
Rabat (folding; page 37)
Shaping into a ball (page 42)
Glazing (page 49)
Creaming butter and sugar (page 284)

IT'S READY . . .

When the brioche is golden. When the cream is thick and white.

STORAGE

2–3 days in the refrigerator.

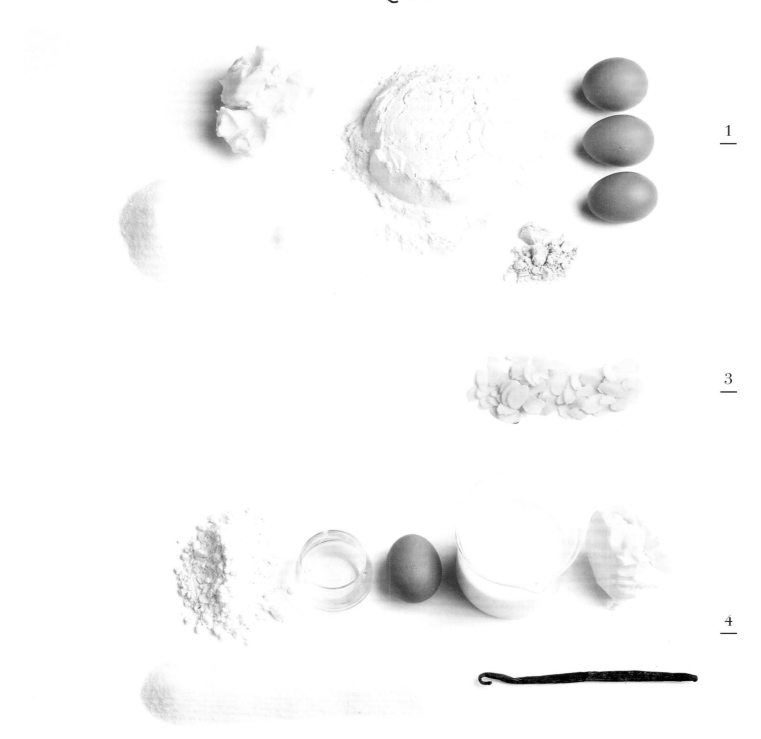

1

3

4

SERVES 8

1 BRIOCHE DOUGH (500 G)

220 g T45 pastry flour
3 eggs
4 g salt
35 g caster sugar
7 g fresh baker's yeast
110 g softened unsalted butter (page 284)

2 GLAZE

1 egg
3 g (½ teaspoon) milk
pinch of salt

3 TO FINISH

10 g flaked almonds

4 GERMAN BUTTER CREAM

1 egg
80 g caster sugar
25 g cornflour
10 g orange blossom water
250 g milk
½ vanilla bean, split lengthways
    and seeds scraped
125 g unsalted butter

THE DAY BEFORE

1 Make the brioche dough (see page 66).

THE NEXT DAY

2 Shape the brioche dough into a ball (see page 42) then roll it out a little with a rolling pin while retaining the round shape and put it in the middle of a tart ring placed on a baking sheet lined with baking paper.

3 Make the glaze (see page 49). Glaze the brioche with a pastry brush. Leave to prove for 1 hour 30 minutes in a warm place (25–28°C).

4 Preheat the oven to 160°C. Glaze again, then sprinkle with flaked almonds. Bake for 35 minutes. Allow to cool.

5 Make the German butter cream: in a round-bottomed bowl, mix the egg, sugar, cornflour and orange blossom water.

6 Bring the milk to the boil in a saucepan with the vanilla bean and seeds. Pour it into the bowl with the egg mixture then return the mixture to the saucepan. Heat for 2 minutes, whisking constantly (the cream thickens very quickly), then remove from the heat.

7 Add half the butter to the warm mixture and mix it in.

8 Transfer the cream to a bowl and cover with plastic wrap (plastic touching the cream; see page 285) so that it doesn't form a crust. Let it cool to room temperature.

9 Using an electric mixer with the beater attachment, add the remaining butter to the cream and mix gently until it increases in volume slightly and turns pale (see page 284).

10 Cut the brioche in half horizontally and cover the bottom with the butter cream using a palette knife. Replace the top of the brioche.

KUGELHOPF

Understand

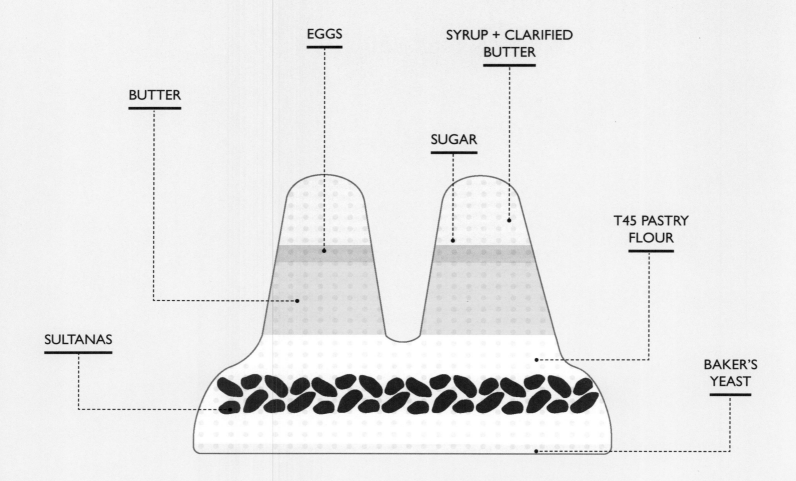

EGGS

SYRUP + CLARIFIED BUTTER

BUTTER

SUGAR

T45 PASTRY FLOUR

SULTANAS

BAKER'S YEAST

WHAT IS IT?

Brioche cake flavoured with sultanas, cooked in a kugelhopf mould, dipped in syrup and clarified butter, and dusted with icing sugar.

CHARACTERISTICS

Weight: 300 g
Size: 15 cm diameter
Crumb: tight

EQUIPMENT

Electric mixer with dough hook (optional)
Pastry brush
15 cm kugelhopf mould

TIME TO MAKE

Soaking: overnight
Preparation: 1 hour
Fermentation: overnight plus 2 hours
30 minutes to 3 hours (30 minutes
resting in the refrigerator, 2 hours
to 2 hours 30 minutes proving)
Baking: 30 minutes

TECHNIQUES TO MASTER

Kneading (pages 30–33)
Rabat (folding; page 37)
Shaping into a ball (page 42)

IT'S READY . . .

As soon as the kugelhopf is lightly browned.

STORAGE

2–3 days, covered with plastic wrap.

WHY MUST THE KUGELHOPF BE DIPPED IN THE SYRUP AND THEN IN THE CLARIFIED BUTTER?

The soakings add taste and moisture. They are done in two steps because sugar doesn't dissolve in fat. If you mix the butter and sugar to dip only once, the sugar won't be absorbed well and will leave crystals that are unpleasant to eat.

1

3

4

MAKES I

1 KUGELHOPF DOUGH

30 g sultanas
140 g T45 pastry flour
2 eggs
3 g salt
20 g caster sugar
4 g fresh baker's yeast
70 g unsalted butter

2 GREASING

10 g softened unsalted butter (page 284)

3 SYRUP

50 g water
50 g caster sugar

4 TO FINISH

20 g unsalted butter
10 g icing sugar

Making kugelhopf

THE DAY BEFORE

1 Soak the sultanas in tepid water. Refrigerate the remaining ingredients.

2 Make the kugelhopf (brioche) dough (see page 66). At the end of kneading, add the drained sultanas. Place the dough on a floured work surface, cover with a clean tea towel and leave to rest for 30 minutes.

3 Make a rabat (fold; see page 37). Transfer the dough to a round-bottomed bowl, cover with plastic wrap (plastic touching the dough; see page 285) and refrigerate overnight.

ON THE DAY

4 Roll the dough on itself and shape into a ball (see page 42). Return to the bowl, covered with plastic wrap (plastic touching the dough), and refrigerate for 30 minutes (see page 285).

5 Grease a kugelhopf mould with the softened butter using a pastry brush. Make a hole in the dough by pushing on the centre with both your thumbs. Turn the dough over and place in the bottom of the kugelhopf mould, pushing hard with your fingers to ensure it fills the mould well.

6 Cover with a clean tea towel and leave to prove in the mould for 2 hours to 2 hours 30 minutes in a warm place (25–28°C).

7 Preheat the oven to 160°C (fan-forced) and bake for 30 minutes. Turn out onto a wire rack to cool completely.

8 Clarify the butter (see page 284) and transfer to a large bowl.

9 Make a syrup by bringing the water and sugar to the boil in a small saucepan. Transfer to a large bowl and sit the kugelhopf in the syrup for 5–10 seconds.

10 Drain the kugelhopf for 30 seconds then sit it in the clarified butter for 5–10 seconds.

11 Drain the kugelhopf for 30 seconds, then leave to rest for 5–10 minutes for the butter to solidify, then sift over the icing sugar.

PANETTONE

Understand

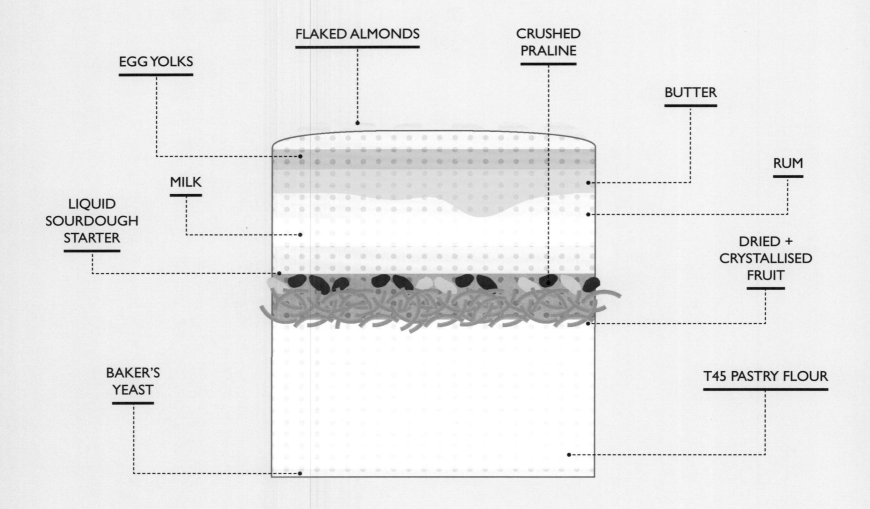

EGG YOLKS

FLAKED ALMONDS

CRUSHED PRALINE

BUTTER

RUM

MILK

LIQUID SOURDOUGH STARTER

DRIED + CRYSTALLISED FRUIT

BAKER'S YEAST

T45 PASTRY FLOUR

WHAT IS IT?

Italian brioche-style cake, flavoured with crystallised fruits, sultanas and rum.

CHARACTERISTICS

Weight: 500 g
Size: 20–5 cm diameter
Crumb: tight, moist

EQUIPMENT

Electric mixer with dough hook
Large (600 g) panettone mould

TIME TO MAKE

Soaking: overnight
Preparation: 45 minutes
Fermentation: overnight pointage,
3 hours proving
Baking: 45 minutes

TECHNIQUES TO MASTER

Kneading (pages 30–33)
Rabat (folding; page 37)
Shaping into a ball (page 42)

DERIVATION

Small panettones: divide the dough into
pieces of about 80 g and bake for 25 minutes.

NON-SOURDOUGH OPTION

For a mixture without liquid
sourdough starter, add an extra 5 g
fresh baker's yeast and 20 g water.

TIP

If the fruit hasn't absorbed all the rum,
drain it before mixing into the dough.

IT'S READY . . .

When the panettone is well browned.

STORAGE

1 week, well wrapped in plastic wrap.

MAKES I

1 DOUGH

180 g T45 pastry flour
50 g milk
40 g caster sugar
3 g salt
5 g fresh baker's yeast
50 g liquid sourdough starter (page 20)
3 egg yolks
60 g unsalted butter, cut into cubes

2 FRUIT

35 g sultanas
70 g crystallised orange peel
15 g dark rum

3 PANETTONE MIX

90 g caster sugar
25 g crushed almond praline (pralinettes)
15 g T55 plain flour
1 egg white

4 TO FINISH

30 g flaked almonds

Making panettone

1

2

3

4

5

6

7

8

9

TWO DAYS BEFORE

1 Soak the sultanas and crystallised orange peel in a bowl with the rum and leave to macerate overnight.

THE DAY BEFORE

2 Knead the flour, milk, sugar, salt, crumbled yeast, liquid starter and egg yolks using an electric mixer (see pages 32–33) for 6 minutes at medium speed. Incorporate the butter and keep kneading at medium speed until the dough pulls away from the side of the bowl.

3 Add the macerated fruit and knead at the lowest speed until well incorporated.

4 Transfer the dough to a round-bottomed bowl, cover with plastic wrap and leave to undergo pointage for 1 hour in a warm place (25–28°C).

5 Make a rabat (fold; see page 37). Return the dough to the bowl, cover with plastic wrap with the plastic touching the dough (see page 285) and refrigerate overnight.

ON THE DAY

6 Shape the dough into a ball (see page 42) and place it in the panettone mould.

7 Cover with a clean tea towel and leave to prove for 3 hours in a warm place (25–28°C).

8 Preheat the oven to 180°C (conventional oven). Make the panettone mix: stir together the sugar, almond praline and flour in a round-bottomed bowl. Add the egg white and stir until the mixture is as smooth as possible.

9 Cover the top of the panettone with the panettone mix using a spoon. Scatter over the flaked almonds. Bake for 45 minutes.

PISTACHIO AND APRICOT
TART

Understand

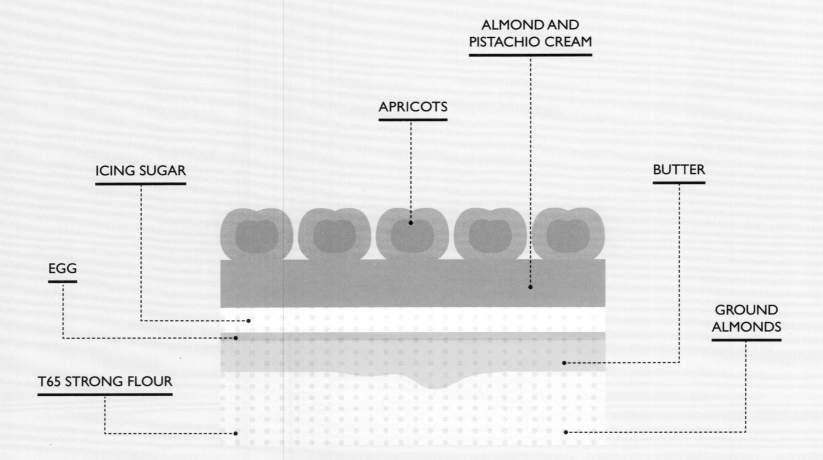

ALMOND AND
PISTACHIO CREAM

APRICOTS

ICING SUGAR

BUTTER

EGG

GROUND
ALMONDS

T65 STRONG FLOUR

WHAT IS IT?

Sweetened pastry case filled with almond
and pistachio cream and quartered apricots.

TIME TO MAKE

Preparation: 1 hour
Resting: 4 hours (2 hours for the pastry
and 2 hours for the almond cream)
Baking: 35–40 minutes

EQUIPMENT

Electric mixer with dough hook
and beater (optional)
Sieve

Whisk
Pastry rolling pin
20 cm tart ring
Piping bag and plain 8 mm nozzle

TRICKY ASPECT

Filling

TECHNIQUES TO MASTER

Kneading (pages 30–33)
Lining a tart ring (page 283)

TIP

If you use tinned apricots, drain them well.

IT'S READY . . .

When the tips of the apricots start to
caramelise and the pastry is golden.

STORAGE

2–3 days in the refrigerator.

WHAT HAPPENS TO THE ALMOND
CREAM DURING COOKING?

*The egg proteins coagulate and the
starch in the cornflour thickens. The
cream swells up and becomes creamier.*

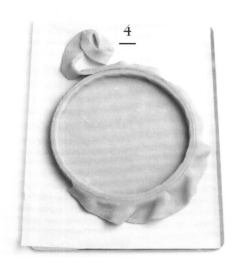

SERVES 6

SWEET SABLÉ PASTRY

155 g unsalted butter, cut into cubes
100 g icing sugar
30 g ground almonds
1 g salt
260 g T65 strong flour
1 egg

ALMOND AND PISTACHIO CREAM

50 g unsalted butter
50 g caster sugar
50 g ground almonds
5 g cornflour
1 egg
20 g pistachio paste

TOPPING

10 fresh apricots or 20 tinned
apricot halves in syrup

TO FINISH

Icing sugar

1 Make the sweet sablé pastry (see page 74) then refrigerate for 2 hours.

2 Make the almond and pistachio cream (see page 78). Add the pistachio paste and refrigerate for 2 hours.

3 Cut the apricots in half then in half again if fresh.

4 Roll out the pastry to 3 mm thick, then use it to line (see page 283) a greased tart ring sitting on a baking sheet lined with baking paper.

5 Preheat the oven to 190°C (conventional oven). Pipe the almond and pistachio cream into the tart base to 1 cm deep.

6 Arrange the apricot pieces on the nut cream in concentric circles.

7 Bake for 35–40 minutes. Allow to cool, then sift over the icing sugar.

FLAN PÂTISSIER

Understand

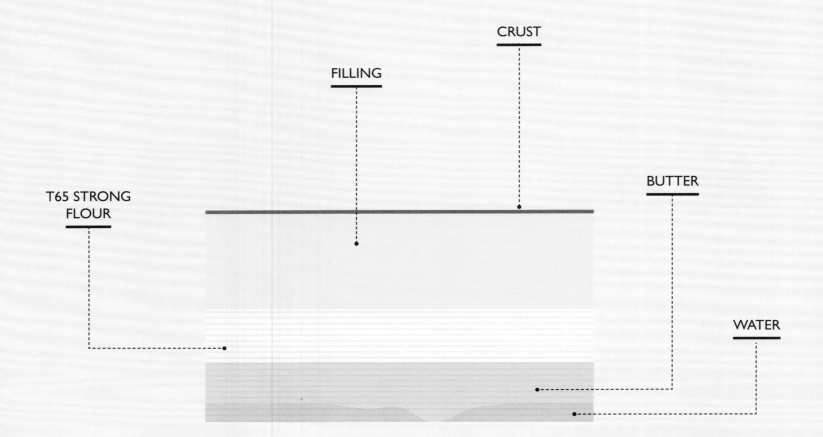

CRUST

FILLING

BUTTER

T65 STRONG
FLOUR

WATER

WHAT IS IT?

Inverse puff pastry base filled with a cooked
cream made with eggs, milk and cornflour.

TIME TO MAKE

Preparation: 1 hour
Resting in the refrigerator: 12 hours
Baking: 35–40 minutes
Cooling: 1 hour 30 minutes

EQUIPMENT

Electric mixer with dough hook and beater
2.5 cm high 26 cm diameter tart ring
Pastry brush
Pastry rolling pin
Whisk

DERIVATIONS

Coconut flan: add 200 g desiccated coconut.
Apricot flan: arrange apricot halves over the
base of the pastry, then pour over the cream.

TRICKY ASPECT

Making the cream.

TECHNIQUES TO MASTER

Kneading (pagse 30–33)
Lining a tart ring (page 283)
Blanching (page 284)

TIP

Allow the filling to cool completely before
baking, so it has a nice crust without cracks.

IT'S READY . . .

When the flan is well coloured, with a few
darker spots.

STORAGE

2 days in the refrigerator.

SERVES 10

INVERSE PUFF PASTRY (300 G)

Beurre manié (kneaded butter)
100 g softened unsalted butter
  (page 284), cut into cubes
40 g T65 strong flour

Détrempe
90 g T65 strong flour
40 g cold water
5 g salt
30 g softened unsalted butter (page 284)
1 g white wine vinegar

GREASING

softened unsalted butter (page 284)

FILLING

3 eggs
200 g caster sugar
80 g cornflour
1 litre milk

1   Make the inverse puff pastry (see page 68).
Roll out the dough (see page 283) to 2 mm thick.

2   Preheat the oven to 170°C (fan-forced).
Grease the tart ring with the softened butter
using a pastry brush. Sit the tart ring on a baking
sheet lined with baking paper and line with
the puff pastry (see page 283). Refrigerate.

3   Cream the eggs with the sugar using a
whisk (see page 284). Mix in the cornflour.

4   Bring the milk to the boil. Loosen the egg
mixture with one-third of the milk, then pour it
all into the saucepan.

5   Whisk for 1 minute over the heat.

6   Pour the mixture into the lined tart ring.
Allow it to cool to room temperature, then bake for
35–40 minutes. Let it cool for 1 hour 30 minutes.

SPICE BREAD

Understand

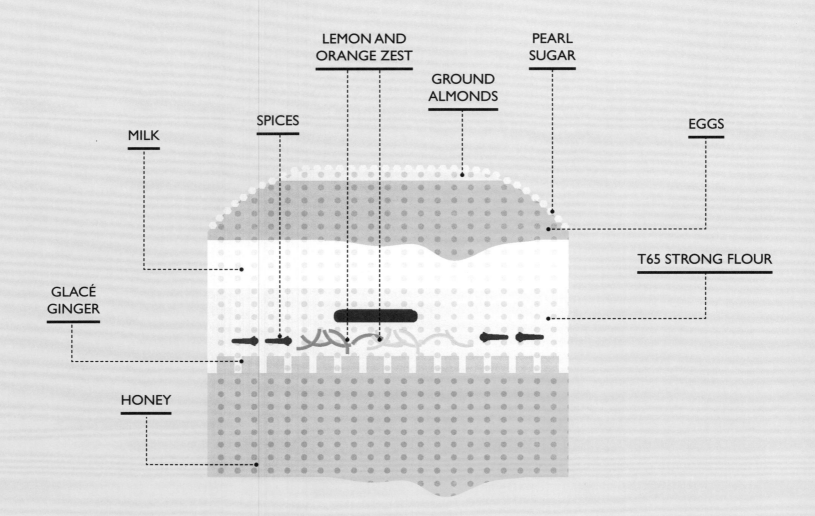

MILK

SPICES

LEMON AND ORANGE ZEST

GROUND ALMONDS

PEARL SUGAR

EGGS

GLACÉ GINGER

T65 STRONG FLOUR

HONEY

WHAT IS IT?

Cake very rich in honey, enlivened with spices and citrus zest.

TIME TO MAKE

Preparation: 30 minutes
Baking: 45 minutes

EQUIPMENT

20 cm long loaf tin
Wooden spoon
Sieve

TRICKY ASPECT

Not letting the milk and honey mixture boil: remove the saucepan from the heat as soon as small bubbles appear.

TIPS

After removing the cake from the tin, wrap it in plastic wrap to keep it moist. If, when the moment comes to add the milk to the mixture it is below 60°C, reheat it over a low heat.

IT'S READY . . .

When the tip of a knife inserted into the cake comes out clean.

STORAGE

1 week wrapped in plastic wrap.

WHY MUST THE MILK NOT BOIL?

So that it doesn't burn the spices as they infuse. If it did, they would release undesirable aromatic notes.

MAKES I LOAF

DOUGH

170 g honey
80 g milk
140 g T65 strong flour
5 g bicarbonate of soda
15 g ground almonds
1 g salt
2 eggs

SPICES

1 g ground ginger
1 g ground cinnamon
1 g whole cloves
3 g orange zest
3 g lemon zest
28 g cubed glacé ginger

TO FINISH

100 g pearl sugar

1   Heat the honey and milk in a saucepan over a low heat and remove from the heat before it boils. Add the ground spices and the whole cloves, then leave to infuse for 15 minutes.

2   Pass the milk through a sieve (see page 285) and discard the whole cloves. Allow to cool.

3   Preheat the oven to 150°C. Sift the flour with the bicarbonate of soda and the ground almonds into a round-bottomed bowl (see page 285). Add the salt, eggs and zests, and mix using a wooden spoon.

4   Carefully pour in the infused milk, stirring constantly to obtain a smooth mixture. Stir in the crystallised ginger.

5   Line a 20 cm long loaf tin with baking paper. Sprinkle in half the pearl sugar.

6   Pour the dough into the tin then sprinkle with the remaining pearl sugar. Bake for 45 minutes. Allow to cool, then turn out of the tin.

FRUIT
CAKE

Understand

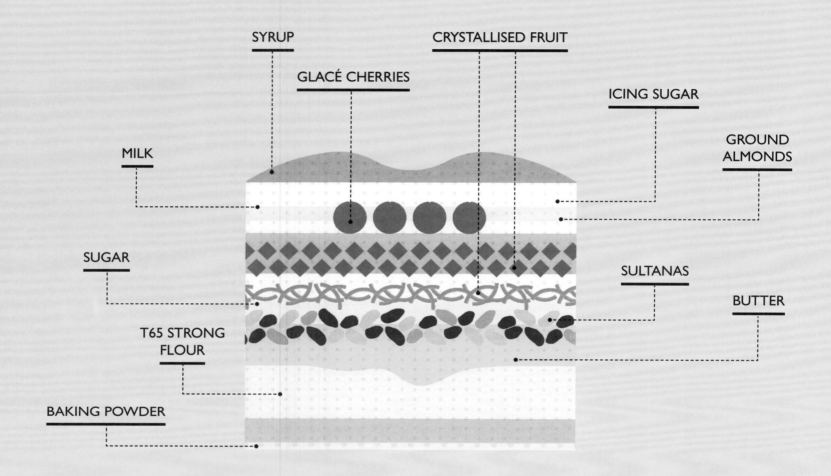

SYRUP

GLACÉ CHERRIES

CRYSTALLISED FRUIT

ICING SUGAR

MILK

GROUND ALMONDS

SUGAR

SULTANAS

T65 STRONG FLOUR

BUTTER

BAKING POWDER

WHAT IS IT?

Cake enriched with crystallised fruits and doused in syrup after baking.

TIME TO MAKE

Preparation: 30 minutes
Baking: 45 minutes

EQUIPMENT

20 cm long loaf tin
Wooden spoon
Sieve
Pastry brush

TECHNIQUE TO MASTER
Creaming butter and sugar (page 284)

TIP
After removing the cake from the tin, wrap it in plastic wrap to keep it moist.

IT'S READY . . .
When the tip of a knife inserted into the cake comes out clean.

STORAGE
1 week, wrapped in plastic wrap.

WHY MUST THE SULTANAS
BE REHYDRATED?

To prevent them absorbing all the water from the dough, which is needed for the starch in the mixture to cook.

MAKES 1

1 GOLDEN DOUGH

80 g softened unsalted butter (page 284)
50 g caster sugar
50 g icing sugar
2 eggs
15 g milk
90 g T65 strong flour
5 g baking powder
20 g ground almonds

2 FRUIT

65 g sultanas
50 g diced crystallised fruit
10 g glacé cherries
15 g diced crystallised orange peel

3 GREASING

10 g softened unsalted butter (page 284)

4 SYRUP

40 g water
50 g caster sugar
40 g dark rum

1 Put the sultanas in a saucepan, cover with water and bring to the boil. Remove from the heat and leave to rest for a few minutes for the sultanas to absorb the water and swell up. Drain on paper towel and allow to cool.

2 Cream the butter, caster sugar and icing sugar in a large round-bottomed bowl using a wooden spoon or an electric mixer with the beater attachment (see page 284).

3 Add the eggs and beat until the mixture is very smooth. Beat in the milk.

4 Sift together the flour, baking powder and ground almonds (see page 285). Fold two-thirds into the egg mixture.

5 Put the drained sultanas in another bowl with the other fruit and add the remaining one-third of the flour mixture. Toss to coat the fruit well.

6 Add the fruit to the cake mixture and fold in gently.

7 Preheat the oven to 65°C. Grease a 20 cm loaf tin with the softened butter using a pastry brush, line with baking paper, then pour in the mixture. Bake for 45 minutes. Remove from the tin and leave to cool completely.

8 Make the syrup: bring the water and sugar to the boil and remove from the heat immediately. Stir in the rum and allow to cool. Soak the cake with the syrup using a pastry brush.

PAIN DE GÊNES

Understand

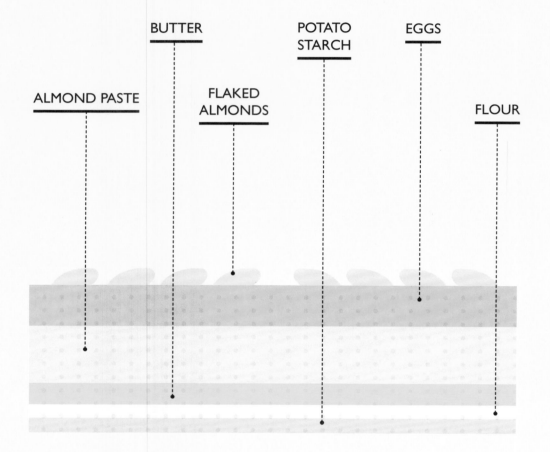

BUTTER

POTATO STARCH

EGGS

ALMOND PASTE

FLAKED ALMONDS

FLOUR

WHAT IS IT?

Very moist cake based on almond paste.

TIME TO MAKE

Preparation: 25 minutes
Baking: 25 minutes

EQUIPMENT

14 cm round cake tin 5 cm high
Electric mixer with whisk and beater
Sieve
Wooden spoon
Pastry brush

CLASSIC USE
Cake base for desserts

TRICKY ASPECT
Baking: if overcooked it loses its moistness.

TIP
Use softened butter to ensure the flaked almonds stick to the tin.

IT'S READY . . .
When the cake is golden.

STORAGE
2–3 days

CAN YOU REPLACE THE ALMOND PASTE WITH GROUND ALMONDS?

With ground almonds, the cake will be less sweet (because almond paste contains lots of sugar). The gluten network will form more easily, yielding an airier crumb less like a cake and therefore less moist.

<u>1</u>

<u>2</u>

MAKES 1

1 CAKE MIXTURE

60 g unsalted butter
200 g almond paste (50% almonds)
3 eggs
20 g T55 plain flour
20 g potato starch

2 PREPARING THE TIN

10 g softened unsalted butter (page 284)
10 g flaked almonds

Making pain de Gênes

3a

3b

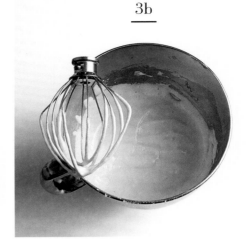

4

5

6

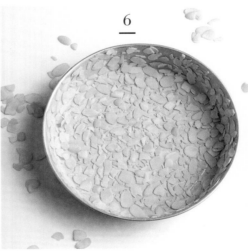

7

1   Melt the butter in a saucepan over a low heat then allow to cool.

2   Put the almond paste in the bowl of an electric mixer with the beater attachment and incorporate two of the eggs at medium speed, adding them one at a time. The paste should be softened and smooth.

3   Add the remaining egg, change to the whisk attachment, then whisk for about 5 minutes to obtain a smooth dough that forms a ribbon (ribbon stage, see page 284) when you lift the whisk.

4   Sift the flour and potato starch together (see page 287) into the mixture and fold in gently with a wooden spoon.

5   Gently fold in the melted butter with the wooden spoon.

6   Preheat the oven to 150°C (conventional oven). Grease the tin with the softened butter (see page 284) using a pastry brush. Scatter over the flaked almonds so they stick to the butter. Tap the tin lightly to remove the excess almonds.

7   Pour the cake mixture into the tin. Bake for 25 minutes. Remove from the oven and cool on a wire rack for 10 minutes, then remove from the tin. Turn over to serve.

SABLÉS

Understand

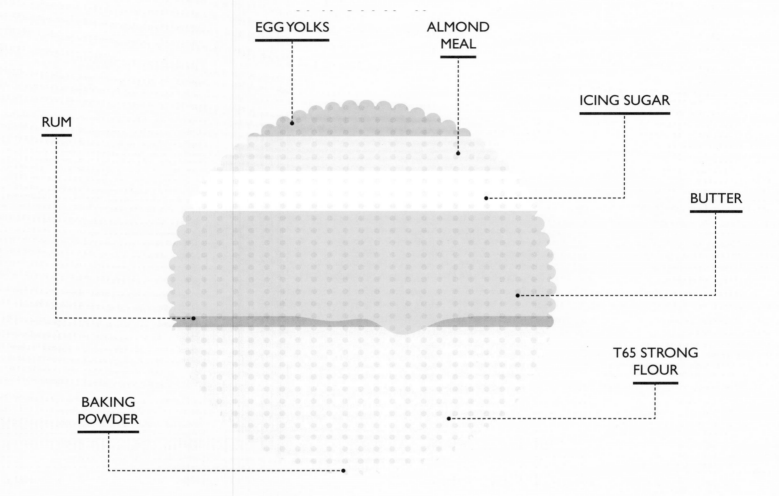

EGG YOLKS

ALMOND MEAL

ICING SUGAR

RUM

BUTTER

T65 STRONG FLOUR

BAKING POWDER

WHAT ARE THEY?

Large dry, crumbly biscuits rich in butter.

TIME TO MAKE

Preparation: 20 minutes
Resting in the refrigerator: 1 hour
Baking: 20 minutes

EQUIPMENT

Electric mixer with beater (optional)
Pastry rolling pin
Fluted 13 cm tart ring
Sieve
Pastry brush

DERIVATIONS
With chocolate chips, slivered almonds

TRICKY ASPECT
Don't overcook the egg yolk.

TECHNIQUES TO MASTER
Glazing (page 49)
Slashing in a lattice (polka; page 51)

TIP
The sablés should be soft when they come out
of the oven; they will harden as they cool.

THEY'RE READY . . .
When the biscuits are golden.

STORAGE
2–3 days sealed in an airtight container.

WHY MUST THE EGG YOLKS
BE COOKED?

*To obtain the characteristic sandy texture.
When being microwaved some of the
egg proteins coagulate. Once they are
incorporated into the dough, they limit the
formation of a gluten network. The looser
the network, the sandier and crumblier
the texture after baking. The tighter the
network, the more compact the texture.*

Learn

MAKES 4

DOUGH

40 g egg yolk (2 yolks), beaten
225 g T65 strong flour
210 g unsalted butter
75 g icing sugar
40 g ground almonds
11 g rum
1 g fleur de sel
1 g baking powder

GLAZE

1 egg
3 g (½ teaspoon) milk
pinch of salt

1 Cook the egg yolk in the microwave on medium heat for 1 minute, then push through a sieve.

2 Mix all the ingredients using an electric mixer with the beater attachment for 5 minutes at the lowest speed. (Alternatively, beat in a round-bottomed bowl using a wooden spoon.)

3 Shape the dough into a ball (see page 42), flatten it roughly, wrap in plastic wrap and refrigerate for 1 hour.

4 Preheat the oven to 180°C (conventional oven). Roll the dough out (see page 283) to 4 mm thick. Cut out four rounds using a 13 cm fluted biscuit cutter.

5 Lay the discs on a baking sheet lined with baking paper. Make the glaze (see page 49). Glaze the sablés using a pastry brush. Score the tops using a fork.

6 Bake for 20 minutes.

PALMIERS

Understand

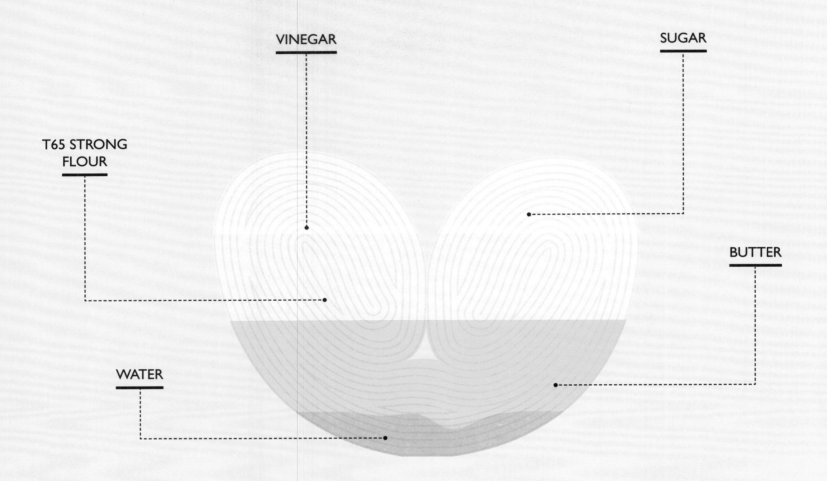

T65 STRONG
FLOUR

VINEGAR

SUGAR

BUTTER

WATER

WHAT ARE THEY?

Puff pastry topped with sugar, rolled
up from both ends then cut into
slices and dried in the oven.

TIME TO MAKE

Preparation: 45 minutes
Resting in the refrigerator: 8 hours 15 minutes
Baking: 15–20 minutes

EQUIPMENT

Electric mixer with beater
Pastry rolling pin

TRICKY ASPECTS

Not rolling the dough too vigorously, or
the layers of butter and dough will mix.
Folding: be sure to make the folds
firmly, to ensure no air remains between
the different layers of pastry.

TECHNIQUES TO MASTER

Kneading (pages 30–33)
Rolling out dough (page 283)

TIP

Dust the work surface with icing sugar rather
than flour; it will caramelise during baking.

THEY'RE READY . . .

When they are well browned and
caramelised.

STORAGE

A few days sealed in an airtight container.

WHY ADD SUGAR WITH
EACH TURN?

*The sugar melts and caramelises during
baking. It acts like glue between the layers,
so the palmiers hold their shape better.*

3

5

6

7

8

MAKES 15

INVERSE PUFF PASTRY (600 G)

Beurre manié (kneaded butter)
200 g softened unsalted butter
(page 284), cut into cubes
80 g T65 strong flour

Détrempe
180 g T65 strong flour
80 g cold water
10 g salt
60 g softened unsalted butter (page 284)
2 g white vinegar

TO FINISH

200 g caster sugar

1 Make the inverse puff pastry (see page 68).

2 Make a simple turn (see page 283): roll out the dough (see page 283) to 60 cm × 20 cm, fold a third of the dough over the middle then another third over the top. Cover with plastic wrap and refrigerate for 2 hours.

3 Make a double turn (see page 283): roll out the dough to 60 cm × 20 cm and fold a quarter of the dough from each side towards the centre. Fold in half across the middle. Cover with plastic wrap and refrigerate for 2 hours.

4 Make a double turn, sprinkling 100 g of the sugar over the dough before folding. Cover with plastic wrap and refrigerate for another 2 hours.

5 Make a simple turn, sprinkling 50 g of the sugar over the dough before folding. Cover with plastic wrap and refrigerate for another 2 hours at least.

6 Roll the dough out to 96 cm × 15 cm. Fold a 16 cm strip from each end over the length of the dough.

7 Fold in the two edges from each end once more, then fold in half to finish.

8 Put the remaining sugar on a plate and roll the dough parcel in it. Wrap the dough in plastic wrap and freeze for about 15 minutes.

9 Preheat the oven to 160°C (conventional oven). Cut the dough into 1 cm slices. Lay on a baking sheet without baking paper. Bake for 15–20 minutes.

RASPBERRY PAILLES

Understand

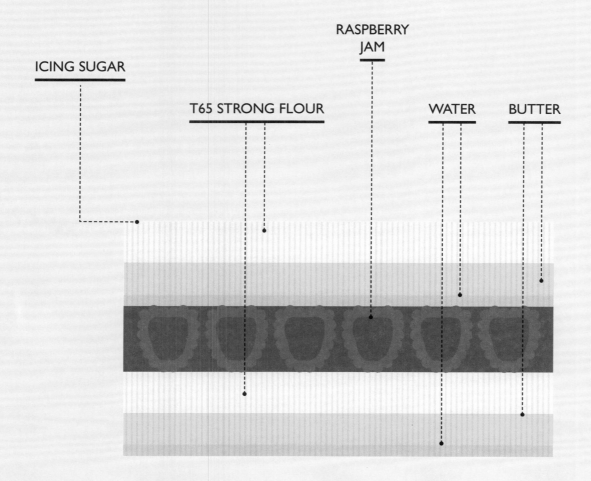

ICING SUGAR

RASPBERRY JAM

T65 STRONG FLOUR

WATER   BUTTER

WHAT ARE THEY?

Squares of puff pastry dried in the oven then filled with raspberry jam.

TIME TO MAKE

Preparation: 25 minutes
Resting in the refrigerator: 12 hours
Baking: 20 minutes

EQUIPMENT

Electric mixer with beater
Pastry rolling pin
Pastry brush
Whisk

TRICKY ASPECT
Achieving uniform caramelisation of the pastry layers.

TECHNIQUES TO MASTER
Kneading (pages 30–33)
Rolling out dough (page 283)

THEY'RE READY . . .
When the pastry is golden.

STORAGE
2–3 days

Learn

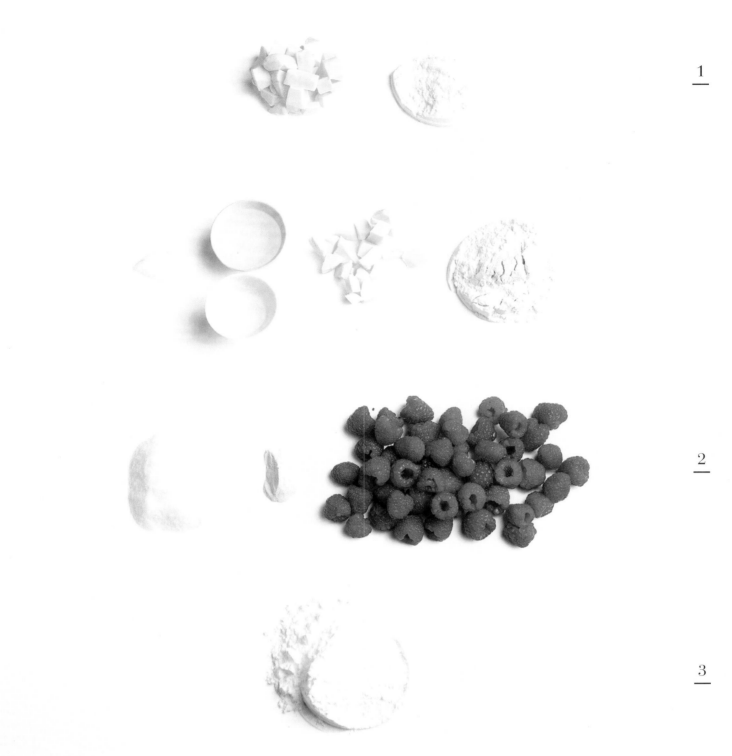

<u>1</u>

<u>2</u>

<u>3</u>

MAKES 5

1 INVERSE PUFF PASTRY (300 G)

Beurre manié (kneaded butter)
100 g soft unsalted butter, cut into cubes
40 g T65 strong flour

Détrempe
90 g T65 strong flour
40 g cold water
5 g salt
30 g softened unsalted butter (page 284)
1 g white vinegar

2 RASPBERRY JAM

60 g caster sugar
1.5 g pectin
125 g raspberries

3 TO FINISH

icing sugar

Making raspberry pailles

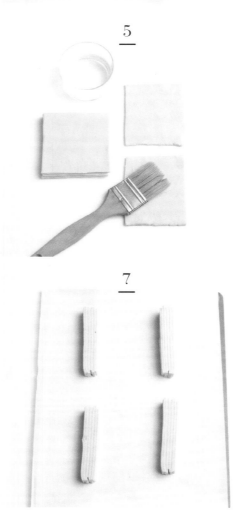

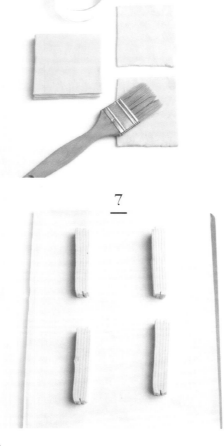

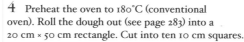

1 Make the inverse puff pastry (see page 68).

2 Make the raspberry jam: mix 10 g of the sugar with the pectin in a small bowl. Put the raspberries and the remaining sugar in a saucepan over a low heat and cook until they form a sauce.

3 Incorporate the sugar and pectin mixture. Whisk then bring to a simmer, whisking and checking frequently. Pour into a bowl and allow to cool.

4 Preheat the oven to 180°C (conventional oven). Roll the dough out (see page 283) into a 20 cm × 50 cm rectangle. Cut into ten 10 cm squares.

5 Brush the puff pastry squares with water using a pastry brush. Put them in two piles of five squares each.

6 Cut the pastry squares into 2 cm slices.

7 Lay the slices with one cut side up on a baking sheet lined with baking paper. Bake for about 20 minutes. Allow to cool.

8 Spread the raspberry jam on one puff pastry slice, then cover with a second slice. Repeat with the remaining puff pastry pieces and raspberry jam. Dust with icing sugar.

FINANCIERS

Understand

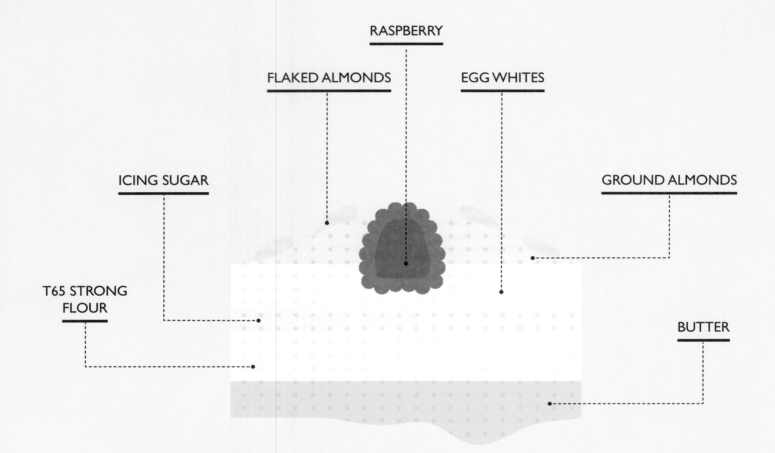

RASPBERRY

FLAKED ALMONDS

EGG WHITES

ICING SUGAR

GROUND ALMONDS

T65 STRONG FLOUR

BUTTER

WHAT ARE THEY?

Small moist cakes like friands, made with ground almonds and egg white.

TIME TO MAKE

Preparation: 15 minutes
Resting in the refrigerator: at least 2 hours
Baking: 20–25 minutes

EQUIPMENT

8 mini loaf tins
Sifter or strainer and fine-mesh sieve
Whisk, pastry brush
Piping bag with plain 8 mm nozzle (optional)

TRICKY ASPECT
Making the beurre noisette.

TECHNIQUE TO MASTER
Piping (page 285)

THEY'RE READY . . .
When the financiers are lightly browned.

STORAGE
2–3 days, covered in plastic wrap.

WHY REST THE DOUGH IN THE REFRIGERATOR?

During whisking, air is incorporated into the dough: it is imprisoned in the mixture thanks to the eggs (which contain proteins that hold the air). Adding the melted butter will coat this structure. While resting in the refrigerator, the butter will harden and set the aerated structure evenly throughout. After baking, the financiers will be more regular.

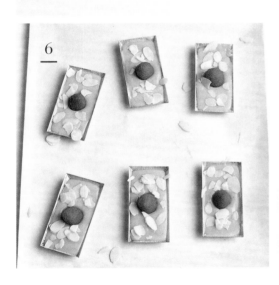

MAKES 8

DOUGH

25 g ground almonds
65 g icing sugar
30 g T65 strong flour
2 egg whites (60 g) at room temperature
45 g unsalted butter

GREASING

5 g softened unsalted butter (page 284)

DECORATION

8 raspberries
10 g flaked almonds

1 Sift the ground almonds, icing sugar and flour together into a bowl (see page 285). Add the egg whites and whisk.

2 Make a beurre noisette: melt the butter in a saucepan over a medium heat and cook until golden. When the butter no longer 'sings' and stops foaming, strain it through a fine-mesh sieve.

3 Add the hot beurre noisette to the ground almond mixture and continue to whisk until very smooth.

4 Cover with plastic wrap (plastic touching the mixture; see page 285) and refrigerate for at least 2 hours, or overnight.

5 Preheat the oven to 150°C (fan-forced). Grease the mini loaf tins with the softened butter using a pastry brush. Fill the tins with the cold mixture using a spoon (or a piping bag).

6 Place one raspberry and some flaked almonds on each financier and bake for 20–25 minutes.

MADELEINES

Understand

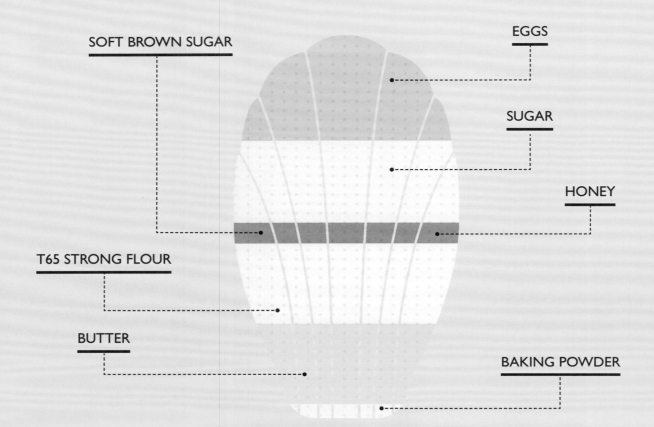

SOFT BROWN SUGAR

EGGS

SUGAR

HONEY

T65 STRONG FLOUR

BUTTER

BAKING POWDER

WHAT ARE THEY?

Little moist cakes in the shape of a shell.

TIME TO MAKE

Preparation: 20 minutes
Resting in the refrigerator: 24 hours
Baking: 8–10 minutes

EQUIPMENT

20-hole madeleine tin
Sieve
Piping bag with plain 8 mm nozzle
Pastry brush

TRICKY ASPECT
Resting the dough sufficiently.

TECHNIQUE TO MASTER
Piping (page 287)

THEY'RE READY . . .
When the madeleines are golden
and have a bulge in the middle.

STORAGE
A few days sealed in an airtight container.

HOW DOES THE BULGE FORM?

*When using cold dough (straight out
of the refrigerator) and a hot oven, the
bulge will be more likely to form:
– the cold increases the viscosity of
the dough, which will tend to spread
less in the mould and rise more
– the high temperature of the oven
stimulates the rapid formation of steam
and thus makes the cakes rise.*

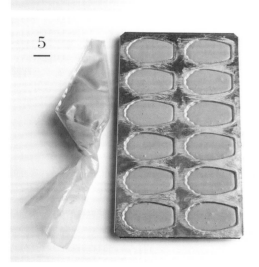

MAKES 20

DOUGH

190 g softened unsalted butter (page 284)
150 g caster sugar
20 g soft brown sugar
4 g salt
30 g honey
4 eggs, lightly beaten
1 vanilla bean
190 g T65 strong flour
7 g baking powder

GREASING

5 g softened unsalted butter (page 284)

THE DAY BEFORE

1   Mix the softened butter, caster sugar, brown sugar and salt in a round-bottomed bowl using a wooden spoon. Add the honey and eggs, then mix until smooth.

2   Flatten the vanilla bean with the back of a utility knife. Split lengthways and scrape the seeds. Add the vanilla seeds to the bowl without the bean.

3   Sift the flour with the baking powder (see page 285) into the bowl and mix one last time.

4   When the mixture is very smooth, cover with plastic wrap (plastic touching the mixture; see page 285) and refrigerate for at least 24 hours.

ON THE DAY

5   Preheat the oven to 210°C. Grease the madeleine tin with the softened butter using a pastry brush. Fill the holes to three-quarters with the mixture using a piping bag (see page 285) or a large spoon.

6   Bake for 8–10 minutes.

ALMOND
TUILES

Understand

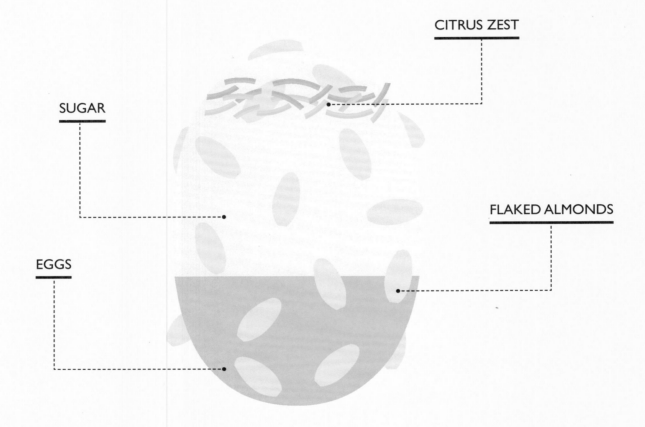

CITRUS ZEST

SUGAR

EGGS

FLAKED ALMONDS

WHAT ARE THEY?
Thin dry biscuits with flaked almonds.

TIME TO MAKE
Preparation: 20 minutes
Resting in the refrigerator: at least 2 hours
Baking: 8 minutes

EQUIPMENT
Yule log cake tin or pastry rolling pin
Palette knife

DERIVATION
Tuiles with crushed hazelnuts

TRICKY ASPECT
Shaping the tuiles.

TIP
Bake the tuiles in several batches: they
must be shaped quickly while they
are still hot or they will break.

THEY'RE READY . . .
When the edges of the tuiles
are lightly browned.

STORAGE
A few days sealed in an airtight container.

WHY MUST THE DOUGH BE
RESTED FOR 2 HOURS?
*During this resting time, the sugar
dissolves in the water provided by the
egg whites. This will limit crystallisation
of the sugar during baking and thus
prevent graininess in the finished biscuit.*

Learn

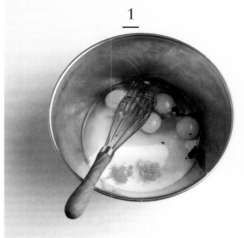

MAKES 25

1 vanilla bean
250 g caster sugar
4 eggs
2 g finely grated lemon zest
2 g finely grated orange zest
250 g flaked almonds

1   Flatten the vanilla bean with the back of a utility knife. Split lengthways and scrape the seeds. Put the vanilla seeds in a round-bottomed bowl. Add the sugar, eggs and zests, and whisk until smooth.

2   Delicately add the flaked almonds and mix gently. Cover with plastic wrap (plastic touching the mixture; see page 285) and refrigerate for at least 2 hours or overnight.

3   Preheat the oven to 170°C (conventional oven). Using a teaspoon, make eight little heaps of the tuile mixture on a baking sheet lined with baking paper or a silicone mat, spacing them widely because the mixture will spread quite a bit.

4   Dip the back of a fork in water and push on the little heaps to turn them into rounds, using circular movements from the centre towards the outside of the tuiles.

5   Bake for about 8 minutes, until the edges of the tuiles are golden.

6   Quickly lift the tuiles with a palette knife and place them in a yule log tin or on a rolling pin. Shape the tuile to the support using your hands. Repeat with the remaining tuile mixture.

CHOUQUETTES

Understand

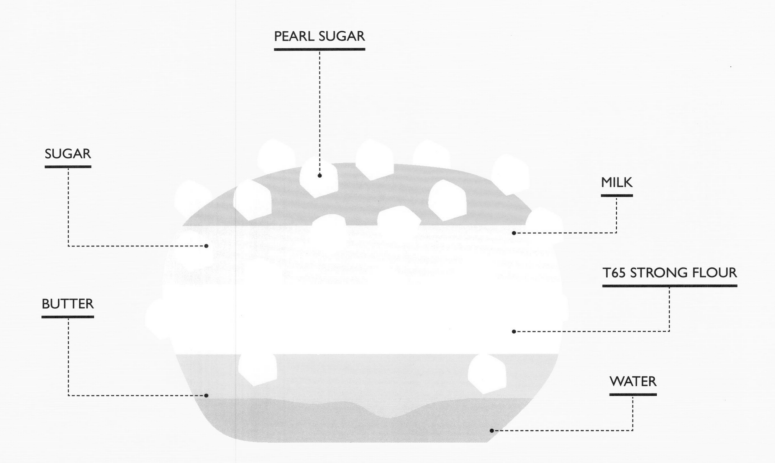

PEARL SUGAR

SUGAR

MILK

BUTTER

T65 STRONG FLOUR

WATER

WHAT IS IT?

Small unfilled choux balls
sprinkled with pearl sugar.

TIME TO MAKE

Preparation: 15 minutes
Baking: 20 minutes

EQUIPMENT

Electric mixer with beater (optional)
Wooden spoon
Dough scraper
Piping bag and plain no. 10 nozzle

TRICKY ASPECTS
Drying the choux pastry well without
burning it.
Baking the choux balls.

TIP
To avoid the balls sinking, make
sure you don't open the oven door
before the crust seems dry.

IT'S READY . . .
When the balls have puffed up nicely
and are golden, and the pearl sugar
has started to caramelise slightly.

STORAGE
For eating quickly.

WHY DOESN'T THE SUGAR MELT
DURING BAKING?

*Pearl sugar is sucrose (as is table
sugar). It melts from 160°C. The baking
temperature of the choux balls is
below this (150°C), so the pearl sugar
retains its shape and doesn't melt.*

Learn

MAKES 50

CHOUX PASTRY

165 g milk
90 g water
110 g unsalted butter
2 g caster sugar
2 g salt
150 g T65 strong flour
4 eggs

TO FINISH

200 g pearl sugar

1   Make the choux pastry (see page 72).

2   Preheat the oven to 150°C (fan-forced). Put the choux in a piping bag with a plain no. 10 nozzle. Pipe 25 round blobs of pastry of 2–2.5 cm diameter on a baking sheet lined with baking paper, working with the nozzle close to the sheet and perpendicular to it. You will have dough left for a second batch.

3   Sprinkle generously with half the pearl sugar.

4   Bake for 20 minutes. Pipe another 25 choux with the remaining dough, sprinkle over the remaining pearl sugar and bake for 20 minutes.

CHAPTER 3
ILLUSTRATED GLOSSARY

1

2

3

4–5

6

9
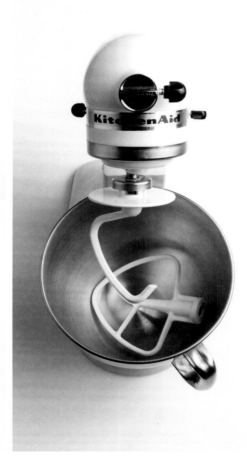

7

8
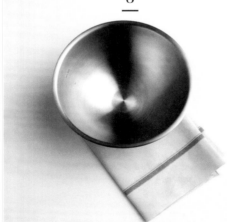

1 DOUGH CUTTER

Tool (plastic or metal) used to divide/cut dough cleanly.

2 DOUGH SCRAPER

Plastic tool used to scrape a mixture from one vessel to another.

3 BREAD LAME (RAZOR)

Sharp blade used to slash bread, to form notches (blooms), peaks and 'ears'.

4 SCISSORS

Used to create particular blooms, such as picot edges or wheat stalks.

5 BREAD KNIFE

Large serrated knife used to cut cooked bread.

6 THERMOMETER

Allows checking of the dough temperature after kneading. It should be between 23°C and 24°C for optimal fermentation.

7 SCALES

For weighing ingredients precisely.

8 ROUND-BOTTOMED BOWL, TEA TOWEL

Stainless-steel vessel used for mixing ingredients or proving bread doughs. We cover it with a clean tea towel while proving to prevent a crust forming on the dough.

9 ELECTRIC MIXER

It allows kneading of bread doughs, which is a long and tiring job when done by hand. It yields stronger doughs because the kneading is more intense. We knead with the dough hook attachment. The beater attachment is used to beat soft or semi-liquid doughs or creams. The whisk attachment is used to increase the volume of creams or egg whites.

UTENSILS

1 LOAF TIN WITH A LID

Rectangular tin for making bread with a square profile. Available from specialist kitchenware suppliers.

2 FLUTED BRIOCHE TINS

Metal mould, round and crinkled, used to cook the body of Parisian brioches. Available from specialist kitchenware suppliers.

3 KUGELHOPF MOULD

Mould traditionally of terracotta used to cook kugelhopf. There are also metal ones.

4 PANETTONE MOULD

Paper mould. There are also metal springform moulds.

5 MADELEINE TIN

Cake mould with numerous shell-shaped holes. A metal one ensures better baking than a silicone one.

6 MINI LOAF TINS

There are single moulds with several holes or individual moulds. Metal ones ensure better baking than silicone ones.

7 BAKING SHEET

Metal tray used to cook bread. Line with baking paper if the surface isn't non-stick.

8 PIPING BAG AND NOZZLES

Used frequently in pâtisserie for piping mixtures in a decorative way (dessert creams). In bread-making, they are basically used for inserting fillings (jam doughnuts, almond croissants), adding a uniform cream layer (Epiphany cake), cleanly moulding small items (financiers, madeleines), or making choux puffs or chouquettes. We therefore generally use plain nozzles, of medium diameter (8 or 10 mm). Disposable piping bags are practical and hygienic.

9 PASTRY ROLLING PIN

Wooden log used for rolling out doughs in a uniform manner. Turn the dough 90 degrees (quarter turn) between rollings to ensure an even thickness.

10 PASTRY BRUSH

Food brush used to glaze Viennese pastries, and apply syrups and liquids for baking.

DOUGHS

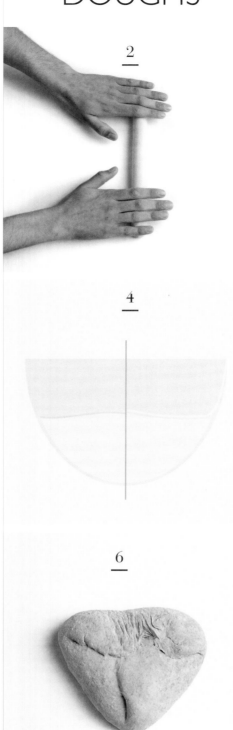

1 BASSINAGE

Extra water added to a dough after kneading to increase its hydration when it is too dense.

2 ELONGATING

Pre-shaping a piece of dough into a log shape. Place both hands in the centre of the dough. Elongate it by rolling it with two hands, working out towards the ends until it reaches the desired length.

3 DEGASSING

Flattening the dough with your hands to remove the gas. This allows better distribution of the air bubbles created during rising. The crumb will have better aeration.

4 FORMING A CRUST

Occurs when a dough or cream hardens on the surface. This happens when the mixture is exposed to the air: it oxidises.

5 SCRAPING OUT

Extracting a dough or another mixture from a vessel using a plastic utensil called a dough scraper ('corne' in French).

6 THE SEAM

Join between two parts of the same piece of dough. For breads the seam is generally underneath during baking. In certain cases, the bread is baked with the seam facing up; in such cases it replaces slashing.

7 SHAPING INTO A BALL

Gently flatten the piece of dough. Gradually bring the sides in towards the centre. Pinch these turned-in edges together to join them, then turn the ball over on a floured work surface (seam side down). Smooth the dough ball by running your palms over the whole surface several times (see page 44 for more detail).

8 FRASAGE

In bread-making: mixing dough ingredients together before kneading. In pâtisserie: crushing pastry dough (sablé, shortcrust) on the work surface with the palm of the hand to complete mixing of the ingredients without overworking the dough.

DOUGHS

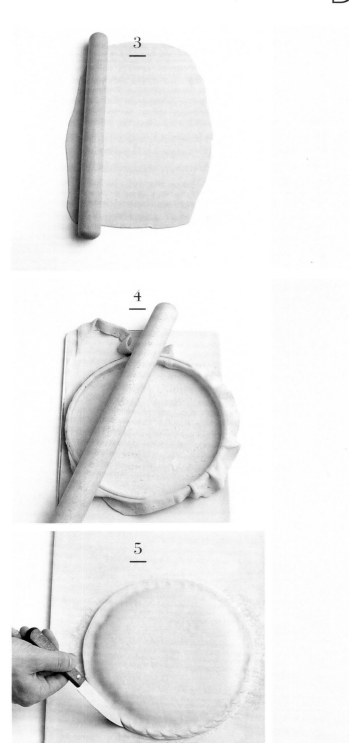

1 EXTENSIBLE DOUGH

Dough that can be stretched easily.

2 ELASTIC DOUGH

Dough that is difficult to roll out: when stretched, it bounces back automatically.

3 ROLLING OUT DOUGH

Spreading out the dough (puff pastry, sablé, shortcrust, pizza, and so on) using a rolling pin. Lightly dust the work surface, rolling pin and dough with flour.

4 LINING WITH DOUGH

Filling a mould or a tart ring with pastry. Use a rolling pin to help stop the pastry breaking: roll the dough around the floured rolling pin, place the rolling pin at the edge of the mould and unroll over the mould.

5 PINCHING THE EDGES

Making small regular score marks all round the edge of pastry using a small knife. This allows the pastry to swell up faster during baking and give a more aesthetically pleasing end result. Make the marks by starting at the outside and moving inwards for 5 mm.

6 A SIMPLE TURN

Folding puff pastry into three thicknesses during the rolling and folding phase. Roll out the dough (with the seam on the vertical) until it is three times longer than wide. Fold one-third towards the middle, then another third over the top. Wrap in plastic wrap and refrigerate to rest.

7 A DOUBLE TURN (OR 'WALLET')

Folding puff pastry into four thicknesses during the rolling and folding phase. Roll out the dough (with the seam on the vertical) until it is three times longer than wide. Fold a quarter of the dough from each end towards the centre. Fold in two across the middle. Wrap in plastic wrap and refrigerate.

BUTTER AND EGGS

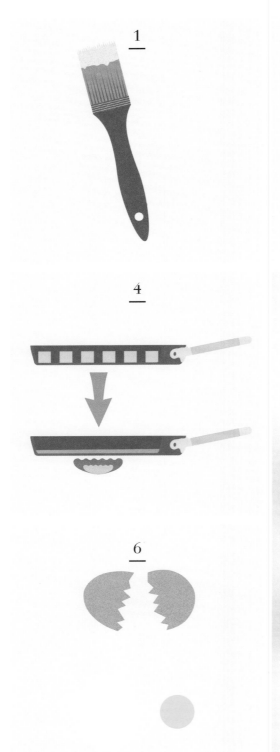

1 GREASING A MOULD

Using a pastry brush, cover the whole interior surface of the mould with softened butter. Greasing the mould makes the cooked item easier to remove after baking.

2 SOFTENED BUTTER

Very soft (but not liquid) butter, worked until supple, with the texture of a cream. Cut the butter into pieces, place in a bowl and leave at room temperature for 1–2 hours before working with a wooden spoon or beating with an electric mixer using the beater attachment.

3 CREAMING

Whisking softened butter with sugar to obtain a pale, fluffy cream.

4 BEURRE NOISETTE

Butter cooked until it turns brown.

5 CLARIFIED BUTTER

Butter in which nothing but the fat remains, from which all the impurities have been removed. Melt the butter over a very low heat. Once it has melted completely, skim the impurities from the surface using a spoon. Pour the butter (yellow) into a bowl, taking care to leave behind the whey (white) in the bottom of the saucepan.

6 SEPARATING (CLARIFYING) EGGS

The French call separating the white from the yolk 'clarifying' an egg.

7 REACHING RIBBON STAGE

Whisking eggs with sugar to obtain a silky smooth mixture. The mixture falls without breaking, like a ribbon folding up on itself.

8 BLANCHING

Vigorously whisking egg yolks or butter with sugar until the mixture turns pale (blanches).

BASIC TECHNIQUES

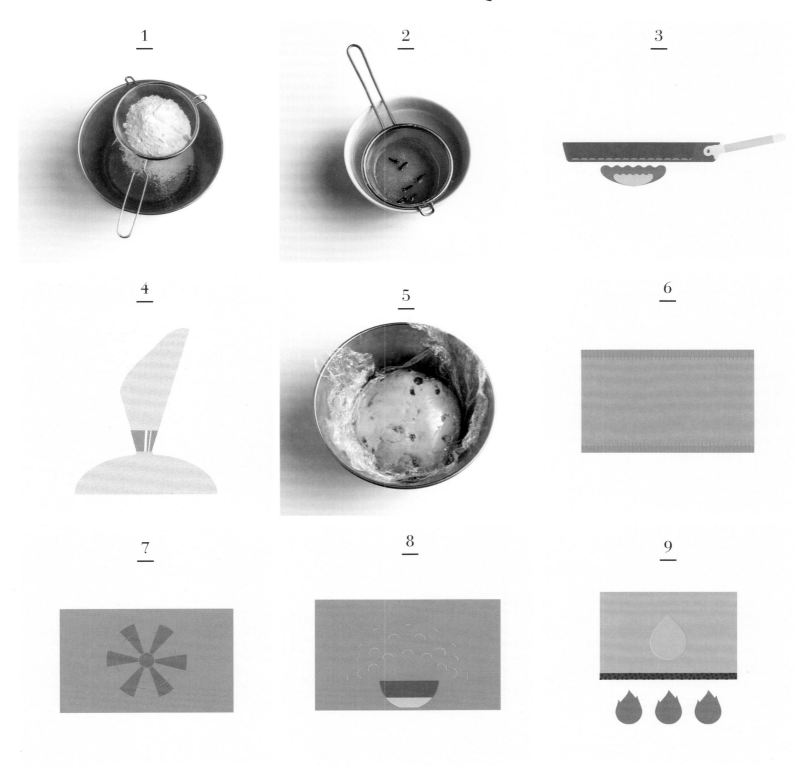

1 SIFTING

Passing a powder through a sieve (or strainer) to remove any residues or lumps.

2 STRAINING

Passing a liquid through a sieve (or strainer) to remove residues or items that are too big.

3 TOASTING FRUITS AND SEEDS

Roasting dried fruits or seeds to bring out their flavours. Place on a baking sheet and bake for about 12 minutes at 180°C. With a frying pan, toast them without any fat, shaking the pan regularly. Watch carefully that they don't burn.

4 PIPING

In pâtisserie, using a piping bag, with or without a nozzle, to make shapes (discs, domes, éclairs, choux puffs) with a dough or decorations.

5 TOUCHING WITH PLASTIC WRAP

Applying plastic wrap to a mixture so that it is in direct contact with it, to ensure the mixture isn't exposed to the air. This prevents a crust forming or the mixture drying out.

6 CONVENTIONAL OVEN

Where the heat is created in an oven equipped with two heating elements (at the top and bottom of the oven). The heat gradually rises. It is not advised for cooking with several baking sheets at the same time.

7 FAN-FORCED OVEN

Where the heat is created in an oven equipped with two heating elements as well as a fan. The heat is distributed evenly throughout the oven.

8 CREATING STEAM

Introducing water into the oven in the form of steam at the beginning of baking, to maintain a humid atmosphere during cooking. This makes a good, shiny crust, aids with the formation of blooms and limits the evaporation of water (so the bread keeps for longer).

9 MAILLARD REACTIONS

Chemical reactions between the proteins and sugars, which start to occur as soon as there are no longer any water molecules at the surface (with bread this is at the end of cooking). They result in a brown colouration and caramelised aromatic notes.

RECIPE LIST

INDEX OF INGREDIENTS